Working in Organisations
Second Edition

For our children:

Sophia, Reeves, Jade, Rebecca, Alex, Nicholas and Daniel, who with luck,
like their parents, will spend most of their working lives
in meaningful organisations.

We can never know what to want, because, living only one life,
we can neither compare it with our previous lives nor perfect it in our lives to come.
There is no means for testing which decision is better, because there is no basis
for comparison. We live everything as it comes, without warning, like an actor going on cold.
And what can life be worth if the first rehearsal for life is life itself?

Milan Kundera, *The Unbearable Lightness of Being*

Working in Organisations

Second Edition

ANDREW KAKABADSE, JOHN BANK
and SUSAN VINNICOMBE

GOWER

Published by
Gower Publishing Limited
Gower House
Croft Road
Aldershot
Hants GU11 3HR
England

Gower Publishing Company
Suite 420
101 Cherry Street
Burlington, VT 05401-4405
USA

Andrew Kakabadse, John Bank and Susan Vinnicombe have asserted their right under the Copyright, Designs and Patents Act, 1988 to be identified as the authors of this work.

British Library Cataloguing in Publication Data

Kakabadse, Andrew
    Working in organisations. – 2nd ed.
    1. Organizational behavior
    I. Title II. Bank, John III. Vinnicombe, Susan
    658

ISBN 0 566 08419 8

Library of Congress Cataloging-in-Publication Data

Kakabadse, Andrew.
    Working in organisations.-- 2nd ed. / Andrew Kakabadse, John Bank, and Susan Vinnicombe.
        p. cm.
    Includes bibliographical references.
    ISBN 0-566-08419-8
    1. Organizational behavior. 2. Organizational behavior--Case studies. I. Title:
    Working in organizations. II Bank, John. III. Vinnicombe, Susan. IV. Title.

    HD58.7.K34 2004
    658.4--dc22

                                                                                        2003025983

Reprinted 2004

Typeset by Adrian McLaughlin, a@microguides.net
Printed and bound by MPG Books Ltd, Bodmin Cornwall.

Contents

List of figures

List of tables

Authors' preface to the Second Edition

In the past 16 years, since the first edition of *Working in Organisations* appeared, the role of the manager has become even more important. As the Greek philosopher Heraclitus said: 'We cannot step into the same river twice.' The river changes, as does everything else. The role of management has undergone cataclysmic changes. We have updated the themes of this book and added new chapters on managing organisations in the twenty-first century.

The content of the book reflects new priorities in the manager's environment. By giving the book a traditional framework, we still attempt to answer fundamental questions about working in organisations. Throughout the book we focus on how managers behave in organisations. We use a device we call a 'reality check' which is a short account of real people in a real situation that illuminates the management theories or practices we are discussing.

Part 1 of the book is about people, jobs and relationships. In Chapter 1, we provide an overview of the challenges managers face in both private and public sector organisations. We identify the five major challenges as:

- establishing business ethics,
- managing globalisation,
- dealing with downsizing,
- valuing employee diversity and
- exploiting new technology.

We look at a manager's job in Chapter 2. First we glance back at the history of managerial work. Then we examine the seminal work of Henry Mintzberg, who has spent his professional life researching the jobs of real managers. We explain some of his recent new thinking about the complex role of the empowering manager.

A managerial career is the focal point of Chapter 3. We show how the concept of career has changed in every aspect. From attraction and selection, to induction and socialisation, to career development, there is a new dynamic between the manager and his or her organisation. Today managers are rarely offered lifetime careers in organisations. They are subjected to continuous assessment and, at times, have to re-apply for their jobs as companies ruthlessly 'cut out the dead wood'. We contrast the new psychological contract that underpins most careers today, with the old psychological contract of the past. We argue for a better matching of a manager's knowledge and skills to the core competencies set out by the organisation. A good match leads to many benefits such as greater flexibility, mobility, horizontal opportunities, a better work/life balance, and a more meaningful, challenging career.

In Chapter 4 we explore motivation at work. What needs do people bring to the workplace that require a manager's attention to achieve peak performances from them? How do managers design jobs to enhance motivation? We describe how men and women at work experience different sources of motivation. Given the speed of change and the pressures of competition, organisations are now searching for ways in which commitment at work can be sustained.

Teamworking to achieve synergies has escalated. Most managers work in teams and are responsible for team performance. Many reward schemes are now based on team (not individual) performance. In Chapter 5 we answer the question: how do virtual teams differ from face-to-face teams? We also look at Meredith Belbin's classic team roles as one form of team analysis and Tim Mills' new approach to team competencies as another. We explore the work of 'hot groups'. We discuss in detail 'group think' (the opposite of synergy), using the launch of the space shuttle Challenger as a case study. Unfortunately, judging from the conclusions of the Columbia Accident Investigation Board (August 2003), into the loss of the second space shuttle in February, there are parallels between both accidents. Flawed management practices were 'as much a cause' of the tragedies as technical faults. NASA managers missed at least eight opportunities to evaluate damage to the shuttle after a piece of foam, the size of a suitcase, from Columbia's fuel tanks, struck a wing after its lift-off (Columbia Accident Investigation Board, Report Volume 1, August 2003, Limited First Printing by the Columbia Accident Investigation. Subsequent Printing and Distribution by the National Aeronautics and Space Administration and the Government Printing Office, Washington, DC).

Valuing employee diversity and individual differences is the theme of Chapter 6. We look at the meaning of diversity and its six primary dimensions: sex, age, race, ethnicity, disability and sexual orientation. In the past the justification for diversity was equal opportunities for all as demanded by social justice. The focus was on ending discrimination in the workplace, shattering glass ceilings and glass walls that keep talented women from advancing in their managerial careers. (It is persistent sex discrimination that results in only a handful of women (about 3 per cent) holding executive or inside director positions on the boards of FTSE 100 companies in the UK and the Fortune 500 companies in the USA.) Today's focus on increasing diversity in the workplace is supported by business reasons. We explore the business benefits of a diverse workplace, the so-called dividends of diversity. We also examine individual differences such as personality, using the Myers-Briggs Type Indicator®. We discuss perception and impression management.

We then explore, in Chapter 7, three very different types of leadership: transactional, transformational and discretionary. Transactional leadership is the application of managerial skills to deal with the day-to-day realities of working life. The manager runs meetings, enforces budgets, appraises staff, designs new projects and so on. We explain the 'situational leadership' model, developed by Paul Hershey and Ken Blanchard, that helps managers in the art of delegation. In contrast, transformational leadership is concerned with how a manager deals with change, through providing a vision for the future and persuading others to share that vision. In this transforming leadership role, managers empathise with employees to raise their awareness of issues, encouraging them to fulfil the leader's vision for the future. Transformational leaders tend to be charismatic, which prompts us to explain the concept of charisma and its opposite, narcissism. The chapter concludes with a discussion of discretionary leadership with its emphasis on choice and changing circumstances that dictate the most appropriate leadership style the different leaders in the organisation may adopt.

Part 2 of the book is entitled 'Making the Organisation Work for You'. It opens with Chapter 8, about communication and conflict, which describes the nature of communications, distinguishing between interpersonal and organisational. We examine a special kind of communication called negotiation, focusing on a principled approach to negotiations devised at the Harvard Law School. We move on to an exploration of conflict at work, where conflict is seen as a natural process arising from the divergence of interests of the stake-holders who form any enterprise.

Politics is sometimes given a bad name, but political behaviour is essential in organisa-tions. We dedicate Chapter 9 to it. We look at shared and unshared meaning as the basis of political behaviour and the ways in which differences and problems arise between people in organisations. Naturally this leads to a discussion of boss and subordinate behaviour, cen-tre versus subsidiary tension and rivalry among colleagues. We offer a number of practical approaches on how to gain political influence.

Power is the theme of Chapter 10. We look at prerequisites for the use of power before giving a detailed description of the seven levers of power: reward, role, personal, knowledge, network, information and corporate memory. We examine each of these levers in different contexts before going on to the topics of behavioural change and organisational change.

Appropriately, we take up the key topic of organisational design in Chapter 11. The shape of an organisation, its structure, influences how people behave. We look at organisational design from two perspectives, the traditional, vertically-integrated hierarchy and the resource-flexible perspective, involving, among other features, outsourcing. We speculate on the best shape of an organisation to meet its present market requirements and the business environ-ment in which it operates. We explore the redesign of organisations as a viable option.

A 'reality check' for this penultimate chapter features Andy Law, the founder and for-mer chief executive officer of St Luke's advertising agency. His words pull together many of the themes of this book:

> *Business is the world's employer and the difference it could make to the lives of so many mil-lions is immense. It can enrich, enliven, teach or entertain. But it rarely does. More often it does the opposite and somewhere along the line the world of business has become a byword for cyn-icism, greed, duplicity and manipulation. The recent US cases of Enron, WorldCom and others clearly reinforce this. But businesses are only collections of people and a mass transformation of attitude and behaviour would lead to super-fast change. Within the current, conventional organ-isational framework of business, only leaders can instigate this.*

> Andy Law (2003), *Experiment at work*, London: Profile Books, pp 19–20.

Perhaps the number one task for these new business leaders is sorting out the gover-nance issues confronting their organisations. Having examined varying design features, Chapter 12, the final chapter, takes an even broader perspective through exploration of the contrasting governance philosophies and practices that profoundly impact the structure and culture of our organisations. Questions such as: what is the ultimate purpose of organ-isations and what contribution do they make to society? and what are they supposed to achieve? are critical themes for examining the contrasting shareholder and stakeholder gov-ernance models. Such scrutiny helps explain why managers face tensions that are difficult to resolve. Nevertheless, ways through distinct challenges have to be found and it is up to the manager to be both innovative and sensitive in their approach to solving organisation-al and societal problems. As Chapter 1 introduces you, the reader, to the world of work through a microscopic analysis of the manager and his job, Chapter 12 takes a macroscop-ic view of the corporate forces that determine our lives today.

Andrew Kakabadse, John Bank and Susan Vinnicombe
Bedfordshire, 2004

Acknowledgements

We deal with management challenges on a daily basis as we interact with managers who are undertaking education programmes. All three authors of this book are faculty members at the Cranfield School of Management, a leading, university-based, international business school. We believe in the Latin axiom: 'We learn by teaching'. We have learned much from interacting with our MBA, MSc, PhD, DBA and executive management students. They come to us as graduate students with 6 to 12, or more, years experience as managers, working in business and industry in many countries. They have chosen to be managers throughout the greatest period of change ever encountered in the business world. We share their dilemmas and learn from their experiences. To them goes our first word of thanks. Likewise we are in debt to our fellow faculty members at Cranfield whose intellectual curiosity and corridor conversation are constant stimuli.

We also learn by engaging in management consultancy for clients and conducting research projects on a global scale. This experience brings a practitioner dimension, an international perspective and, we believe, a strong sense of reality to our writing. We are grateful to these many organisational clients who unwittingly have contributed their wisdom and insights to the book.

Our Cranfield colleagues include our secretaries, Jean Hutton, Sheena Darby and Karen Surrall, who worked hard to produce the manuscript for the book from over-written drafts. They chased references and kept us on schedule. Karen in particular, as Project Manager, drew on her reservoir of patience, energy and skill to complete the book. Thank you.

Rachel Campbell, Heather Peake and Mary Betts-Gray from the Management Information Resource Centre at Cranfield School of Management provided us, on short notice, with data used in the text and searched for facts we needed to verify. Many thanks.

Malcolm Stern, now a retired publisher from Gower, was involved in the first edition of *Working in Organisations* and sold the paperback rights to Penguin. His fondness for the title inspired us throughout the year it took to practically rewrite the entire book. He worked closely on the text as a freelance first editor and made a heroic effort to keep the language of the book as free of academic jargon as possible. We are grateful, Malcolm!

We are also thankful to Jo Burges, Director of Publishing Systems at Gower, and to Guy Loft, editor and Publishing Manager, whose penetrating comments have significantly improved this title.

Our final vote of thanks goes to you, the reader, for buying the book, which is a little like opting for the casual car pool in the Bay Area of San Francisco as 10 000 commuters to the city do daily. Anonymity is part of the transaction in the car pool and gives reciprocal benefits. (It is unlikely that you know us, the authors, or that we know you, the reader.) The driver of the car gets to use the fast lanes on the freeways that are reserved for car pool commuters and the passengers avoid the congestion of public transit in favour of the comfort of a private car. We all arrive swiftly and safely at our destination – an understanding of how managers work in organisations.

AK, JB and SV, London 2004

1 *People, Jobs and Relationships*

1 *Challenges*

Critical challenges facing managers

Managers must understand how to lead and why people at work behave the way they do in order to accomplish the goals of their organisation. Understanding organisational behaviour becomes a prerequisite of good management. But there is nothing static about this process because the science of management is forever evolving and the context in which managers work is in continual flux. People change too; they change their aspirations and expectations, their hopes and dreams, their lifestyles. All of these changes – environmental changes and personal changes – converge to produce particular challenges for managers today.

Five of the most critical challenges in the role of management at the start of the twenty-first century are:

- establishing business ethics,
- managing globalisation,
- dealing with downsizing,
- valuing employee diversity and
- exploiting new technology.

Although we can analyse each of these aspects of management separately they are joined, interlinked like Olympic circles. They share common causes and are affected by the convergence of economic, political, scientific, social and competitive factors.

BUSINESS ETHICS

Good management of organisations goes on all the time quietly unnoticed. It is usually the cases of bad management that grab the banner headlines and causes grief for tens of thousands, perhaps millions, of people. When Estelle Morris dramatically resigned from the Government as Education Secretary in October 2002 she cited among the reasons for her resignation her inability to handle both the 'modern media' and the 'strategic management of her department'. She took responsibility for the A level debacle that left thousands of English students confused about their grades and some with lower marks than they expected, thereby disqualifying some of them from the universities of their choice. She also accepted blame for the failure of her department to achieve its targets on literacy and numeracy tests.

On the global scene, TV images of Enron's top managers, the directors of Anderson's and WorldCom's chief executive officer, Bernard Ebbers, being led off by the authorities to face charges of serious mismanagement offered visual evidence of the urgent need for greater corporate responsibility and business ethics in America. An initial report ordered by the bankruptcy-court judge to 'examine wrongdoing, mismanagement and incompetence' at WorldCom found that a further restatement beyond the US$7.2 billion in fraudulent accounting may be required.

The consequences of bad management leading to the failure of these three colossal, global companies – one in energy, the second in accountancy and the third in telecommunications – have affected the lives of millions of employees and investors. They have also contributed to creating a crisis of confidence that has shaken financial markets around the world. In one swoop, the three discrete events demonstrate the need for principled management and codes of conduct and the interconnectivity of today's world. These and other examples of unethical behaviours in major organisations have shaken people's trust in aspects of the entire economic system. Trust is a belief that people – in this case, managers – will deliver on our positive expectations of them. When this trust is shattered, it is extremely difficult to have it restored.

Who is responsible for the ethical management of organisations? It is the primary responsibility of directors and senior managers who set the policies, establish values and develop the strategies to deliver goods and services to their customers. But everyone in the organisation shares collective responsibility for his or her part of the business and this often leads individual employees to play the role of whistle blower when they are otherwise powerless to stop unethical or incompetent practices within their own organisations. It was a unique event to have the *Time* Magazine 'Person of the Year' 2002 shared by three women whistle blowers, Cynthia Cooper (WorldCom), Coleen Rowley (FBI) and Sharon Watkins (Enron), who risked their careers to call attention to unacceptable practices in their organisations.

It is the scale of poor practices and unethical behaviour and the magnitude of the consequences of such unprincipled actions that have accelerated the importance of business ethics. The end does not justify the means and ethical leaders all over the world must sort out the Machiavellians in their organisations who think it does. As Tonge, Greer and Lawton (2003) have documented in their account of the Enron saga, it is easy for organisations to be hypocritical.

It is generally considered that the key determinant of ethical culture of an organisation is the example set by senior management. Enron is no exception. In principle Enron claimed to subscribe to a morally worthy set of values insofar as respect, integrity, communication and excellence are at the core of its mission statement. Respect is defined as 'We treat others as we would like to be treated ourselves. We do not tolerate abusive or disrespectful treatment. Ruthlessness, callousness and arrogance don't belong here.' As our account . . . demonstrates, these latter qualities belonged precisely there, along with bullying, manipulation and lying!

Tonge, A., Greer, L. and Lawton, A. (2003), 'The Enron Story, you can fool some of the people some of the time', *Business ethics: a European review*, **12**(1), January, p 10

Other examples of unethical behaviour from the Enron case include: a greed for profits, negligence at board level, an intricate corporate web of financial dealing, conflicts of interest, insider trading and other betrayals of shareholders' trust, false accounting, and the destruction of documents. It was a high-octane mix of these unethical behaviours that led to the downfall of both America's seventh largest corporations and one of the world's leading accountancy firms.

Survey data from the US indicates that the problem of poor adherence to business ethics may lie in part in the absence of personal ethics. In a survey by the organisation, 'Who's who among American high school students', a sample of these bright students were asked, 'Do you cheat to pass important exams? Do you fraudulently turn in papers? Do you plagiarise?' An alarming 80 per cent of the students said, 'Yes, isn't that what you have to do?' (Kidder, R. (1999), 'Global ethics and individual responsibility', *RSA Journal*, (1 April), pp 40–41).

Postgraduate students did not do much better. Donald McCabe (Kidder, 1999) at Rutgers University surveyed graduates who were going on to do postgraduate studies. He asked them, 'Did you cheat as an undergraduate so you could get into the graduate programme of your choice?' and found that 57 per cent of the students going to colleges of education answered, 'Yes, I cheated to get here.' The numbers rise: in law schools, 63 per cent; in medical schools, 68 per cent; in schools of engineering, 71 per cent; and with MBA students in business schools, 76 per cent.

REALITY CHECK

CHERNOBYL'S NEAR MELTDOWN WAS CAUSED BY A MORAL MELTDOWN

Did you know that:

- Chernobyl is the largest industrial accident in the world.
- 32 people were killed.
- The health of 3500–150 000 people was/is affected.
- It ruined large areas of fertile land in the Ukraine.
- The damaged reactor core has to be encased in concrete for thousands of years.
- Cracks in the encasing concrete have already appeared because of the freezes and thaws of the lake on which the reactor core sits.

The accident at Chernobyl was caused by two engineers working late into the night 'fiddling with reactor number four'. Their actions were officially referred to as 'conducting an unauthorised experiment'. They wanted to find out how long the turbine would freewheel if they took the power off it. To run the experiment the two engineers had to manually override six separate computerised alarm systems. Each system issued a warning to stop what they were doing because it was dangerous. But the engineers ignored each of the warnings to continue their experiment. They had to padlock valves in the open position to keep them from automatically shutting down in a failsafe mechanism. Their actions were 'deliberate and unconscionable'. 'Before there was a meltdown at the core of reactor number four there had already been a moral meltdown.'

Source: Kidder, R. (1999), 'Global ethics and individual responsibility', *RSA Journal,* (1 April), pp 39–40.

Whilst business ethics can be studied on their own as a special subject, it is perhaps better to highlight the ethical dimensions of various areas of business activity from accountancy to fair trading practices, from mergers and acquisitions to sourcing raw materials from developing countries. Business ethics examines the consequences of business decisions. As demonstrated in the Robert Maxwell case, decisions made by a rogue chief executive officer not only destroyed the company and cheated all of its stakeholders but robbed the Mirror Group's pension fund of over £400 million and thereby jeopardised the retirement of thousands of loyal employees. Societal ethics are about decisions that are both legal and morally acceptable to the wider community. Fundamental principles and values about the worth of life and respect for people are the bedrock of ethics. Since business is a type of society, it too needs commonly held norms, values and meanings. Businesses have an obligation to contribute to the communities they serve, rather than plunder them.

But when management is done extraordinarily well, it too attracts media attention and applause. The former mayor of New York City, Rudolph W. Giuliani, won global recognition, including an honorary knighthood from the Queen, for his leadership in handling the September 11th terrorists' attacks on the World Trade Center. His masterful demonstration of crisis management has given managers everywhere a positive case study of how to lead a team in extreme emergency situations. His was a visible leadership as he was leading from the front in the street with his staff and the rescue teams.

'Then the second plane hit', Giuliani recalled. 'All I saw was a big flash of fire. By that point we were at Canal Street, which marks the beginning of Manhattan's southern tip. Initially I thought it was the first tower experiencing a secondary explosion, but Patti got a call from Police Command saying the south tower, Tower 2, had also been struck, by what turned out to be the United Airlines Flight 175, a 767 en route from Boston to LA. This convinced us it was terrorism. We redoubled calls to the White House switchboard but cellphone service was now becoming difficult. We continued rushing south toward the scene. Driving by, I could see the stunned expression on every face as people stared up at the nightmare unfolding before their eyes.'

Giuliani, R.W. with Kurson, K. (2002), *Leadership*, London: Little, Brown, p 5.

At the time of the attack, Giuliani had been pulling together his ideas for a book on leadership based on his experiences of managing New York City. He is now an international consultant to other cities and companies that want to measure, benchmark and improve their performance.

Barbara Cassani, who is now chairperson for London's 2012 bid for the Olympic and Paralympic Games, had a bad experience with unethical behaviour on the part of her employer, British Airways, when she was a marketing manager for the airline stationed in the USA. Virgin Atlantic exposed its rival's unethical behaviour in a lawsuit that won extensive damages and embarrassed British Airways. A member of British Airways' sales team invented the scam in which they used Virgin's confidential computerised bookings, hacked from the computerised reservation system, run by British Airways, which other airlines fed into. British Airways used the data to try to poach passengers away from its rival airlines. As a middle-level marketing manager Barbara Cassani became enmeshed in the dirty tricks affair in a minor way. 'The statistics were being gained completely illegally, yes, completely,' she said, 'but I had no idea at the time they were being collected. If I had known they were being collected illegally I would have stopped the activity immediately. You do the best you can and when you find out that something is being done improperly you just stop it.' (Vinnicombe, S. and Bank, J. (2003), *Women with attitude: lessons for career management*, London: Routledge, pp 23–24).

GLOBALISATION

For good or ill, the actions of many managers have a global dimension that reflects the interconnectivity of today's world. 'Think globally, act locally!' has been the dictum for over three decades. Begun in the 1970s, globalisation is the 'phenomenon of the transition of industries whose competitive structure changes progressively from multinational to global. Industries such as telecommunications, processed food, personal care and retail are in the process of globalisation.' (Lasserre, P. (2003), *Global strategic management*, Basingstoke: Palgrave Macmillan). Examples of global companies include: Coca-Cola, Pepsi, McDonalds, Sony, Citibank, Asea Brown Bovery, Ford, Nissan, General Electric, Microsoft, Dell, BT and Benetton; any company that sells into the main markets of the world in an integrated and co-ordinated way. This is achieved through an organisational structure and integrated management processes that pull together various activities in different parts of the globe into an interdependent whole. For example, global manufacturing integration means that the sub-assembly parts of a Nissan car made in specialised factories across Europe, are cross-shipped from the different production sites to a final assembly plant in Wearside, England. Global product development, likewise, pulls together research and development units and marketing teams from across the world. Global products, like Microsoft Windows XP, are launched simultaneously on the world market.

Rosabeth Moss Kanter, a Harvard Professor with a global vision, writes about the urgency for managers to develop a global dimension to their local community enterprises.

Globalisation is surely one of the most powerful and pervasive influences on nations, businesses, workplaces, communities and lives. Information technology, communication, travel and trade that link the world are revolutionary in their impact. Global economic forces – and desire – are causing regimes to topple, enemies to bury the political hatchet in a common quest for foreign investment, large corporations to rethink their strategies and structures, governments to scale back their expenditure and privatise services, consumers to see the whole planet as their shopping mall and communities to compete with cities worldwide for prominence as international centres that attract the best companies and jobs.

Kanter, R.M. (1995), *World class: thriving locally in the global economy*,
New York: Simon & Schuster, p 11.

REALITY CHECK

CRISIS IN THE COFFEE MARKET

When Vietnam decided to turn its Central Highlands, 200 miles north of Ho Chi Minh City, into a coffee growing region with global aspirations, within a decade (1990–2000) the country's farmers planted more than a million acres of coffee in fertile, rainforest soil. Its annual production of coffee increased over tenfold from 84 000 tons to 950 000 tons making Vietnam the second largest producer of coffee in the world, pushing Colombia into third place. With Brazil's production pegged at 1.4 million tons, Vietnam produces more than a quarter of the world's supply. In 1997, a frost in Brazil decimated the crop and drove prices on the New York Commodities

Exchange above US$3 a pound. The Vietnamese coffee growers saw their profits rocket in the short-term. But in 1999 world coffee prices began a three-year free fall sinking in December 2001 to the lowest prices in a century at 42 US cents a pound, a price that did not cover the cost of production. The quality of coffee suffered; many of the world's 25 million coffee growers were financially damaged and the US Agency for International Development estimated that at least 600 000 coffee workers lost their jobs in Africa, Central and South America and Southeast Asia.

Source: Stein, N. (2002), 'Crisis in a coffee cup', *Fortune*, (16 December), p 24.

It is the sweeping scope of globalisation, with its social, political, economic and environmental consequences that makes it a target for critics. These critics argue that globalisation increases the North–South divide, widening the gap between rich and poor people. Global companies, in the critics' eyes, are allowed to exploit the developing nations and are guilty of damaging the environment through global warming and pollution. They use child labour, corrupt politicians with their bribes, disregard human rights and use their power and market dominance to the disadvantage of their global suppliers, customers and competitors. Anita Roddick OBE, founder of The Body Shop, with nearly 2000 outlets worldwide, is both an advocate of social responsibility for business and an opponent of the abuses of globalisation. In her third book, *Take it personally: how globalisation affects you and powerful ways to challenge it* (2001, HarperCollins, London), she cites the evils of globalisation and action points for campaigners. 'I'm probably one of the few international retailers to be baton-charged and tear-gassed by American policemen during the World Trade meeting in Seattle in November 1999,' she said (Vinnicombe, S. and Bank, J. (2003), *Women with attitude: lessons for career management*, London: Routledge, p 160).

Anita Roddick's message, however, is not always that dramatic and strident. 'Beautiful Business', a speech calling for corporate leadership founded on social and political action, delivered to the Royal Society of Arts (RSA) on 29 March 2000, was published by the *RSA Journal* on 4 April. In her speech she said, 'Leaders in world business are the first true global citizens. We have worldwide capability and responsibility. Our domains transcend national boundaries. Our decisions affect not just economies but societies; not just the direct concerns of business, but world problems of poverty, environment and security.' ('Beautiful Business', a speech calling for corporate leadership founded on social and political action, delivered to the RSA on 29 March 2000, published by the *RSA Journal* on 4 April (2000).

'Open up a typical management book and you will find it hard to avoid words like leadership, team-building, company culture or customer service,' she said. 'However, you will be lucky to find words like community, social justice, human rights, dignity, love or spirituality – the emerging language of business.' (Vinnicombe, S. and Bank, J. (2003), *Women with attitude: lessons for career management*, London: Routledge, p 160).

Eight hundred workers at Dyson Technology in Malmesbury, Wiltshire, were made redundant as the assembly plant for James Dyson's bagless vacuum cleaners was shifted to Malaysia where wages are much lower. The UK site is still used to make Dyson washing machines. James Dyson maintained that he needed the lower labour costs to be able to market his vacuum cleaner in America. Dyson, whose company is 100 per cent owned by Dyson and family trusts, has been outspoken in defending British design and manufacturing (Dyson, J. (1997), *Against the odds, an autobiography*, London: Orion Business Books).

It took 20 years, about 5000 prototypes and a series of setbacks before finding success with his colourful, smartly designed, high-tech vacuum cleaners that have captured over half of the UK market. Even then he had a number of legal battles with other vacuum cleaner companies over his advertising of the bagless product and had to defend, in court, his patents of the centrifugal force process used to separate dirt from air as other major vacuum cleaner manufactures infringed his patents with their 'me-too' models.

Today he is listed among the top 100 richest people in the country, according to the *Sunday Times* Magazine Rich List 2003. Despite his success and wealth, he has not been able to resist the forceful impact of globalisation.

Naomi Klein, (2002) an award-winning journalist from Toronto, has become one of the strongest voices putting the case against globalisation. Since the publication of *No logo: taking aim at the brand bullies*, she has opposed the excesses of global companies from a worldwide platform. An anti-corporation activist, she has been directly involved in the major demonstrations opposing globalisation's excesses. Klein's major articles and speeches have been published in *Fences and windows* (2002). She writes:

Opponents of the World Trade Organization – even many who call themselves anarchists – are outraged about a lack of rules being applied to corporations, as well as the flagrant double standards in the application of existing rules in rich and poor countries . . . They came to Seattle because they found out that World Trade Organization tribunals were overturning environmental laws protecting endangered species because the laws, apparently, were unfair trade barriers. Or they learned that France's decision to ban hormone-laced beef was deemed by the World Trade Organization to be unacceptable interference with the free market. What is on trial in Seattle is not trade or globalisation but the global attack on the right of citizens to set rules that protect people and the planet.

Klein, N. (2002) *Fences and windows: dispatches from the front lines of the globalization debate*, London: Flamingo, HarperCollins, p 5.

Surprisingly the winner of the Nobel Prize for Economics 2001, Joseph Stiglitz, also puts the case against globalisation as it is practised by many in words similar to the activist Klein. 'Globalization today is not working for many of the world's poor. It is not working for much of the environment. It is not working for the stability of the global economy. The transition from communism to a market economy has been so badly managed that, with the exception of China, Vietnam and a few Eastern European countries, poverty has soared as incomes have plummeted,' Stiglitz wrote (Stiglitz, J. (2002), *Globalisation and its discontents*, London: Penguin, p 214). In addition to the Nobel Prize, his credentials include having been the chief economist at the World Bank and chairman of former President Clinton's Council of Economic Advisors. He is currently Professor of Finance and Economics at Columbia University.

He argues that, 'It is the trade unionists, students, environmentalists and ordinary citizens marching in the streets of Prague, Seattle, Washington and Genoa who have put the need for reform on the agenda of the developed world.' But as one would expect of a serious economist, Professor Stiglitz does not take a pro-globalisation or anti-globalisation position. Instead he analyses the complex economic realities in terms of what self-regulation of market forces should be allowed and what interventions governments must make. His solutions are tough-minded ones that involve substantial shifts of power between the developed and developing nations. 'To some there is an easy answer: abandon globalisation. That is neither feasible nor desirable ... Globalisation has brought huge benefits – East Asia's success was based on globalisation, especially on the opportunities for trade and increased access to markets and technology. Globalisation has brought better health, as well as an active global civil society fighting for more democracy and greater social justice. The problem is not with globalisation, but with how it has been managed.' (p 214.) As Stiglitz explained: 'We are a global community, and like all communities have to follow some rules so that we can live together. These rules must be – and must be seen to be – fair and just, must pay due attention to the poor as well as the powerful, must reflect a basic sense of decency and social justice. In today's world, those rules have to be arrived at through democratic processes; the rules under which the governing bodies and authorities work must ensure that they will heed and respond to the desires and needs of all those affected by policies and decisions made in distant places' (p. xv).

Drawing on his own experience of the major economic events, Professor Stiglitz explained the Pacific Rim financial crisis. 'When the Thai baht collapsed on July 2, 1997, no one knew that this was the beginning of the greatest economic crisis since the Great Depression – one that would spread from Asia to Russia and Latin America and threaten the entire world. For ten years the baht had traded at around 25 to the US dollar; then overnight it fell by about 25%. Currency speculation spread and hit Malaysia, Korea, the Philippines and Indonesia. By the end of the year what had started as an exchange rate disaster threatened to take down many of the region's banks, stock markets and even entire economies. The crisis is over now, but countries such as Indonesia will feel its effects for years. Unfortunately, the IMF [International Monetary Fund] policies imposed during this tumultuous time worsened the situation' (p 89).

The debate about globalisation will continue with strong arguments for and against. At the heart of the debate lies the fundamental questions of inequalities and unfair rules governing trade. These issues were highlighted by a half-page banner headline in Britain's *The Independent* when world leaders opened a summit to discuss poverty – 'We do our best for the world's poor. Perhaps our aid budgets are not as large as they could be, but we do what we can. Wrong! Through the complex web of taxes, tariffs and quotas that governs trade, we take far more from the poor than we give them. For every US dollar we give in aid, we take two through unfair trade. Unfair trade costs the world's poor US$100 billion a year. In September 2003, ministers from around the world begin a five-day World Trade Organization meeting in Cancun, Mexico. There are terrible inequities that need to be addressed if the 2.7 billion people in the world who live on less than two US dollars a day are to be enabled to stand on their own feet' (*The Independent*, 10 September 2003).

The collapse of the Cuncan Round of talks, engineered by some two dozen developing countries, may have been a self-inflicted wound to the nations. Nihal Kaneira observed: 'With no new WTO pact now in sight, most of the countries in the Gulf and Middle East as well as Asia and Africa will now have to wait indefinitely to gain access to the lucrative US market for their farm products and industrial goods, like readymade clothes' (*Financial Times*, 20 September 2003).

DOWNSIZING

Developments in terms of international competition, economic deregulation, trade agreements and industrial restructuring have irrevocably altered the experience of doing business for most managers. It will never be the same. Just one consequence for managers is the now common practice of regular downsizing of their organisations. Motorola, a company that downsized 22 000 employees between December 2000 and May 2001, then required each of its remaining 17 000 US employees to take an average of a mandatory two weeks paid or unpaid holiday before the end of the second quarter of 2001. Another US firm, Lucent Technologies, got rid of 54 000 employees in the years 2001–2003 at an average cost of US$78 000 for each person. Ericsson, the Swedish maker of telecommunications equipment, during the same two-year period, cut its workforce from 45 000 to about 30 000 due to falling sales. Worldwide, Ericsson has downsized from a peak of 107 000 in early 2001 to less than 65 000 in early 2003. The French telecom-equipment maker Alcatel SA cut its workforce from 110 000 to 77 000 in two years by using an early retirement ploy and by selling operations to other companies. Downsizing has been particularly prevalent amongst technology companies over the last three years. However, downsizing impacts all enterprises that seek competitive gain through cost advantage.

Downsizing – begun in the mid-1980s as a one-off, traumatic event to drastically cut costs to help organisations survive fierce global competition or sharp declines in their business – has now become a permanent feature on the world's economic landscape. There is a powerful inter-relationship between the three main drivers of downsizing – global competitive pressure, new technology and the demands of customer requirements, including database-driven marketing and other customer-focused activities. Certain industries, like banking, financial services and telecommunications, that were well-protected businesses in the past, are experiencing wave after wave of downsizing with its unsettling consequences for directors, senior managers and employees alike. Other industries, such as steel, shipbuilding and some sectors of manufacturing, which have experienced structural unemployment, are no strangers to systematic downsizing. Corus, the UK steel company, announced the closure of another of its major steel-making plants in March 2003, the second in a few months, leaving only two plants still operating, with job losses in the thousands. Mergers across the financial, car manufacturing and chemical sectors have resulted in job losses from their global operations. The European Aeronautic Defence and Space Company downsized by 1600 jobs in 2002 and at the start of 2003 added another 1700 redundancies to the toll.

The statistics confirm the ubiquitous use of downsizing as a required method of sustaining competitiveness. In the UK, for example, between 1991 and 1995, workforce reductions in companies such as Rolls-Royce, British Telecom (BT) and British Petroleum (BP) are estimated to have been between 34 and 43.6 per cent. In the USA, the first half of 1990 saw the loss of 3.1 million jobs as a result of downsizing; the total figure since 1979 is estimated at 43 million. AT&T at the start of 1990 employed 945 000 people, but by March 2000 the number had shrunk to 140 000.

The major reason for downsizing is to save money. Employees' costs make up between 30 and 80 per cent of total business costs, depending on the industry (Cascio, 1993). But there are other reasons for downsizing. Technological advancements leading to productivity increases, more efficient product designs and the better quality of materials have all increased sales output per hour. Unless companies downsize in the face of these productivity improvements, they lose their competitive edge.

The benefits that downsizing brings to companies include making companies leaner and fitter, an increase in shareholder value, lower overheads, less bureaucracy, swifter decision-making and increased productivity. Various surveys confirm productivity rises. The Cranfield survey pointed to improvements in quality, customer service and more willingness in risk-taking (Sahdev and Vinnicombe, 1998). Within BT, where the workforce was slashed from 265 000 to 127 000 within eight years, downsizing is reported to have improved employees' external focus and a positive shift from the organisation to natural work teams (Doherty, Bank and Vinnicombe, 1996).

Of course, the positive aspects of downsizing have to be weighed against the negative aspects of the technique. Stephen Roach, the US economist credited with initiating downsizing as a management technique, gave warning about the way downsizing was being handled in many organisations. He claimed it was being misused. At the extreme, by excessive downsizing companies can cause 'organisational anorexia', where companies, like young people with the slimming disease anorexia, go too far with downsizing, therefore depleting their organisation of the necessary experience, skills, competencies and knowledge required for survival.

Then there are the survivors – those employees who remain in their organisations after downsizing. Their condition has a number of shared characteristics that give rise to the psychological phenomenon known as the 'survivor syndrome'. Often these employees who remain are shattered by the experience and left with no trust in their managers and too much work to do, as workloads double and triple in some cases. The survivors experience added stress. Trust can disappear, taking commitment with it and sending motivation in a downward spiral.

One of the main causes of the survivor syndrome is that the people left in the company feel betrayed. They feel that the company has torn up the psychological contract it has with each employee. By the psychological contract we mean that unwritten, voluntary, subjective, informal agreement between the employee and the employer about their expectations at work. When employers radically change the conditions of the contract unilaterally as in downsizing, surviving employees can view it as a violation of the contract. As such it leaves them angry and mistrustful of the organisation. They are often saddened by the loss of so many colleagues at work, some of whom had become friends, and they are left uncertain and anxious about their own future in the downsized organisation. They are also usually left with much bigger jobs to handle.

Managing a downsizing is a challenge for most managers. They need to communicate to everyone – the leavers and the survivors – the reasons for the downsizing (breaking the news to their employees before they hear it on the media or on the grapevine), the fairness of the redundancy selection procedures and the compensation awarded to the leavers. Moreover managers need to develop strategies for creating a resilient workforce. They need to shift the energies of the survivors away from the negative, draining, emotional reactions to seeing the change as a challenge, an opportunity for growth and personal gain.

The task of achieving positive outcomes from downsizing for every manager may differ. But most cases will include the manager first understanding thoroughly the context of downsizings and their underlying causes, to seek to mitigate the most damaging effects of it for both leavers and survivors by communicating clearly the rationale behind the downsizing. Building trust and taking positive measures to create a resilient workforce then becomes a priority for managers, employees and their representatives.

EMPLOYEE DIVERSITY

Globalisation highlights the fourth major change in the manager's world – the need to manage diversity actively. (Chapter 6 is devoted entirely to this topic, so the challenge will be dealt with briefly here.) Only part of this change can be put down to globalisation. The argument links diversity with inclusiveness and greater equality in sharing out the benefits of globalisation and the control of resources and the sprawling companies capable of exploiting the resources.

The challenge of employee diversity has been thrust upon organisations by the convergence of factors other than increased globalisation. These include demographic changes, particularly negative population growth. The traditional pool of labour in the West is shrinking and changing in composition. For not much longer will white, Anglo Saxon males dominate in the workforces of the USA or the UK. In the USA, by 2008, women are expected to make up 48 per cent of the US workforce. Minority groups like Hispanics (13 per cent by 2008) and Asians (5 per cent by 2008) are entering the mainstream labour force in increasing numbers (The source for all of these predictions is found in 'Charting the projections: 1998–2008', *Occupational Outlook Quarterly*, (Winter, 2002).

The so-called 'war for talent' is adding to the momentum for change in the racial, ethnic and sex makeup of tomorrow's workforce. Any organisation serious about its future in an increasingly global and competitive marketplace will survive only if it can attract employees with the skills and talents in rare supply. To do so these organisations will have to establish track records for dealing positively with employee diversity. They will have to demonstrate, in action, that senior positions and boardroom seats are open to women, people of colour and people with different ethnicity. For a company legitimately to claim to be global and diverse, its managerial profile will have to be different from one English firm whose middle and senior managers were all white, males, public school educated, with military backgrounds and a proclivity to play golf.

For example, in 2003 British hospitals solved the problem of a shortage of nurses by recruiting on a global basis. One NHS hospital in London tabulated that it has nurses from 49 different countries. Despite a ban on the practice imposed in 2001, Britain is continuing to poach skilled medical staff from the poorest nations in the world. To shore up the NHS, 3472 nurses from countries on the 'banned' list were registered in the UK, according to the Nursing & Midwifery Council (2002).

The business case for increasing employee diversity goes beyond the recruitment issues and the search for new talent, although this is a source of competitive advantage. It comprises other benefits of a diverse workforce such as: better decision making from heterogeneous teams, more creativity from diverse perspectives and less conformity to norms of the past, richer marketing inputs from diverse employees, such as the woman director on Nike's board who suggested the creation of a line of running shoes designed especially for women. Ethnic employees likewise have marketing inputs rooted in their own cultures than can help create new products and market existing ones. Greater system flexibility will result from managing diversity in that the system will become less determined, less standardised and more fluid.

In the West, the workforce is ageing and people are being told to expect to work longer. In the US by 2008, a full 40 per cent of the labour force will be older than 45. (It was 33 per cent in 1998.)

Across the spectrum of employees there has been a remarkable change in employees' expectations from work and career. When Virgin Airlines was faced with the first downsizing and layoffs in its history, a meeting of the employees revealed that many of Virgin's thrusting, young employees voluntarily welcomed time off from work to travel, making compulsory redundancies unnecessary. A few years later, however, with its airline business suffering the downturn in air travel, Virgin made 1200 employees redundant to offset losses.

Lifestyle changes mean that people often frame their lives very differently from their parents. Under the new psychological contract at work, people may appear less loyal to their organisations, but they are simply responding to the 'new deal' at work, which encourages them to assess continually how their skills fit what organisations need. They have little expectation of lifetime employment or careers in one company that were traditionally on offer a few decades ago, but have been withdrawn unilaterally by many organisations. Flexible portfolios, including movable pensions, have made it easier for them to move from one organisation to another to acquire new experience and competencies or to take a break from work for travel, career changes or more formal education, like a Master of Business Administration.

Flexible working is a growing demand to fit jobs into a broader work/life balance. With dual-career couples, there is more effort to share child-rearing responsibilities more evenly. Employees want challenging work that fulfils their needs for participation and involvement. Employees want empowerment on the job to make work more meaningful and satisfying. They want to contribute their unique talents to organisations that acknowledge their contribution. Their expectations need to be managed by more senior employees, who themselves may have changing aspirations and similar wants and values.

NEW TECHNOLOGY

The exploitation of new technology is the fifth critical area of dramatic change affecting managers today. J.F. Rayport, an associate professor at Harvard University, said:

> *The success of e-commerce business will hinge largely on the art of management even as it is enabled by the science of technology.*

Rayport, J.F. (1999), 'The truth about internet business models', *Strategy and Business*, **16**, p 5.

There are two major aspects of the impact of new technology as it affects the manager today. One is the use of information technology to transform the manager's way of working in terms of producing traditional products and services and dealing with the processes used to administer these businesses. This development has been underway since the early 1970s. The second is the manager's growing involvement in e-commerce business itself. E-business began in earnest and flourished wildly from 1995 to 2000, before hitting the buffers as the dot.com bubble burst. It is now on course again for spectacular growth worldwide and is labelled the 'new economy' to contrast it with the traditional economy that is referred to as 'the bricks and mortar economy'. Broadband capabilities, connectivity, standard languages (html, xml), wireless communication and portability have all come together to give the world the digital age and its most visible embodiment – the internet or the World Wide Web (WWW) or simply, the 'web'. This aspect of new technology is having an astonishing impact on how managers do business. E-commerce is predicted to total US$12.8 trillion by 2006.

Henry Mintzberg's early work identified the roles of the manager as that of: interpersonal role, decision-making role and informational role (Mintzberg, H. (1975), 'The manager's job: folklore and fact', *Harvard Business Review*, **53**(4), p 49). It was not surprising that the world of the manager would be turned upside down with the information technology explosion. Its impact on the manager's informational and decision-making roles is profound. In many cases, the widespread use of new technology completely eliminated the role of the manager as the conduit of information. De-layering added to the decimation of middle management as some went from 27 levels in a managerial hierarchy to only four levels.

Managers have always had a need for information, but it is surprising to see how in the past they settled for imperfect information. Managers assumed that they had to get on with the absence of timely information. No one has worked harder to correct this misconception than Bill Gates. He continues to think, talk, write and produce software so kindly in the manager's interest that one almost forgets he is selling. 'As I was preparing my speech for our first chief executive officer summit in the spring of 1997,' Gates wrote, 'I was pondering how the digital age would fundamentally alter business. I wanted to go beyond a speech on the dazzling technology advances and address questions that business leaders wrestle with all the time. How can technology help you run your business better? How will technology transform business? How can technology help make you a winner five or ten years from now? If the 1980s were about quality and the 1990s were about re-engineering, then the 2000s will be about velocity. About how quickly the nature of business will change. About how quickly business itself will be transacted. About how information accesses will alter the lifestyle of consumers and their expectations of business' (Gates, B. (1999), *Business @ the speed of thought: using a digital nervous system*, Harmondsworth: Penguin Books, pp xiii–iv).

As Bill Gates then pointed out, 'People have lived for so long without information at their fingertips that they don't realize what they're missing. One of the goals of my speech to the chief executive officers was to raise their expectations. I wanted them to be appalled by how little they got in the way of actionable information from their current IT investments. I wanted chief executive officers to demand a flow of information that would give them quick, tangible knowledge about what was really happening with their customers.'

Even companies that have made significant investments in information technology are not getting the results that they could. What's interesting is that the gap is not the result of a lack of technology spending. In fact, most companies have invested in the basic building blocks: PCs for productivity applications; networks and electronic mail (e-mail) for communications; basic business applications. The typical company has made 80 per cent of the investment in the technology that can give it a healthy flow of information, yet is typically getting only 20 per cent of the benefits that are now possible. The gap between what companies are spending and what they're getting stems from the combination of not understanding what is possible and not seeing the potential when you use technology to move the right information quickly to everyone in the company.

The job that most companies are doing with information today would have been fine several years ago. Getting rich information was prohibitively expensive, and the tools for analysing and disseminating it weren't available in the l980s and the early 1990s. But here on the edge of the twenty-first century, the tools and connectivity of the digital age now give us a way to easily obtain, share and act on information in new and remarkable ways.

Gates, B. (1999), *Business @ the speed of thought: using a digital nervous system*,
Harmondsworth: Penguin Books, p xiv.

REALITY CHECK

ROOTS: THE INVENTION OF SILICON VALLEY

The beginning of the new technology revolution can be traced to 1947 when William Shockley invented the transistor at Bell Telephone Laboratories in New Jersey. The US Army wanted to exploit this new invention for weapons and space exploration, but Shockley's early germanium transistor ceased to operate when it heated up. The Army gave Shockley US$15 million to invent a better transistor for the demands of war and space.

He left Bell in 1955 and chose eight of the country's top scientists for the research project that he based at Stanford University in California, his home state. But after two years the group of scientists found Shockley impossible to work with. (Lest anyone doubt the importance of leadership style and its role in teamworking, the consequences for Shockley were disastrous.) They pushed him out of the group but kept together under their new leader, Robert

Noyce. They found a new sponsor, the Fairchild Camera Company, and moved their research operation to bean fields at the south end of the San Francisco Bay area. There this team invented the silicon chip. Shockley received a Nobel Prize for his invention, although he was excluded from the discovery of the silicon chip. Under Robert Noyce's leadership, the team immediately set out to exploit their invention. They set up a string of high-tech companies for the manufacture of silicon chips for microprocessors that became know as the Silicon Valley, making them and some of their employees multimillionaires.

Source: Larsen, J.K. and Rogers, E.M. (1984), *Silicon Valley fever: growth of high-technology culture*, London: George Allen and Unwin, pp 37–38.

The advent of the microprocessor was heralded by some as the most important invention of all time. The impact of information technology was predicted to be greater than any other technological developments including the invention of steam power, the telephone and electricity itself. Within a decade the availability of cheap computer power had begun to transform the modern world. From banks to supermarkets, schools to hospitals, offices to factories, cars to aeroplanes, health aids to children's games, entertainment rides to weapons of mass destruction, telecommunications to space exploration – practically anything we could think of could be improved by microprocessors and computers. Suddenly managers had both computer-aided administration devices and computer-aided manufacturing devices to enhance the speed and efficiency of their work. Later the information superhighway would add a worldwide, new dimension to the digital revolution.

In the last 25 years most of the population in general, and managers in particular, have become computer-literate – accustomed to working with computers. They now have laptops and personal computers (PCs) putting more information power at their fingertips than the massive mainframe computers of the past could generate. The impact on the administration side of business alone has been astonishing. Many managers no longer have any need for secretaries. Today, managers book their business flights online, make rental car and hotel reservations online, and use computers in their cars to plan cost-effective routes. They input their requirements for meetings directly to their PCs or laptops, which have software programs that automatically check the availability of their colleagues for the meetings. Letter writing and memos have been supplanted by instant e-mail. They have broadband access to the internet with its unlimited sources for reference, discussions, debates or global shopping. They conduct e-management activities – planning and controlling, data-base-sharing, recruiting, training, other Human Resources admin, discuss issues with virtual teams, and conduct commercial transactions such as B2B (Business to Business) buying and selling deals online. They also use the Web for e-partnering, benchmarking, information-sharing, research and development, dealing with political issues and other strategic matters with their partners. As if state-of-the-art laptops are not portable enough for managers on the move, the new third generation of mobile phones, in addition to video calling and the luxury of photo messaging, will put internet access in the manager's pocket or handbag.

The Web has given rise to the dot.com companies phenomena. These so-called 'pure players' are companies that have been created specifically to facilitate Web transactions. Their products and services help organise transactions, serve as intermediaries and provide software platforms. The e-commerce companies facilitate sales that can be B2C (Business to Consumer), B2B (Business to Business) or C2C (Customer to Customer). The intermediaries provide tools for transactions such as e-payment, security, search engines (such as Google™, Yahoo!®, or AltaVista™), domain names and browsers such as Internet Explorer.

REALITY CHECK

AMAZON.COM: 'EARTH'S BIGGEST SELECTION'

Jeff Bezos left his job as a successful Wall Street investor and borrowed money from his parents to found Amazon.com in 1995. He started up as a small online bookseller, giving himself a 30 per cent chance of success. Just eight years later he is at the head of the most successful cyberspace business in the world with daily sales of books and other merchandise of more than US$3 million. Using customer-relationship technology Amazon.com treats customers as individuals, and tailors offerings to meet their unique profiles. The messages are put personally in the particular custom interest. As in, 'People who have bought Nadezhda Mandelstam's *Hope against hope* have also bought these three Russian poets. Would you like to add them to your shopping basket, as new or used books?'

His vision for Amazon.com is built on his own identification of future trends. 'Three such trends are especially noteworthy.

• Whether a company's base of operations is strictly in its home country or across the globe, connecting people is the key to building the synergies necessary for success.

• Consumers are not a homogenous group; to market a product effectively, a company must target customers based on their multiple characteristics, including their race, age and ethnicity.

• Technology will continue to have an enormous impact on business.' (Stroh, L.K., Northcraft, G.B. and Neale, M.A. (Eds) (2001) *Organizational behaviour: a management challenge* 3rd ed., Mahwah, New Jersey: Lawrence Erlbaum Associates, p 7).

He keeps a high profile in the dot.com company and the high visibility led to his being *Time* Magazine's Person of the Year. Millions of Amazon's global customers are kept in touch with the founder and chief executive officer of the company by personalised e-mails in which Jeff Bezos discusses his efforts to improve customer service. His letter in February 2003, for example, announced that the free Super Saver Delivery was now permanent. He wrote: 'For more than a year, we've been testing free Super Saver Delivery in the United States. We introduced it as a long-term test because we weren't sure we could afford it. In the process, we learnt two things: firstly, it is definitely expensive for us (it cost us more than US$30 million over the past three months alone!) and secondly, customers love it.' Bezos' letter then went on to extend the free mailing service to his UK customers on purchases over £39.

'I think the main thing that has differentiated Amazon.com from conventional retailers, and it's been this way since the very first day, is its obsessive-compulsive focus on the end-to-end customer experience.'

Bezos explained. 'It includes having the right products, the right selection and low prices' (Keefe, C. (2003), Jeff Bezos, founder and CEO, Amazon.com *Dealerscope,* 45(1), p 76).

Instead of taking years to get going as they expected, Amazon.com had served customers in all 50 States and 45 other countries within the first 30 days of operation. Bezos' original plan was for selling only books. But he discovered by asking his customers what other products they wanted – besides the 3 million active books in print and readily available from Amazon.com – that they were also interested in music and films, and electronics, computer and networking products.

'In electronics today we are approaching 100 000 items in our electronics selection,' Bezos said. 'We're going to keep working on that. What we have been doing for the last seven years has worked well for us, and there's really no reason to change it' (Keefe, 2003). Far from changing the formula, he has just added sales through

the website of clothing from a range of retailers including Gap and Eddie Bauer. 'Customers are now shopping at Amazon.com as much for our lower prices as for our selection and convenience,' Bezos said, announcing that the addition of clothing had been its most successful new business ever. (Buckley, N. (2003) 'Amazon reports higher profits than expected.' *The Financial Times Companies & Finance The Americans Edn,* (24 Jan))

Amazon's reduced profits for 2002 reflected Bezos's free delivery on orders in the USA over US$25, but the company continued to grow in sales by 28 per cent from US$1.12 billion to 1.43 billion, above analysts' expectations (Buckley, 2003). Bezos is surprised by the speed of growth. 'It's been astonishingly fast growth, quicker than any sane human being would have predicted,' he said. 'Seven years ago the internet was a pretty small place and we had ten employees and today we have 8000. Nobody would have predicted that' (Hunt, B. (2002) 'Getting bigger even faster: view from the top: Jeff Bezos of Amazon.' *The Financial Times FT Report//FTIT//Asian IT Edn,* (4 Dec)). Bezos is totally dedicated to keeping Amazon.com in pole position in an online industry that is expanding. 'In the last 12 months I think we had 27 million people purchase from us. That's a big number but it's small compared to the number of people there are,' he says (Hunt, 2002). Online shopping accounts for up to 23 per cent of sales of books, music, videos, electronics, computers and toys. '"Long term you're going to have high-band wireless connectivity everywhere you go or almost everywhere. And you'll have a great little device that you can keep in your pocket that has a screen that's actually big enough to do something and a better input device," he says. And no doubt such devices will be available at an Amazon portal near you.'

Managing in the new world order

Managers in particular and people in general are facing an extraordinary moment of promise of the new world order with unrivalled prosperity in the offing. Technology has already delivered on its first promises to create wealth and improve services and to make work more efficient and enjoyable. In the developed world people will soon have the opportunity to be online all the time while working in offices, riding in cars or trains, walking city streets or country lanes, or in the comfort of their homes. People in the developing nations will also be able to join in the online experiences although with perhaps only a fraction of the buying power of the richer global shoppers. The entertainment and news, products and services, personal needs and political agendas that will keep people online all the time will need carefully managing from a new generation of managers used to the tools and techniques of e-business.

E-business has already changed the shape of selling, making it faceless. Even hugely expensive items that a short while ago would have required relationship-building, face-to-face selling are now sold on the Web. For example, radiologists and doctors, who use General Electric's computed tomography scanner and magnetic resonance imaging machines, are able to go to the Web to try out the General Electric software that improves the machines' efficiency on spinal examinations.

If they like the new upgrade to these diagnostic machines, they can buy it on the Web for US$65 000 without seeing or speaking to or having any physical contact with a salesperson. Sixty five per cent of them do (Colvin, G. (2001), 'Shaking hands on the web', *Fortune European Edition*, **25**(14 May)).

The goals of Amazon.com, TimeWarner and Yahoo!® are similar: creating a customer experience superior to anything their competitors can create. Somehow a selling relationship with no human contact – for their millions of online customers – is experienced as a great relationship. But the chief executive officers behind these three major online companies – Jeff Bezos, Steve Case and Jerry Yang – are among the first e-managers to survive the first internet firm shakeout. Oddly enough when asked about 'the source of their competitive advantage', they talk more about creating that customer experience than they do about technology (Colvin, 2001). Each of these chief executive officers has his team to lead, his staff to motivate, his business strategies to develop, his conflicts with the stakeholders to sort out, his risks to take. The stakes in the global management game could not be much higher.

REALITY CHECK

BILL GATES' GLOBAL VISION FOR MICROSOFT

Competitive advantage is one of the benefits of globalisation – to dominate world markets, to have a global vision at the beginning and to carry it through, as Bill Gates has done with Microsoft. As he said: 'People often ask me to explain Microsoft's success.

'They want to know the secret of getting from a two-man, shoestring operation to a company with more than 21 000 employees and more than US$8 billion a year in sales. Of course, there is no simple answer, and luck has played a role, but I think the most important element was our original vision.'

His vision was of the ubiquitous power of cheap computers and the new software that would be needed to exploit it. 'Our initial insight made everything else easier. We were in the right place at the right time. We got there first, and our early success gave us the chance to hire more and more smart people. We built a worldwide sales force and used the revenue it generated to fund new products. But from the beginning, we set off down a road that was headed in the right direction.'

Source: Bill Gates (1996), *The road ahead*, London: Penguin Books.

Summary

Five major challenges confront managers today. They are:

- developing business ethics,
- managing globalisation,
- dealing with downsizing,
- valuing employee diversity and
- exploiting new technology.

DEVELOPING BUSINESS ETHICS

Essential for any manager. Although it is the direct responsibility of the chief executive officer, directors and senior managers of companies who set the policies, determine the values and develop the strategies to deliver goods and services to their customers, they have the primary duty to establish ethical policies and practices in their organisations. But everyone should feel responsible for carrying out ethical behaviours at his or her level.

High profile failures in ethical standards by Enron, Anderson's and WorldCom and other companies have alerted people everywhere to the scale and far-flung consequences of unethical behaviour in modern corporations. All the stakeholders suffer losses as a result of unethical practices. In all three notorious cases managers at many levels engaged in fraudulent activities and it was left to whistle blowers to alert the public to the corporations' widespread deceptions. *Time* Magazine's Person of the Year was shared for 2002 by three women whistle blowers.

A lack of personal ethics is a possible contributing cause in the general failure to adhere to business ethics. Research students in the USA revealed a lack of personal ethics with regard to cheating in their programmes of studies. Postgraduate business students had the worst results. The greatest industrial accident in history – the near meltdown at the nuclear power plant in Chernobyl – was due to unethical behaviour on the part of two engineers who recklessly over-rode a half dozen safety systems to conduct an unofficial experiment that directly caused the accident.

Perhaps the best advice for dealing with ethically doubtful practices comes from Barbara Cassani, who when her marketing team at British Airways got caught up with dirty tricks that took unfair advantage of competitor airlines, said: 'You do the best you can and when you find out that something is being done improperly, you just stop it.'

MANAGING GLOBALISATION

Since the 1970s globalisation has been gathering momentum. It is the process of transition of industries where competitive structure changes progressively from multinational to global.

Globalisation affects industries like telecommunications, processed food, personal care and retail. Any company that sells into the main markets of the world in an integrated and co-ordinated way is a global company.

Globalisation has widespread social, political, economic and environmental consequences. Not surprisingly it is controversial and has led to street protests wherever world leaders meet. Critics of globalisation say that it widens the gap between rich and poor people. It allows companies to exploit the developing nations, whilst damaging the environment through global warming and pollution. Many global companies are charged with acting outside existing laws, using child labour, corrupting politicians with bribes, disregarding human rights and ruthlessly using their power and market dominance to the disadvantage of their global suppliers, customers and competitors. Activists like Naomi Klein and the Winner of the Nobel Prize for Economics 2001, Joseph Stigliz agree that in its present form globalisation is not working for the world's poor.

Proponents of globalisation argue that global companies create wealth and development for everyone. These companies breed a healthy interdependence and foster an interconnectivity that brings benefits of opportunities for trade and increased access to markets and technology. They lead to more democracy and greater social justice and better health for the world. Professor Stigliz analyses the complex economic realities in terms of what self-regulation of market forces should be permitted and what interventions governments must make. He argues that it is not feasible or desirable to abandon globalisation. The key is to manage it better, to strive to eliminate inequalities and unfair rules governing trade.

DEALING WITH DOWNSIZING

Downsizing, begun as a short term management strategy in the mid-1980s, has become a permanent feature on the world's economic landscape. It was first devised to deal with the financial consequences of international competition, economic deregulation, trade agreements, re-engineering and other forms of industrial restructuring some of them due to new technology. Downsizing in which large numbers of employees are dismissed en masse now impacts all enterprises that seek competitive gain through cost advantage.

The three main drivers of downsizing are:

1) global competitive pressure,
2) new technology and
3) the demands of customer requirements, including database-driven marketing and other customer-focused activities.

The main reason for downsizing is to save money. Labour costs, depending on the industry, range from 30 per cent to 80 per cent of the total business costs. Companies that downsize become leaner and fitter, increase their shareholder value, have lower overheads, less bureaucracy, swifter decision making and increased productivity. They may also improve quality and customer service, and be more willing to take risks. In certain companies, downsizing has also improved employees' external focus and enhanced natural work teams.

But the positive aspects of downsizing must be weighed against its negative aspects. Excessive downsizing can lead to 'organisational anorexia' where companies go too far with downsizing and so deplete their organisations of the necessary experience, skills, competencies and knowledge required for successful operations. In addition there is an effect called 'the survivor syndrome', a psychological phenomenon in which employees who remain are shattered and betrayed by the experience and left with little trust in their managers and too much work to do as workloads may double or triple with the loss of so many colleagues. Survivors also feel added stress and a fall-off of motivation and commitment. They are frequently sad over the loss of their workmates, many of them friends, and they are unsure of their own futures in the organisation.

Managing downsizing well demands talent, skill, understanding and empathy. It is critical for the manager to break the news to the workforce before they hear it elsewhere; to develop a fair redundancy selection procedure and a compensation package for the leavers. The challenge for the manager is to shift the energies of the survivors from the negative aspects of the survivor syndrome to helping create a more resilient workforce.

VALUING EMPLOYEE DIVERSITY

Valuing employee diversity is a behaviour expected of today's managers. This expectation, in part, springs from globalisation. Companies that work all over the world should reflect their global intent in the ethnic and racial make up of their workforces – at the top managerial level as well as at the managerial level. It also arises from necessity. Demographic changes, including negative population growth among the majority communities of nearly all western nations mean that most companies will have to cast their recruitment nets wider than traditionally done, if they are to obtain sufficient skilled employees. Companies with good reputations for diversity and inclusion will have competitive advantage over those without proven track records for valuing diversity.

But it is not only in recruitment in times of skill shortages that companies benefit from a diverse workforce. Diversity brings with it other benefits than winning battles in the war for talent. Diverse work teams are more creative, better at problem solving and often provide insights into marketing when, for example, ethnic employees provide insights to understand cultural effects on buying decisions and map strategies to respond to them. They are more sensitive to work/life balance issues. Flexibility at work is often prompted by employees trying to achieve a better work/life balance for family or lifestyle reasons. In addition to these business case reasons for increasing and valuing employee diversity and inclusion, companies may be motivated by ethical arguments such as the social justice case against all forms of discrimination, the need to create a level playing field for all, and the moral argument that talent and merit are the criteria for career advancement. There is also the good citizen argument for organisations to be role models in keeping the laws of the land enacted to protect minority and racial groups, the disabled and ageing workers.

EXPLOITING NEW TECHNOLOGY

Managers' ability to manage e-commerce and other forms of new technology may be their most important critical success factor. Managers need to concentrate on two areas:

- using technology to transfer ways of working for producing traditional products and services and processes for dealing with administrative processes and
- creating e-commerce business itself. E-commerce companies facilitate sales that can be

B2C (Business to Consumer), B2B (Business to Business) or C2C (Customer to Customer). The Web has given rise to the dot.com companies phenomena. These are the so-called 'pure players' – companies that have been set up simply to facilitate Web transactions.

Despite a hiccup over the unrealistic expectation of the initial wave of dot.com companies and the subsequent shake out, the future is bright for the survivors. E-commerce is now ready for a global growth spurt that will need careful managing. This so-called 'new economy' is in contrast with the 'bricks and mortar economy' of the past.

2 *The Manager's Job*

Traditionally the job of the manager involved the direct management of a team of people. Increasingly managers act as 'singletons', they have no direct teams, but have an important role in indirectly supporting the work efforts of others. Managers usually have specific performance targets to hit. Managers help other people get their work done in efficient, high quality and personally satisfying ways. In the past managers were often seen as 'planners', 'controllers', 'thinkers', 'communicators' or 'organisers' (see reality check: three takes on the job of the Chief Executive Officer). Today managers are more often referred to as 'coaches', 'team leaders', 'recruiters of talent' or 'player managers' (see reality check: managed professionals)

REALITY CHECK

THREE TAKES ON THE JOB OF THE CHIEF EXECUTIVE OFFICER

1. 'The job of the chief executive officer is to think', she says. "That's one of your big jobs, to think the company into its strategy, and into its plans for execution; not thinking would be a bad thing. In fact, I used to schedule in a certain amount of time to read . . . I read things that might be provocative, that I never would have read, things from other industries, to get me to think.'

   Source: 'Inside the mind of a CEO. Interview by Stefan Stern with Marjorie Scardino, CEO of Pearson, the global media company', *RSA Journal*, (October 2002), p 39.

2. ' . . . the difficult and never-ending responsibility of a chief executive officer and the members of the company's senior leadership team to communicate to every employee in every way possible just what it is that the company is in business to accomplish and what its immutable values are. That means communicating by site visits, town hall

   staff meetings, breakfasts, lunches, and dinners with business unit leadership, web casts, intranets, video conferences, staff memos and on and on until you are blue in the face from talking about this stuff . . . and then you simply go out and do it all over again. It is a message that cannot be repeated often enough.'

   Source: 'New York Times Company President and Chief Executive Officer Russell Lewis, on "The CEO's lot is not a happy one"', *Academy of Management Executive and Address*, (11 August 2002).

3. 'Growing up, I had a lot of chores to do, tasks that were my sole responsibility as an individual contributor, but I was also contributing to the entire family. I learned very quickly that all the chores, in addition to my own, must get done even when a brother was gone. Whether working on the farm or playing on the sports field, I discovered early on that success centres on people responsibility,

playing different roles at different times for the greater good. As the chief executive officer of Lockheed Martin, I've seen that kind of teamwork makes all the difference.'

Source: 'Lockheed Martin, Chairman and CEO, Vance Coffman on achieving mission success, interview by Hal. B. Gregersen and Jeffrey H. Dyer', *Academy of Management Executive*, **16** 3 August 2002), p 33.

REALITY CHECK

MANAGED PROFESSIONALS

Encouraged by the new corporate governance environment that grew up in the 1990s, professional organisations strengthened and formalised their management. More full-time managerial positions were created, particularly in the areas of operations, finance, information technology and human resources as these functions were expanded to meet the growing complexity of the firms. Administrators and executives from outside the professions were appointed to roles such as 'practice manager', 'marketing director', 'chief operating officer' and occasionally 'chief executive', and the incorporation of partnerships became more widespread . . .

In most professional service firms, team leaders and even business unit and division heads still combine client interface with team management, and now they have to interact with the central management framework as well. They are still player managers, operating in a culture where it is their performance as players rather than position in the management structure that wins the respect of the people they are managing.

Source: Augar, P. and Palmer, J. (2002), *The rise of the player manager: how professionals manage while they work*, Penguin, p 24.

In order to capture the array of tasks and challenges within any manager's job, this chapter examines the characteristics of managerial work, how managers can empower other people to perform to even higher levels, the nature of the competencies and skills required of managers, the stress managers experience and the key considerations in educating managers.

Characteristics of managerial work

At the turn of the twentieth century well known writers like Max Weber, Henri Fayol and Frederick Taylor saw managerial work as rational, subject to planning and governed by the principles of time and motion to achieve efficiency with employees. Fredrick Taylor, an engineer himself, thought that all managers had to behave as engineers and break down jobs into their components to find the best way of doing each bit, using time and motion study to establish a standard time for each job. His approach was called scientific management, or Taylorism. Today leading management writers agree that effective managers need to move far away from this impersonal, mechanistic approach to management in the work place.

In a classic study of managerial behaviour, Mintzberg (1975) identified several key characteristics of a manager:

- *Managers work long hours*. The notion of working a 35 hour week is a myth for most managers. With the popularity of laptops and mobile phones, work can become a round-the-clock, seven-days-a-week activity, particularly in global organisations. Despite organisational efforts on work/life balance it is individual managers who have to impose the boundaries to really create a balanced life.
- *Managers are busy people*. Managers have always been over-worked. Over the past 15 years there have been many pushes towards creating an ever-increasing lean and agile organisation. Downsizing has been widespread with the result that the managers who survive downsizing and de-layering often have to do the work of two or three people.
- *The manager's work is fragmented and done in short bursts*. The work is varied and the trivial mixes with the consequential, requiring managers to shift gears frequently.
- *Managers are frequently interrupted*. In most offices managers no longer have private secretaries, who serve as gate-keepers or buffers between the manager and those who make instant demands on his or her time. Managers are usually in charge of all their communications. E-mail, whilst giving managers instant communications, has compounded this problem with many managers confessing to spending excessive time – up to several hours a day – just processing their e-mails. Managers appear to prefer interruption to their work. Superficiality is common.
- *Managers like action*: things that are current, specific, well-defined, routine and concrete. They enjoy a stimulus-response approach.
- *Managers spend most of their time with other people*. Actually, most managers have little time alone in their offices to think up strategies for the organisation. (Not surprisingly the practice of team away-days is often taken up in an effort to protect space for thinking about the future and building more effective teams.) They spend most of their time in meetings.
- *Managers spend up to half their time with external contacts*. These include customers, suppliers, associates, press and others.

Twenty years after Mintzberg's original study of chief executives he returned to extend his study of managers, this time across a wide variety of roles and organisations (Mintzberg, 1994). The outcome is an integrated model of managerial work examining the person in the job, the frame (or structure) of the job and how to manage at three different levels.

THE PERSON IN THE JOB

Individuals come into managerial jobs with personal histories. They have values, for example, honesty, integrity or morality. They also bring a body of experience, which expresses itself in terms of a set of skills or competencies and knowledge. An individual's knowledge may be used directly or indirectly to help interpret the various work situations encountered, for example, when an employee's absence from work becomes a pattern requiring attention. Mintzberg asserts that each individual has a set of mental models to interpret the world. All of these individual characteristics come together to influence how the manager approaches his or her job. This is referred to as the manager's style of managing.

THE FRAME OF THE JOB

Once the individual is placed in a managerial job, Mintzberg suggests that he or she creates a frame for the job – a type of mindset that includes strategy and vision. There are three

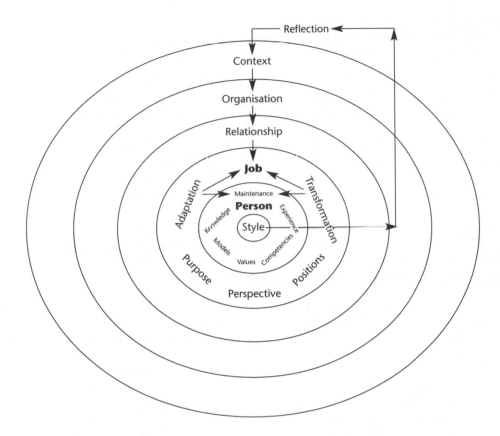

Figure 2.1 Capturing Mintzberg's person/job/organisation context inter-relationship (developed by the authors)

aspects as to how they interact with the job. First is 'purpose' – what is the manager trying to do with the department he or she is managing? A manager may create, maintain or adapt the unit to new circumstances or entirely transform the department. To use the image of a rail track, the manager may construct the rail track layout or keep the department on the track (or put it back on track) or improve or redesign the track layout, or completely rebuild the track, transforming it. Critical therefore is the 'purpose' a manager ascribes to the job (Figure 2.1).

On a broader base is the 'perspective' a manager adopts. Perspective is the overall approach to the management of the department, including notions such as 'vision' and 'culture'. An additional, but more tangible, consideration is that of 'positions', which include the location of the department in its environment, the specific products or services offered, the markets served and the systems and processes designed.

How a manager ultimately performs in a job is determined by how he or she conceives its frame. The frame can be imposed by senior management or left to be developed by the manager, thereby encouraging entrepreneurship. Secondly, the frame can be sharp or vague, for example 'increase sales by 30 per cent by the end of the year' or 'update this product portfolio'. The frame of any managerial job determines the set of issues the manager will be concerned with and this necessarily dictates how time is allocated.

MANAGING ON THREE LEVELS

The essences of Mintzberg's model are the three levels managers engage to take action:

- managers can manage action directly (the most tangible level),
- they can manage people to ensure that the necessary actions get done or
- they can manage information to influence people to take the necessary actions.

The ultimate goal of managerial work is the taking of action that can be managed directly, indirectly through people or even more indirectly by information through people. Managers perform all of these but the level a particular manager actually prefers becomes an important determinant of managerial style as is the case with Steve Jobs.

REALITY CHECK

STEVE JOBS – MANAGEMENT ROLE MODEL

The reaction of Steve Jobs to the drop in demand for personal computers in the autumn of 2000, was four-fold:

- Continue with the new product plans with the expectation that demand would pick up in 2001.
- Restructure the company so that Apple would continue to be viable as an annual revenue basis of US$6 billion, as opposed to US$8 billion.
- Not lay off people.
- Protect Apple's cash reserves.

The challenge was the paying of penalty fees for cancellations and providing rebates to manufacturers, retailers and distributors for orders already agreed. However, the positive note was that Jobs had already outsourced a considerable proportion of Apple's manufacturing to various subcontractors and despite the penalty fees, the opportunity arose to clear out an '11 week inventory glut'.

Despite the sizing down, Steve Jobs was as inspiring as always in the promotion of Apple Macs, particularly so at the Macworld trade shows in San Francisco and Japan (Apple has approximately 4 per cent of the US PC market and 3 per cent of the global market).

'Jobs kicked off each show with a keynote that was an amalgam of stand-up routine, magic show and pep rally. For all his showmanship, the message was subtle . . . He had to demonstrate that in a world of networks based on industry wide standards, Apple computers are powerful enough to do everything Windows PCs can. Yet he had to distinguish Macs to warrant their premium prices. As a subtext, he wanted to keep wooing loyal Apple users by stroking their snobbery, reminding them that they weren't mere worker bees twiddling spreadsheets, but intelligent people who like to have fun and be creative with their computers.'

Apple is still around, still innovative and probably has one of most fiercely loyal users. Steve Jobs' vision, discipline and power of inspiration neatly integrated Macs with the internet and the digital multimedia.

Source: Schlender, B. (2001), 'Steve Jobs: the graying prince of a shrinking kingdom', *Fortune*, (14 May), pp 84–90.

A well-established view of the manager's roles is the manager as doer, someone who is directly involved in the action. Doing involves action both inside and outside the organisation. Doing inside involves projects and problems. Managers champion change to gain competitive advantage, handling problems and crises, often with 'hands on' involvement. Managers 'do' because they feel their judgement is required in the situation. Alternatively they may be substituting for someone else! Directly doing is also an effective way of staying in touch with the department's work. Doing outside involves negotiations and arranging deals. Managers often have to do these things themselves because the situation requires their authority and their expertise.

When managers manage through other people they are one step removed from the action. As with 'doing', managers manage people both internally and externally. Mintzberg refers to the internal role as leading and the external role as linking. Managers lead at the individual, group and organisational level. They lead on a 'one-to-one' basis by motivating, inspiring and mentoring staff. They lead on a group level by building and managing teams. Lastly, they lead on the organisational or department level by creating and sustaining a dynamic culture. Externally, the manager spends a lot of time networking, building contacts with suppliers, clients and maybe also competitors with a view to a joint venture or partnership.

To manage by information is to sit two steps away from managerial action. Here the manager focuses on information as an indirect way to make things happen. In recent years this approach has become very popular and known as the 'bottom line' approach to management. Mintzberg refers to two roles in managing by information – communication and controlling. Communicating refers to the collecting and disseminating of information. Here oral information conversations form a critical part of the information. Controlling refers to the use of information in a directing way to provoke action. Managers do this by developing systems, designing structures and imposing directives. The controlling role is what people think of when they refer to the 'administrative' side of managerial work.

THE EMPOWERING MANAGER

Empowerment is a management technique that is the arsenal of managers at all levels of an organisation. Empowerment is a strategic option for senior managers. They can choose to free employees from rigorous controls to take responsibility for their own ideas, decisions and actions and in that way release hidden resources that would otherwise remain inaccessible both to the individual and to the organisation. Senior managers can make it a high priority to create an environment in which individuals take greater control over more responsibility for the results of their work within clear guidelines, can use more of their talents and creativity on the job, and increase their knowledge. Senior managers write the policies that either promote or block empowerment from the top. They set the agenda for middle and frontline managers to follow that reaches down to the shop floor, the call centres and the offices.

Research contrasts the characteristics of an empowered workforce with a disempowered one. Empowered workforces display high levels of morale, entrepreneurial spirit, recognition, teamwork, participation, commitment, creativity and trust, whereas, disempowered individuals show boredom, tension and stress, frustration, cynicism, lack of ownership, poor motivation, lower productivity and lower levels of satisfaction.

Empowered individuals take risks, gain knowledge and develop new skills. They grow and are responsible and accountable. They choose and make decisions and behave like adults. They are creative, innovative and entrepreneurial.

Empowerment creates competitive advantages. For it is impossible to get people's best efforts, involvement and concern for things that are important to their customers and the long term interest of their organisations, when senior managers write policies and procedures that disempower their employees. The strategic objective is to make organisations a place where people can use their expertise, innovation and energy and take initiatives to do what is right for their customers to retain business in the face of global competition.

Managerial competencies and skills

Boyatzis' book *The competent manager* (1982) triggered the popularity of the term 'competency'. Competencies are 'the set of behavioural patterns that the incumbent needs to bring to a position in order to perform its tasks and functions with competence'. Over the past few years there has been increasing recognition that there is a need to match the competencies of managers with the business context, and that as conditions change, so does the importance of different competencies. Equally, the relative importance of competencies varies across the different levels of management.

Technical competencies/skills are considered most important at entry levels of management. This is an ability to perform specialised tasks, for example, word processing, database management, e-mail and spreadsheet analysis. Some of these technical skills are acquired through education, others are acquired through training or on the job experience.

Human skills are the ability to work well with other people. They are central to management work. Examples of such human skills are presentation, communication, negotiating, team leading and coaching. An important new development in this area is emotional intelligence, defined by Daniel Goleman (1996) as the ability to manage both oneself and one's relationships effectively. Emotional intelligence can matter more than IQ when it comes to being successful. It is now considered an important managerial competence. Examples of emotional intelligence are self-awareness, motivation, empathy, persistence, trust, stress management and supporting others.

REALITY CHECK

THE WHISTLE BLOWERS

Sharon Watkins was the Enron vice president who wrote a letter to chairman Kenneth Lay in mid 2001 warning him that the company's methods of accounting were improper. Coleen Rowley is the FBI staff attorney who caused a sensation with a memo to FBI Director, Robert Mueller, about how the bureau brushed off pleas from her Minneapolis field office that Zacarias Mousaouri, who was indicted as a September 11th co-conspirator, was a man who must be investigated. One month later in 2002 Cynthia Cooper exploded the bubble that was WorldCom when she informed its board that the company had covered up US$3.8 billion in losses through the prestidigitations of phoney book-keeping. They were people who did right just by doing their jobs rightly – which means ferociously, with eyes open and with the bravery the rest of us always hope we have and may never know if we do.

Source: Time Magazine, 6 January 2003, p 38.

As Daniel Goleman discovered, 'academic intelligence offers virtually no preparation for the turmoil – or opportunity – life's vicissitudes bring. Yet even though a high IQ is no guarantee of prosperity, prestige, or happiness in life, our schools and our culture fixate on academic abilities, ignoring *emotional* intelligence; a set of traits – some might call it character – that also matters immensely for our personal destiny. Emotional life is a domain that, as surely as maths or reading, can be handled with greater or lesser skill, and requires its unique set of competencies. And how adept a person is at those is critical to understanding why one person thrives in life while another, of equal intellect, dead-ends: emotional aptitude is 'meta-ability', determining how well we use whatever other skills we have, including raw intellect." (Goleman, D. (1996), *Emotional Intelligence*, London: Bloomsbury, p 36).

At the most senior levels managers need to have conceptual skills in order to analyse the complex issues facing the organisation. Conceptual skills are used to identify problems and opportunities, gather and interpret relevant information and make good decisions.

Managers and stress

Too much stress at work can break down a manager's physical and emotional systems, causing mistakes, accidents, reduced performance, absenteeism, dissatisfaction and illness. Pfeffer (1992) criticised organisations for creating 'toxic workplaces'. A toxic company implicitly says to its employees, 'We're going to put you in an environment where you have to work in a style and at a pace that is not sustainable. We want you to burn yourself out. Then you can leave.'

Research on 'hardiness' reveals how managers can cope with stress. The 'hardy' personality comprises three aspects: commitment, control and challenge. Each hardiness characteristic is believed to offer different appraisal and coping mechanisms. 'Commitment' results in the person appraising events as meaningful and aligning with their personal values. 'Control' assists the person in approaching events as the initiator of action. 'Challenge' implies energy and the ability to rise to new situations. Past research has indicated that 'high-hardys' reported greater desirable events and perceived more control over these events than 'low-hardys'.

Hardiness has been associated with the perception of high physical energy. Another study shows that hardiness and its components are associated with rigorous mental health. Few studies have been examined directly how hardy people behave in stressful situations. A study at Cranfield took on this aim. The study was carried out with managers in a UK division of a global pharmaceutical company that had recently gone through significant organisational change. A group of 'high-hardy' managers were interviewed and compared to a group of 'low-hardy' managers (using Kobassa's scale (Kobassa, S.C., Maddi, S.R. and Khan, S. (1982), 'Hardiness and health: a prospective study', *Journal of Personality and Social Psychology*, **42**(1), pp 168–177.). The 'high-hardy' managers demonstrated a number of specific coping characteristics not elicited from the 'low-hardy' sample:

- Stressful encounters were tackled straight away rather than letting them escalate.
- An ability to put the problem situation into a wider perspective, thereby taking a positive stance.
- They get other people's support. Getting along easily with other colleagues and establishing good relationships were essential to them.

- An ability to put an issue on one side until it can be addressed.
- An ability to switch off at the end of the workday.
- A balanced life, hence avoiding long working hours or taking work home.
- They like to have fun at work.
- A deep sense of self-worth.

The degree of self-worth that the 'hardy' managers exhibited offers the potential to reduce the degree of stress that these people feel; self-worth moderates the effect of potentially stress-provoking situations such as conflict and criticism. Confidence was frequently cited as the most important reason for failing to feel pressurised. They do not worry and have sufficient faith in themselves that they will overcome problems.

Educating managers

Management education today is synonymous with the MBA (Master of Business Administration). MBA programmes are often criticised for their over-emphasis on analysis at the expense of both integration and developing wisdom, as well as leadership and inter-personal skills. It was often said that MBA programmes equip students for only one job – being chief executive officer. The MBA teaches students to analyse business situations but doesn't prepare them to be good leaders, actually implementing change. A number of MBA programmes have begun to address this issue of practical relevance in the following ways:

- They choose only students who have had management experience. Students are more discerning about what they learn and are more likely to see the transferability of knowledge.
- The design is multidisciplinary. These programmes recognise that the real world of business is inter-related, instead of falling into traditional functional categories.
- Their focus is not only on learning concepts and techniques, but also on how people think about business issues. Changing how people think is an essential step in changing what people do and how they manage. It is the philosophy that underlines many development approaches, such as 'total quality management'.
- They are oriented towards action learning, which means they are action oriented, particularly when it comes to driving through demanding projects.

REALITY CHECK

REFLECTION ON FLEXIBILITY

Victor: 'The idea of long-term employment is a thing of the past. A job is no longer for life . . . Paul, you are the modern man. You embody the ideal. Experience becomes a ceaseless search for experience . . . Slap! It goes on your C.V. "I worked for Victor Quinn." It now seems incredible. My father had a job and the expectation of the same job for life. Now we live longer, we expect to live many lives, not one. Freelance culture persuades us to believe we may start again. But is it true?'

Source: Hare, D. (2000), *My zinc bed*, London: Faber & Faber.

Mintzberg believes that everything effective managers do is sandwiched between reflection and action at three levels. The first level concerns people and interpersonal relationships, where the orientation has to be collaborative. The second is organisational, where the primary orientation is analysis. The third is context, encompassing the different demands of varying stakeholders and the pressure they place on the organisation. Here, managers need to understand global issues. Mintzberg pulls together what he calls the five frames of the managerial mind – the five mind sets:

- Managing self: the reflective mindset
- Managing relationships: the collaborative mindset
- Managing organisations: the analytical mindset
- Managing context: the global mindset
- Managing change: the action mindset.

The implication is that for mangers to be 'well' educated, they need to be challenged on all five mindsets (Figure 2.1).

Summary

Managers are people who directly or indirectly support the work efforts of others.

CHARACTERISTICS OF MANAGERIAL WORK

Mintzberg, in his classic study, identified several key characteristics of managerial work:

- Managers work long hours.
- Managers are busy people.
- The manager's job is fragmented and done in short bursts.
- Managers are frequently interrupted.
- Managers like action.
- Managers spend most of their time with other people.
- Managers spend up to half their time with external contacts.

In 1994 Mintzberg developed an integrated model of managerial work.

THE PERSON IN THE JOB

The individual comes to the managerial job with a personal history of values, experience and competencies. All of these characteristics influence a manager's style of managing.

THE FRAME OF THE JOB

Once the individual is in the job he or she creates a frame – a type of mindset that includes strategy and vision. There are three aspects as to how managers interact with their jobs. The first is purpose – what is the manager trying to achieve? The second is perspective – this is the overall approach to management and includes vision and culture. The third aspect is positions – it locates the department the manager is managing in its environment (both internal and external). The frame of the job determines the set of issues handled by the manager.

MANAGING ON THREE LEVELS

There are three levels managers engage to take action:

- Managers can take action directly.
- Managers can manage people to ensure the necessary actions get done.
- Managers can manage information to influence people to take the necessary actions.

EMPOWERMENT

Empowerment is a management technique that frees employees from rigorous controls to take responsibility for their own ideas, decisions and actions. Empowered employees show high levels of morale, entrepreneurial spirit, recognition, teamwork, participation, commitment, creativity and trust. Empowerment creates competitive advantage.

MANAGERIAL COMPETENCIES AND SKILLS

Competencies are 'the set of behavioural patterns that the incumbent needs to bring to a position in order to perform its tasks and functions with competence'. There are different kinds of competencies. Technical competencies are the ability to perform specialised tasks such as word processing. Human skills are the ability to work with people. A new development in this area is emotional intelligence, defined by Goleman, as the ability to manage both oneself and one's relationships effectively. Conceptual skills are needed to identify problems, gather and interpret information and make good decisions.

MANAGERS AND STRESS

Too much stress can break down a manager's physical and emotional systems, causing mistakes, accidents, reduced performance, absenteeism, dissatisfaction and illness. Research on 'hardiness' reveals how managers can cope with stress. The 'hardy' personality comprises of three elements, commitment (events are seen as meaningful and aligning with personal values), control (the person approaches events as the initiator of action) and challenge (implies energy and the ability to rise to new situations).

EDUCATING MANAGERS

Management education is synonymous with the MBA (Master of Business Administration). MBA programmes can be criticised for their over emphasis on analysis, at the expense of integration and developing leadership skills. In a similar vein, Mintzberg believes that effective managers continually move between reflection and action. He talks about the five frames of the managerial mind:

- Managing self: the reflective mindset
- Managing relationships: the collaborative mindset
- Managing organisations: the analytical mindset
- Managing context: the global mindset
- Managing change: the action mindset.

3 *The Manager's Career*

Wilensky defined 'career' in 1961 as a succession of related jobs, arranged in 'a hierarchy, through which people move in an ordered sequence'. This definition of career is now out- dated. Today a career can consist of many unrelated jobs. Most hierarchies have been severely flattened so that individuals advance their careers through job enlargement or lat- eral moves as opposed to vertical moves. There is little predictability about career development in the twenty-first century. Instead we witness career sabbaticals, flexible working, downshifting and short stays in organisations. We also see tremendous worka- holism and material greed. This chapter not only looks at the traditional aspects of a manager's career, but also discusses, in some detail, the shift from the old psychological con- tract to the new deal at work.

The whole process of joining a new organisation can be viewed from two contrasting points, that of the new employee and that of the organisation. From the employee's point of view, the process comprises highlighting one's skills and attributes, working out how to progress in the organisation, learning to perform well and, more generally, squaring the commitment involved in all of this with the commitment to one's home and family life. The same process from the organisation's point of view concern's attraction and selection, induction and socialisation, career development and work/life balance. The two processes are two sides of a complicated negotiation which will lead to an understanding whereby the contribution of each party aims to address the other's expectations. This understanding may be renegotiated many times by either party, as expectations change over time.

Any such understanding between two parties has both quantitative and qualitative ele- ments. The quantitative elements refer to tasks, output and hours to be worked. The qualitative elements are such factors as fit, commitment, energy, drive, trust and identity. Do the individuals identify with their employing organisation? Are they committed to what they are doing? Do they trust their bosses, colleagues and subordinates both as people and as creditworthy professionals? Are the individuals willing to commit the drive and energy required to make themselves successful? Equally, are the individuals' bosses, or other key managers, willing to offer them jobs or tasks of substantial responsibility? Do they trust them from what they have seen of their performances? Because of the qualitative nature of such an understanding, the parties may not be clear as to its exact elements, but at least they feel that some form of agreement has emerged.

The manner in which such tacit agreements develop is highlighted by examining the following four areas:

- Attraction and selection
- Induction and socialisation
- Career development
- Work/life balance.

Early experiences in an organisation can have one of two outcomes. Either the individual feels content and well matched with the organisation (in which case we say they are well socialised), or the individual feels disappointed and out of place, which rests very much on the extent to which the individual feels the organisation reinforces their personal feelings about how people should be treated at work. In periods of economic growth, where job mobility is easy if the individual feels uncomfortable in the organisation, they can leave. In periods of economic recession, where job mobility is difficult, there is increasing pressure on the individual to conform to the organisation. This in itself sets up all kinds of personal dilemmas. Sufficient attention to the processes of entry and socialisation can turn potentially negative experiences into an exciting and stimulating learning phase.

Attraction and selection

Talent management is now a key responsibility for many managers. In the top ten non-financial measures used by investors to analyse company performance ability, 'to attract and retain talented people' was recently rated more highly than 'market share'. By 2006, the number of 16–24 year olds in the UK labour market will have shrunk by one million compared to 1987. As a result Ewing et al. (2002) suggest 'it is a distinct possibility that in coming years competition for talent among firms will be even more fierce than competition for customers'. This fierce competition has been called 'the war for talent' and has led many organisations to offer a variety of incentives, or 'golden hellos', to entice undergraduates into their organisations.

A major international management consultancy firm embarked on a study to increase the number of female undergraduates who applied to it, since they were unable to attract as many female undergraduates as male undergraduates (30 per cent versus 70 per cent). The study showed that female undergraduates favour organisations that:

- employ people with whom you feel you have things in common,
- have a friendly, informal culture,
- provide you with an internationally diverse mix of colleagues,
- use your degree skills,
- really care about their employees as individuals,
- offer variety in your daily work,
- require you to work standard working hours only and
- offer a relatively stress-free working environment.

The one organisational attribute that male undergraduates attach significantly more importance to, compared with female undergraduates, is 'a high starting salary'.

This 2003 study indicates that organisations need to look at the image they project to male and female undergraduates, who may be picking up different messages.

In the recruitment process both the employer and the prospective employee are trying to find out if there is a match: the employer is seeking a candidate who can be integrated into the job and the organisation; the candidate is looking for a job and organisation that will satisfy their needs and expectations.

These needs and expectations are entirely subjective. They exist in the perception of the individual, who perceives the congruence of the offered rewards and the satisfaction of their needs, expects to perform the job successfully, believes that they will fit into the culture of the organisation and will enjoy working with the people there. Add to these a liking for the organisation and a desire to take up a job offer flows naturally.

Interviews alone are notoriously unreliable as predictors of future job performance. Some people are good performers and can project a favourable and professional image in an interview. Some selection interviewers are not well prepared or briefed, or have not developed the skills of gathering the information about candidates that enable them to arrive at a sound decision. It is easy to see how poor decisions at the selection stage can be made. Below are listed problems to which attention should be paid, so that the entry process can be effectively managed.

PROBLEMS IN THE MANAGEMENT OF ENTRY

The recruitment/selection and job-hunting processes are problematic both for the individual and the employing organisation.

- *Obtaining inaccurate information in a situation of mutual selling*. Since the organisation is trying to attract the best candidate and the applicant is trying to secure the best job, there are strong incentives on both sides to exaggerate. Both want to emphasise their strengths and disguise their weak points. Careful questioning at the interview stage can help elicit an accurate picture.
- *Unconsciously colluding in creating unrealistic expectations about the early career*. There may be a tendency in the interview to concentrate on the long-term prospects available in the organisation, rather than thoroughly reviewing the demands of the immediate job. Hence the applicant joins the organisation on the basis of what it offers in one or two years' time, rather than the reality of the first job.
- *Incorrect image of the organisation*. If recruiters emphasise to the applicant how much they value his or her abilities and subsequently he or she does not feel fulfilled in the first job, disillusionment may set in. Van Maanen (1978) has shown that there is a relationship between the toughness of the recruitment and selection process and the positive self-image and commitment of the individual. The harder it is to get into an organisation, the more highly the individual values membership of it.
- *Uncertainty about the future*. Choosing to offer a job to an applicant or deciding to take up a job offer is an expensive decision and may involve a long-term commitment. Applicants should be as clear as they can be about their abilities, needs and values. They must communicate such information accurately to others. At interview they should ask the questions that will tell them what they need to know about the potential job. Similar principles apply to the organisation. Recruiters must know the organisation's needs. They must be able to communicate the nature of the job and organisation now, and the prospects for the future. They should be able to diagnose the applicant's potential against the competencies required. It is often helpful to involve the prospective employee's immediate supervisor in the selection and recruitment process.

Induction and socialisation

It is very important that new individuals are assimilated smoothly into the organisation. This section looks at the issue of person–organisation fit, which is increasingly attracting research attention, the problems of induction and some mechanisms for effective induction. Additionally, we examine the learning people experience in entering and being socialised into the organisation.

PERSON–ORGANISATION FIT

Person–organisation fit refers to the compatibility between the individual and the employing organisation. The fit includes not only the competencies of the individual but also personal characteristics (for example, someone who generates respect) and personal values (for example, honesty, ethical). Person–organisation fit is usually assessed during the interview process and a perceived lack of fit may well lead to a rejection, even if the individual applicant has all the competencies necessary for the job.

Whether there is good person–organisation fit has important implications for both organisational and individual outcomes. A good fit between the employees' values and those of the organisation has been shown to predict job satisfaction and organisational commitment. It may also be correlated with improved performance and retention.

SOCIALISATION

'Organisational socialisation is the process by which employees learn about and adapt to their workplace, including new responsibilities and roles and the organisation's culture.' Ed Schein goes on to describe five key elements in this process (1978):

- Accepting the reality of the organisation (that is, the constraints governing individual behaviour).
- Dealing with resistance to change (that is, the problems involved in getting personal views and ideas accepted by others).
- Learning how to work realistically in the new job, in terms of coping with too much or too little organisation and too much or too little job definition (that is, the amount of autonomy and feedback available).
- Dealing with the boss and understanding the reward system (that is, the amount of independence given and what the organisation defines as high performance).
- Locating one's place in the organisation and developing an identity (that is, understanding how an individual fits into the organisation).

The five elements combine together to give an individual a certain orientation towards the organisation (Schein, E.H. (1978), *Career dynamics: matching individual and organisational needs*, Reading, Mass: Addison-Wesley, pp 94–111).

The knowledge, values and skills that individuals learn from being socialised differ for two reasons. First, individuals are different, holding contrasting values and attitudes and having acquired and developed varying levels of skills. The values, attitudes and skills level of different people will strongly influence the way they each view the new organisation, their new job and new colleagues. Second, the actual experience of induction and socialisation into the organisation will vary according to the prevailing circumstances.

Three assumptions underlie this discussion of socialisation. First, individuals in a state of transition experience anxiety. They want to learn about their new role as quickly as possible to reduce this anxiety. Second, when an individual moves into a new job the surrounding colleagues, subordinates, superiors and clients play active roles in the socialisation process by giving them information about what really happens in the organisation. Third, the productivity of any organisation depends upon how individuals learn to perform in their new positions.

To appreciate the impact of socialisation on individuals, we shall first examine the typical problems that emerge during a person's induction into the organisation. Then we shall review the practices organisations use to socialise newcomers, namely the mechanisms for effective induction and, lastly, we shall look at how individuals cope with the emotional stages involved in such a transition.

PROBLEMS WITH INDUCTION

Just as there are problems in the attraction/selection/job-hunting process, so there are in the early induction and socialisation period. The main questions typically facing any individual are:

- Will the job test me?
- Will my contribution be valued?
- Will I be able to maintain my individuality and integrity?
- Will I be able to balance my job with my family and outside interests?
- Will I have the opportunity to develop in the job?
- Will I feel proud to belong to this organisation?

The main issues facing organisations are:

- Will this individual fit in with our organisation?
- Will this individual make a real contribution?
- Will this individual be able to develop within the organisation?

Organisations spend considerable time and money on the induction of employees. Usually the direct costs of induction programmes are substantial. There are indirect costs as well, since new employees generally work below capacity whilst they are learning their jobs. The possibility of reducing costs provides an important incentive for management to learn how to improve socialisation.

MECHANISMS FOR EFFECTIVE INDUCTION

Three American researchers Meryl Louis, Barry Posner and Gary Powell (1983) conducted a study to compare socialisation practices and to investigate how they might affect employee attitudes. They were interested in the availability and helpfulness of various socialisation practices and about their impact on newcomers' job satisfaction, commitment and intention to stay with the organisation.

The most representative practices and influences which emerged were: formal on-site induction, off-site residential training, meeting other new recruits, relationships with more senior colleagues, mentor or sponsor relationships, or both, positive supervisor/boss, secretary or other support staff interactions, daily interactions with peers while working, social/recreational activities with people from work, and business trips with others from work.

The three most important socialisation practices were interaction with peers, supervisor and senior colleagues. Interaction with peers on the job was reported to be the most widely available aid, and was viewed as most important in helping newcomers become useful employees. The fourth most important practice was mentoring.

Mentoring

Ragins and Cotton (Ragins, B.R. and Cotton, J. (1991), 'Easier said than done: gender differences in perceived barriers to gaining a mentor', *Academy of Management Journal*, **34**, pp 939–951) define mentors as 'individuals with advanced experience and knowledge who are committed to providing upward support and mobility to their protégés careers' (p 939). Mentoring can be informal, where the relationships develop spontaneously, or formal, where there is some form of intervention to match or even monitor the process. Informal mentoring based on interpersonal attraction seems to be more successful than formal mentoring.

Mentoring is an increasingly popular practice for supporting junior managers, particularly women, towards senior roles. Indeed, in one major study of senior female managers and their chief executive officers, 91 per cent of female managers mentioned having a mentor and many saw this as the 'single most critical piece to women advancing career-wise'. The benefits of mentoring to the protégé may be career focused, with the mentor acting as a sponsor, coach, protector, challenge-giver and exposure-provider. It may also be psychosocial, with the mentor acting as friend, social supporter, parent, role model, counsellor and acceptance giver. There are also benefits for mentors. They report rewarding experiences, improved job performance, a loyal base of support, organisational recognition and 'generativity' (a sense of continuity and regeneration for mentors).

Mentoring is acknowledged to be of benefit to protégé, mentor and the organisation. 'The mentor gives, the protégé gets and the organisation benefits.' There has been little research on measuring the benefits of mentoring to the organisation. A case study of a local government's informal mentoring process in 2001, by one of the authors, did reveal a number of benefits to the organisation (Vinnicombe, S. and Bank, J. (2003), *Women with attitude: lessons for career management*, London: Routledge, pp 159–160), as shown in Figure 3.1.

Human resources management benefits
- spots talent,
- develops talented managers,
- develops pool of managers,
- helps trapped managers,
- grooms future leaders,
- invests in future success,
- helps retention and recruitment.

Culture and change
- strengthens culture,
- helps management of change,
- gives stability in times of change,
- gives competitive edge,
- increases capacity to handle diversity.

Communications benefits
- helps communication,
- helps induct new staff,
- early warning system.

Figure 3.1 Perceived benefits of mentoring to the organisation (compiled by John Bank)

STAGES OF TRANSITION

Two researchers at Cranfield School of Management, Chris Parker and Ralph Lewis, consider that all managers go through phases in the process of entry and socialisation into the organisation. Whether the manager has accepted a new job in a new organisation, been promoted within an organisation, or had a sideways move, Parker and Lewis indicate that the manager will undergo a transition. In essence, the person has to learn what it really means to perform effectively in the new job and organisation, and that process takes time. During the period of transition the person will experience problems, failures and frustrations. How well new managers contend with these problems depends significantly on the degree of perceived change required on their part, their capacity to adapt, and the support and guidance provided for them during the process.

A person's capacity to adapt to a new environment and the support provided is critically important. Many organisations operate a 'sink or swim' philosophy. Casualties occur because individuals take too long to reach the required level of competence. The time taken to move through the transition phase varies, depending upon the degree of perceived change. Below are the phases of the 'transition curve', illustrated in Figure 3.2.

Phase 1: Getting used to the place

A person has just changed job. The individual was probably competent in the last job and that is why they were appointed to this next one. In other words, they were seen as effective.

On entering the new organisation or job, work effectiveness drops slightly. Many aspects can be different, unintelligible and overwhelming. The way things are done in the new place is so unfamiliar that the individual is likely to feel that he or she cannot make a contribution or even function adequately.

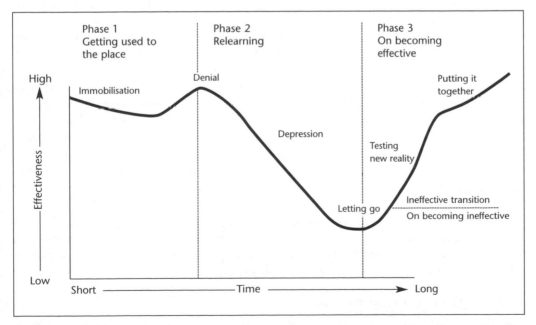

Figure 3.2 Changes of work effectiveness during transition (From Kakabadse, A. (1983), *The politics of management*, Gower, p 150.)

However, within a matter of a few weeks, the person becomes used to the new place. They have found people to talk to and to ask for assistance if required. If they are skilled at handling people, then the old hands at the new place are more likely to give them a chance.

The old hands may make strenuous efforts to ensure that the tasks handed to the new person are not too complex. People may go out of their way to offer advice and guidance on particular jobs or even how to handle particular people, especially troublesome superiors.

Within a short time the initial shock and immobilisation have gone. The individual may now be working quite well. Other people have given them a chance, so our new person is now showing what they can do. The person is, in fact, utilising the same variety of skills as in the last job. After all, they worked there; why should they not work here? The person has entered the stage of denial in that they believe no great changes are required. Their attitude is: 'OK, so I've got a new job. But I don't have to become a different person!'

Phase 2: Relearning

The initial immobilisation and denial stages of phase 1 give way to phase 2 when others begin to make real demands on the person involved.

Denial provided time for a temporary retreat. It allowed the individual to gather strength by using the skills that worked well in the past. However, within a fairly short time after entering the new job, denial can no longer work, for people cease to treat the individual as a 'rookie'. They want them to become part of the team.

For the individual, the realities of the change and the resulting stresses become obvious. New job skills have to be learnt. Additional responsibilities taken on in the new job mean acquiring knowledge that has to be applied to a specified standard.

Most certainly, the individual will have to relearn how to interact with the superiors/subordinates/colleagues around them. Departments, units and whole organisations have their own particular identity, their own culture. Hence people and teams will have their own way of doing things and no individual can deviate too far from the accepted norms of behaviour.

The individual will have to learn how to 'play the system'. Being effective at work involves knowing who and what to take note of, as well as competence at task skills. The covert skills of playing the system take time to learn. Most people learn by the unexpected mistakes they make. It is only when problems have arisen that the individual can appreciate why those challenges occurred and how they could be handled better in the future.

During phase 2, the individual experiences depression. They can no longer effectively apply their old skills. Naturally the new manager wonders, 'What is wrong with me?'

This depression is the first real step to relearning. The person is facing the fact that they have to change. They realise that their performance is deteriorating dramatically and only they can do anything about it. Although frustrated and depressed, the individual can see that it is time to let go of the past and face the future.

Phase 3: On becoming effective

What does one become – effective or ineffective? In other words, how well has the individual negotiated the transition?

After letting go of the past, the person accepts the new reality, the new challenge. The new person is now likely to become more pro-active. They may try out new behaviours, new work styles and new approaches, and apply newly learned skills. The testing stage is as frustrating as the depression stage. The individual is bound to make mistakes, becoming angry with him or herself and irritable with others. These negative feelings have to be coped with.

From the high energy of the testing phase, the individual attempts to put a new world together, and seeks for new meanings as to how and why things are now different.

The final part of the process is one of internalisation, whereby new behaviours and attitudes are incorporated into what is left of the old attitudes and behaviours. The individual has consolidated their position and is operating better than on the day when first appointed.

The initial results of research indicate that this process can take, on average, eighteen months for middle managers and up to three years for top management. However, some people do experience ineffective transitions. They end up operating at their level of incompetence. Some people are appointed to jobs beyond their capacity. Perhaps their depression during phase 2 became intolerable; they could not pull out. Perhaps they also had to tolerate unforgiving superiors and colleagues who could not ignore the mistakes they made.

Career development

Many organisations have developed fairly elaborate systems of career planning and development, for two sound reasons. First, individuals in the organisation should have an opportunity to experience training or some other form of development in order to equip them for their present or future jobs. Second, the organisation gains the full benefit of the actual and latent skills of its employees by providing training and sufficient experience of the total activities of the business, in order to adequately prepare those persons promoted to positions of responsibility. It makes sense to identify, prepare and nurture, on the job, people who will make significant contributions to the development of the organisation.

Equally, career planning and development may tip the balance between good and bad management. What are the differences between those managers considered to have succeeded and those who failed? Essentially, the differences are small but important. Managers considered to be consistently effective are able to admit they were wrong, learn from their mistakes and still maintain good working relationships with all types of people. Hence, adequate and sensitive training, as part of an integrated career planning system, can help executives to minimise their failings, capitalise on their strong points and thereby create a pool of competent executives.

CAREER ANCHORS

A systematic approach is important to career development so that relevant learning opportunities are provided on the job. As the individual acquires further and further job experience, they learn about themselves: their strengths and weaknesses, their needs and desires and, most of all, whether they hold a particular orientation or inclination in terms of the work they undertake. Ed Schein terms this orientation a career anchor; in effect, the individual is anchored into pursuing a particular type of career for themselves and thereby develops a particular occupational self-concept. This self-concept has three components, which together, make up an individual career anchor:

- self-perceived talents and abilities,
- self-perceived motives and needs and
- self-perceived attitudes and values.

The anchors act as internal driving and constraining forces on career decisions so that, if an individual moves into a work environment that fails to comply with his talents, needs or values, they will be 'pulled back' into something more congruent: hence the metaphor 'anchor'. The concept emphasises the interaction between abilities, needs and values. In essence, individuals tend to want and value things that they are good at and improve their abilities on those aspects of work they want and value.

Because of this dominant interaction of abilities, needs and values, an individual's career anchors can be discovered only after a number of years of experience. A person's self-concept will be influenced by the career options available to that person. The concept is designed to explain that part of our lives which grows more stable as we develop more self-insight from increased life experience.

Ed Schein defined eight separate career anchors:

- *Technical/functional*. The self-image of individuals in this group is tied up with their feelings of competence in their particular technical or functional area. It is the intrinsic work which interests them. Such individuals tend to disdain and fear general management.
- *Managerial*. Individuals in this group have management *per se* as their ultimate goal. They see their competence as lying in a combination of three general areas: analytical competence, interpersonal competence and emotional competence. The latter means being able to deal with risks, uncertainty and crises.
- *Security/stability*. Individuals in this group tend to behave as their employers wish in order to maintain job security, a reasonable salary and a stable future. They rely heavily on the organisation to look after them.
- *Creativity*. Individuals here have an overwhelming need to build or create something of their own. Such individuals continually initiate new projects. They are very visible people. They may also have a variety of motives and values that overlap with other anchors, for example, they want to be autonomous, managerially competent and able to exercise their own talents.
- *Autonomy/independence*. Individuals in this group wish to be as free of organisational constraints as possible to pursue their professional/technical competence. Their primary need is to be on their own, setting their own pace, life styles and habits.
- *Entrepreneurial creativity*. Individuals in this group want to create an organisation or enterprise of their own, built on their own abilities and willingness to take risks and to overcome obstacles.
- *Challenge*. Individuals in this group love to work on solutions to seemingly unsolvable problems, to win out over tough opponents or to overcome difficult obstacles.
- *Lifestyle*. Individuals in this group seek a position that permits them to balance and integrate their personal needs, family needs and the requirements of their career. They would want to make all of the major sectors of life work together towards an integrated whole, and therefore need a career situation that provides enough flexibility to achieve such integration.

REALITY CHECK

PERSONAL DEFINITIONS OF CAREER SUCCESS

A study, which investigated how 36 male and female managers, across their 20s, 30s and 40s, saw career success, indicated four types of manager:

1 The *climber* sees career success chiefly in terms of the level of organisational seniority and pay achieved, is status conscious and competitive, but often wants to combine material success with enjoyment at work.
2 The *expert* defines career success as being good at what you do and receiving personal recognition for this accomplishment, is not particularly goal-oriented, and values the content of a job more than its status.
3 The *influencer* associates career success with the degree of organisational influence achieved and may seek hierarchical advancement to gain greater influence but does not value status *per se.*
4 The *self-realiser* defines success in terms of achievement at a very personal level, which usually involves personal challenges and self-development, and sees having the ability to balance work and personal life as an integral part of career success.

Important differences were found between the male and female managers' conceptions of career success, exemplified by the fact that three of the categories identified were dominated by a single sex: the group of 'climbers' consisted of seven men and no women; the group of 'experts' comprised seven women and two men; the group of 'self-realisers' consisted of six women and one man. (There were six male 'influencers' and five female 'influencers'.) This suggests that external criteria such as pay and position may be far more central to men's conceptions of career success, whereas women define their own career success much more in terms of internal criteria such as accomplishment and achievement, and subjective criteria such as influence, personal recognition and respect.

Source: Sturges, J. (1999), 'What it means to succeed: personal conceptions of career success held by male and female managers at different ages', *British Journal of Management,* **10**, pp 239–252.

THE NEW PSYCHOLOGICAL CONTRACT

A contract of employment is a document, legally binding on both parties, that sets out the terms of employment. It may specify, for example, hours of work, holiday entitlement and rules of conduct. In addition to that formal contract, however, there exists an informal, broader, dynamic, underwritten contract – the psychological contract – that indicates what employees and organisations want and expect of each other. There is nothing formal or legal about the psychological contract.

Since the late 1980s this psychological contract has been changing. 'As a result of all sorts of pressure and trends on both sides,' Jean-Marie Hiltrop explained, 'such characteristics of corporate employment as stability, permanence, predictability, fairness, tradition and mutual respect are out. In are new features of self-reliance, flexibility and adaptability' (Hiltrop, J.M. (1995), 'The changing psychological contract: the human resource challenge of the 1990s', *European Management Journal,* **13**(3), pp. 286–294).

The term 'psychological contract' was first used by Chris Argyris and Harry Levinson in the 1960s to describe the subjective nature of the employee's interpretation of the employment relationship. How do you integrate the needs of normal individuals and the task demands of competitive organisations? It is a dilemma that still requires attention especially as the balance of power in the matter has shifted to the employers. It is the employers who have the upper hand and dictate the terms of the new psychological contract or the new deal at work.

The uniqueness of the psychological contract is that it is voluntary, subjective, informal, individually oriented and reciprocal. It evolves and flourishes with time. When this unwritten contract is violated it affects the employee more than the employer, as he or she is unable to influence the fundamental issues. When employers impose widespread redundancies, for example, the terms of the contract are changed unilaterally and that understandably results in feelings of anger and mistrust on the part of the employees if they are victims of downsizing. A similar betrayal of the contract can occur even for people who keep their jobs and experience the survivor syndrome (see Chapter 1). Thus, in order to appreciate the depth and extent of feelings concerning the new psychological contract, two perspectives are examined, the employers and their view concerning jobs for life and that of the employees.

The end of jobs for life

The idea of a lifelong career in one company – quite common in the past – seems increasingly remote today. Organisations are not offering it. Equally, many people would not be interested in such an offer! That is how far we have come from the working conditions of most of our parents.

To take an extreme but amusing example. One day in the 1980s a young man joined an international oil company. In his first week he had a meeting with the 'career planning department' at which he was asked where he wanted to retire to. The question caught him completely off guard as this was his first job after university, but not wanting to be found lost for words, he said, 'Devon!' He had been there several times as a youth on holiday with his family and it seemed an attractive place to retire to. The career planners then mapped for him a career in the company in which he would progress from one position to the next increasing in responsibilities until he reached the height of his career. From then on his responsibilities would start to lessen until he found himself, age 60, running an oil refinery in Devon, where he had five years to ease himself into a comfortable retirement.

Today, instead of developing detailed long-term career plans, employees are encouraged to jump off career ladders, especially when their competencies no longer meet the organisation's requirements. The elaborate career ladders of the past have in many cases been removed. Many of the remaining ones contain only three or four rungs (instead of, say, 27) as organisations have been flattened.

Jack Welch, when chief executive officer of General Electric, took the unilateral rewriting of the psychological contract to extreme. He called it the 'one-day contract', in which all that counted was the current value each party to the contract contributed to the relationship. Managers would expect their employees to be loyal only as long as today's expectations were being met. But the company's commitment to the employee was likewise governed by the current need for that person's skills and performance. Throughout General Electric's enterprises he applied his ruthless measurement system. One per cent of the top contributors won bonuses and promotions while the 10 per cent estimated to contribute the least had their job terminated. That practice, together with his proclivity for closing down unprofitable subsidiaries, earned him the nickname of 'Neutron Jack', as after his visits only the building remained unscathed as the people were 'vaporised'.

Employees are changing too

Not all the changes originate at the top; employee expectations are also evolving to reflect changes in the environment. The high unemployment resulting from downsizing, re-engineering and fierce global competition has combined with demographics to alter the economy – and hence people's expectations. Now more than ever before, they want to know what is going on in the organisations they work for – why certain decisions are made and strategies enacted. Better educated than employees of earlier eras, they insist on making their own contribution to decision making. They expect to be valued and recognised for their creativity, energy and efforts that are indispensable to the success of the enterprises for which they work.

Many have risen to the challenges posed by cross-cultural team-working and by a more open management style. They enjoy empowerment and relish the system of accountability required by new performance management. They celebrate the freedom of portable benefits and the resulting mobility. They develop new competencies and stay with an organisation only as long as they find it challenging. They are struggling to avoid cynicism and disillusionment. They want to discover how to rebuild trust between themselves and their organisations, engendering loyalty but more on their terms. In exchange for a renewed commitment they expect personal and professional development.

COMPARING OLD AND NEW CONTRACTS

Analysing both the old (see Table 3.1) and the new (see Table 3.2) psychological contracts in terms of implicit assumptions, strategies and positive and negative outcomes will help to illustrate how different they are and why they have been adopted unevenly across various industries at different times. (Naturally, assigning a positive or negative value to an outcome implies a judgement on the part of the authors; an outcome like having an older work force can be considered either positively or negatively depending on one's viewpoint.)

Table 3.1 Old psychological contract (compiled by John Bank)

Implicit assumptions (based on old environment)	Strategies	(+) Positive and (–) negative outcomes
Employment relationship is long-term	Benefits and services that reward tenure Employee recognition processes that reinforce long term relationship	(+) Older work force is strong (–) Demographically restricted work force (+) Experienced workforce
Reward for performance is promotion	Linear compensation systems Linear status symbols Fixed job descriptions Static performance standards	(–) Plateaued workforce (–) Demonstrative (betrayed) workforce (+) Loyal workforce (+) Clarity of expectations

Management is paternalistic	Excessive and duplicative support services Long-term career planning systems	(−) Dependent workforce (+) Committed workforce
Loyalty means remaining with the organization	Approved career paths only within the organisation Voluntary turnover penalised Internal promotion, discouragement of external hiring	(−) Narrow workforce (−) Mediocre workforce (−) Non-diverse workforce (−) Complacent workforce (+) High performers retained
Lifetime career is offered	Fitting in Relationships	(+) Co-dependent workforce (+) Contentment

Table 3.2 New psychological contract (compiled by John Bank)

Implicit assumptions (based on new environment)	Strategies	(+) Positive and (−) negative outcomes
Employment relationship is situational	Flexible and portable benefit plans Tenure-free recognition systems Blurred distinctions between full-time, part-time and temporary employees	(+) Flexible work force (−) Lack of continuity (−) Lack of security (−) Uncommitted work force (−) Worried employees (−) Lack of loyalty
Reward for performance is acknowledgement of contribution and relevance	Job enrichment and employee participation The philosophy of quality Self-directing work teams Non-hierarchical performance and reward systems	(+) Motivated work force (+) Task-focused work force (−) Path to promotion now unclear (−) Frightened work force (−) Higher turnover
Management is empowering	Employee autonomy No 'taking care' of employees No detailed long-term career planning Tough love	(+) Empowered work force (−) Resentful work force (−) Isolated subgroups (−) Work overload
Loyalty means responsibility and good work	Non-traditional career paths In/out process Employee choice Accelerated diversity recruiting	(+) Responsible work force (−) Cult of individual
Explicit job contracting is offered	Short-term job planning Not signing up for life No assumption of lifetime caretaking	(+) Employee and organisation bonded around good work

IMPLICATIONS FOR HUMAN RELATIONS

The changing psychological contract is having a far-reaching impact on human relations policy and practice. Areas of current concern include:

- **Reconciling two sets of expectations**. What can employees expect of their organisations when faced with growing professional risks, uncertainty and demands to continually improve productivity, efficiencies and competitiveness? What can employers expect of their employees when they are faced with requirements of globalisation, integration of functions and the need to increase competitiveness?

- *Finding new ways to attract, retain and motivate talent*. When people exhibit a new kind of loyalty to their professions and skills, traditional methods and ways of attracting and retaining talent need to be revamped. Instead of traditional career ladders and the promise of job security, new incentives need to be on offer.
- *Creating new ways of avoiding stress and burnout*. Retraining schemes, relocation efforts (outplacement) and counselling programmes (career guidance) will be needed as older workers yield their jobs to younger, more flexible employees both in the internal and external labour markets.

PROTEAN CAREERS

'The career as we once knew it – as a series of upward moves, with steadily increasing income, power, status and security – has died,' Douglas T. Hall writes. 'Nevertheless, people will always have work lives that unfold over time, offering challenge, growth and learning. So, if we think of the career as a series of lifelong work-related experiences and personal learning, it will never die' (Hall, D.T. and Associates (1996), *The career is dead, long live the career: a relational approach to careers*, San Francisco: Jossey-Bass, pp 1, 20, 21, 344).

Careers that are driven more by individuals than organisations have been given the name 'protean careers'. Such careers are propelled by a need for psychological success rather than by traditional, external measures of success. They involve reinvention and continuous change and self-assessment. As Hall remarked, 'Our career focus has shifted inward. The driving questions are now more about meaning than money, purpose than power, identity than ego and learning than attainments. When no one was looking the protean career sneaked up on us!' (p 1).

The name for this new type of career derives from the Greek god, Proteus, who could change his shape whenever he wanted to, from a handsome young man to a wild boar, from a raging fire to a green tree, and so on infinitely. The flexible, ever-changing career is very much in keeping with the new psychological contract.

One definition of the protean career is, 'A process which the person, not the organisation, is managing. It consists of all the person's varied experiences in education, training, work in several organisations, changes in occupational field, and so on. The protean career is not what happens to the person in any one organisation. The protean person's own personal career choice and search for self-fulfilment are the unifying or integrative elements in his or her life. The criterion for success is internal (psychological) not external.

In short, the protean career is shaped more by the individual than by the organisation and may be redirected from time to time to meet the needs of this person' (p 20).

There are three kinds of flexibility associated with the protean career:

- It provides a new approach to time over the span of one's career. Unlike the traditional sequence of upward moves or predictable phases, the protean career does not follow a linear course. For the protean career person there is no idealised career path; he or she creates a flexible, idiosyncratic course, as unique as a voice print or the image of one's iris used as a PIN code.
- There is also an enlargement of career space. Careers can move out from the narrow

boundaries of paid work in a formal organisation. The distinction between work life and home life becomes blurred as work and non-work roles overlap.

- There is a reversal in the way we think about the relationship between the employee and the organisation. The protean career requires a different perspective, with the individual in the foreground and the organisation in the background. The person pursues his or her personal aspirations within the context of the organisation. When the context is no longer conducive to further development, the protean career person leaves the organisation in search of a better place or a change of scene.

Many of the changes in career management today involve an element of risk for the individual, the organisation and career professionals. But it is an unavoidable risk, a calculated one. As Douglas T. Hall questions, 'How exactly do you help people be whole at work (and at home)? How do people have careers when they are barely staying afloat in the white water? How do you help them make sense of work when the world seems to have gone awry?

'The answer is in the white water. The current chaos provides the two prime ingredients for career growth: challenging growth and relationships. Other people and seemingly impossible tasks provide rich ground for learning. Furthermore, this learning must take place in the context of work (or an organisation) to whose overall purpose the individual can commit her or himself with pride' (p 344).

Work/life balance

It is not just career couples with children but also single individuals who are seeking to achieve a better balance between work and personal life. Those who cannot find balance, particularly women, are jumping out of corporate life and starting their own businesses.

Work/life balance means the harmonious and holistic integration of work and non-work in our lives, allowing individuals to fulfil all their life tools. People seek balance for many reasons – quality of life, childcare, elderly care, voluntary work, education, travel, sports, hobbies and time with friends. Men and women in relationships have to negotiate not only with their respective organisations, but also with each other.

Strategies for managing work/life balance are:

- use technology to work from home some days,
- work efficiently for set hours,
- hold back ambition,
- sort out constraints with partner,
- employ help at home, for example, nanny, cleaner, gardener,
- use concierge services at work,
- postpone having children,
- use up all holiday entitlement and
- negotiate constraints with manager, using flexibility.

In a study of 303 managers in 2001 (most with Masters of Business Administration degrees), 75 per cent of them said work/life balance was very or extremely important. In fact, 49 per cent of the women saw it as extremely important, compared to 37 per cent of the men. For those with dependent children, 85 per cent said it was very or extremely important. Forty per cent of all respondents aged between the age of 25 and 40 said they might turn down promotion for balance, but none had actually done so before the age of 36. This last statistic indicates that managers feel they must have established their careers before they take action to achieve balance. The struggle to achieve balance is so great that many women decide to remain childless. Whilst two thirds of senior male managers have children, only one third of senior female managers do.

REALITY CHECK

WORK/LIFE BALANCE

So many companies report that work/life balance is now one of the key reasons for people leaving, because of the need to manage work and other commitments, and that this affected both men and women. The high workload, long hours culture was making it difficult for people to cope. Interestingly, more enlightened, international companies, such as IBM, have stressed that solutions should be local, as different areas have differing needs. For example, in most of Europe, employees appreciate a laptop computer to enable them to take work home, whilst the French prefer to keep work at work. As well as offering flexibility in terms of work arrangements, often facilitated by new technology, more companies are supporting day-care for children and elders, as well as summer camps in Europe for school age children in holiday periods.

THE BUSINESS CASE FOR EMPLOYERS

The UK Department of Trade and Industry suggests the following reasons for organisations to consider work/life balance:

- as a recruitment tool to attract the best talent,
- to retain employees,
- to improve customer service,
- to increase the return on training investment,
- to create a more diverse workforce, to reflect the customer base,
- to reduce absenteeism, sickness and stress,
- to improve morale, commitment and loyalty and
- to improve organisational flexibility and change competency.

The UK has the longest working hours in Europe, with little and expensive provision of childcare and elderly care. Women employees have wanted flexible ways of working for the past decade. Now, as male managers are also putting work/life balance high on their agenda, the issue becomes critical to employers.

REALITY CHECK

BARBARA CASSANI

Barbara Cassani's first proper job after university was as a management consultant, and then as a senior consultant with Coopers & Lybrand in Washington DC from 1984 to 1987. The consultancy firm was filled with sharp, young MBAs who made up their lack of business experience with brashness. She fitted in nicely. Personally she had her doubts. 'I was doing something described as international business, yet I had never lived or worked abroad (apart from summer jobs in Stockholm).' She and her husband decided to return to his native UK. She tried to arrange a transfer with Coopers & Lybrand to the London office, but the US branch of the company baulked at it, not wanting to pay her moving costs, she felt. So she had to join the firm afresh in London. It was a different company in London from the US firm, with much older consultants who based their advice on 10 to 20 years' experience. She stayed with it for just a year. Ultimately she was not happy with management consultancy as a career. 'Too much observing; not enough doing. You tell people what you think they should do and then you leave.' she said. 'You write reports, you analyse problems and make recommendations and in 80 per cent of the cases sadly nothing happens. Either your report was written for political purposes or there was a problem of implementation.'

She decided she wanted to work in a company. 'I was so arrogant, I had great ideas that needed a real company for testing. I wanted to work somewhere I could figure out what needed to be changed and then implement the change.' She answered an obscure wanted ad in the *Sunday Times* from a company looking for a strategic marketing person with imagination. 'It read: "Do you want to be a marketing challenger in a global service business?" And I said, "Yes please!" I thought it was a bank, because it was at the time of the big bang in the financial sector. You could have knocked me over when I found out after my third interview that it was British Airways.'

After working in a variety of senior manager jobs over ten years with British Airways, Barbara Cassani accepted an invitation from the chief executive officer, Bob Ayling, to do a feasibility study for the start-up of a low-cost airline under British Airways' umbrella. She was British Airways' top marketing manager at the time, based in New York City, living with her banker husband and their two small children. To undertake her research involved many trips between New York and London on Concorde. She recommended the start up of Go Fly Airlines and won £60 million from British Airways. In its first two years Go Fly Airlines lost £20 million each year and then turned in a profit. But by that time British Airways had a new chief executive officer who wanted to sell 'Go'. It did not fit with the British Airways brand and was a distraction to management – that summed up his view. Cassani persuaded him to let her put together a management buyout. A deal was done with British Airways for £110 million. Under her 'hands on' direction as chief executive officer, Go Fly Airlines became more profitable and expanded its routes. She won the Veuve Clicquot Business Woman of the Year Award for 2001.

3i became the largest venture capital partner; next was Barclaycard. Cassani herself was given a 4 per cent share, her plan was to grow the business and then float it as a public company. Eleven months later, though, the venture capital partners accepted an offer – against her advice – for £380 million from rival low-cost airline Easyjet. Cassani's share was nearly £10 million.

While she waits for her next career move, Barbara Cassani has bought a wine bar in South London called 'The Bridge' and is writing a book about her experiences.

Source: Vinnicombe, S. and Bank, J. (2003), *Women with attitude: lessons for career management*, London: Routledge, p 38. (Reprinted with permission of Routledge Publishers.)

Summary

A career is the series of jobs held by an individual over a lifetime. The whole process of joining an organisation can be viewed from two different points – that of the employee and the organisation. Early experiences in an organisation can either make the individual content and well matched or disappointed and out of place.

ATTRACTION AND SELECTION

In the top ten non-financial measures used by investors to analyse company performance, ability to attract and retain talented people was rated more highly than market share. Companies need to be aware of the images they project to potential employees, and men and women may be attracted by different attributes.

Selection is a difficult process due to the subjectivity involved. Problems include:

- inaccurate information due to mutual selling,
- unconscious colluding in creating unrealistic expectations,
- incorrect images of the organisation and
- uncertainties about the future.

INDUCTION AND SOCIALISATION

It is important that individuals are assimilated smoothly into the organisation. Person organisation fit refers to the compatibility between the individual and the employing organisation. It includes competencies, personal characteristics and personal values. Organisational socialisation is the process by which employees learn about and adapt to their new workplace. Just as there are problems in the attraction/selection process, so there are in the induction/socialisation process. The most important socialisation practices are interaction with peers, supervisor and senior colleagues, and mentoring. Mentoring is an increasingly popular practice for supporting junior managers, particularly women, towards senior roles. Mentoring is acknowledged to help protégé, mentor and organisation.

Managers go through different stages in making the transition into an organisation:

- getting used to the place,
- denial,
- depression,
- letting go,
- testing new reality and
- putting it together.

CAREER DEVELOPMENT

Many organisations have well-established systems of career planning and development. As people acquire more and more work experience they become clearer as to their career orientation. Schein called this a career anchor. It contains three components: self-perceived talents and abilities, self-perceived motives and needs, and self-perceived attitudes and values. Schein identified eight career anchors: technical, managerial, security, creativity, autonomy, entrepreneurial, challenge and lifestyle.

A critical element of meaningful career progress is the nature of the psychological contract, namely the unspoken contract, which expresses what employees and organisations expect from one another. The new psychological contract has five implicit assumptions:

- employment relationship is situational,
- reward for performance is based on contribution,
- management is empowering of its employees,
- loyalty means responsibility and good work and
- explicit job contracting is offered.

As a result people will move organisations regularly (this is known as the 'Protean career').

WORK/LIFE BALANCE

This means the harmonious and holistic integration of work and non work in our lives. Work/life balance is important for everyone, especially women. There are many strategies individuals and organisations can employ to achieve a better work/life balance. The Department of Trade and Industry has put forward a powerful business case in favour of work/life balance. At the moment the UK has the longest working hours in Europe and little provision of childcare and elderly care.

4 *Motivation*

The subject of motivation covers the fundamental question, 'What stimulates people at work?' What drives people to do the things they do in their job? Can such energy be harnessed to help individuals to improve their performance at work? Motivation is a familiar concept and the word is used in a way that is close to its Latin root '*movere*', meaning to move. People are motivated to lose weight, to exercise weekly, to read more, to shop less, to give up something for Lent. Highly motivated people may decide to run a marathon or a 10km race. Difficulties at work are attributed to poor motivation, and poorly motivated individuals generate a substantial number of work problems.

Motivation implies *action* and, in order to act, *energy* and *effort* are required. The level of individual motivation is determined by the amount of energy and effort people invest in their work. For people to generate such energy and effort, they need to be stimulated by the work they do, the job they hold and the people they work with. In general, people are highly motivated when they are well matched to their jobs. It is the fit between person and job that determines an individual's level of motivation.

In this chapter we examine these two crucial factors, the individual and the job. We shall focus on individuals and look at what determines individual motivation and how this varies across male and female managers. We shall also examine jobs and analyse those properties of jobs that are regarded as motivational. We finish the chapter by looking at the broader topic of commitment.

REALITY CHECK

THE SUNDAY TIMES 'BEST COMPANY TO WORK FOR' 2003

'It is the best company to work for in Britain,' explains Maxine Edwards.

Despite its 'negative' reputation in certain quarters, Microsoft is rated as a 'best company to work for' by its employees for many reasons, including the sense of 'well-being' that people feel.

Special thank yous are offered to staff in terms of staying at luxury hotels especially at times of launching new products.

'We work long hours but it doesn't feel like work most of the time: it is cool stuff and very upbeat,' she says. 'One of our

directors sent an e-mail saying he doesn't want to see us after 6pm. I've never heard of anything like that before.'

In an internal survey, '93 per cent of staff feel proud to work for the company and say it "makes a positive difference to the world we live in", 92 per cent are excited about where it is going and would miss it if they left.'

Under the direction of Neil Holloway, managing director, the latest in flexible working technology has been introduced. Wireless links exist across their Reading campus, allowing people to utilise their laptops anywhere, have their mobile phone linked to e-mail and have broadband available at home.

'The business park in Reading is spectacular, with a lake where charity rowing teams train, a forest and picnic tables.'

Additionally, there is a well-being clinic, offering everything from a mechanical massage chair to well-man clinics (including classes on how to detect testicular cancer). There is a 'bump' club to help pregnant mothers before their 18 weeks' fully paid leave, on-site nurses and doctor, and even a facility to donate bone marrow.

The firm has opened a crèche with 50

places for £35 a day (£37 for the under 2s), has four cafés, a subsidised restaurant and Xbox games terminals for entertainment (if television stations including the own-brand 'UTV Station' are not enough). Sports are given a boost with a £260 000 social budget, and the firm subsidises outings to shows or trips abroad. There is free private healthcare (including 'life partners' and family), and a four-month sabbatical (unpaid) after four years.

Source: The Sunday Times – 100 best companies to work for, 2003, *The Sunday Times*, 2 March, 2003.

What determines an individual's motivation?

An individual's motivation is the result of the interaction of needs, incentives and perceptions. Figure 4.1 indicates the motivational process for an employee in an organisation. Quite simply, individual motivation is determined by the extent to which the needs that employees bring to the job are matched by the incentives (such as rewards) provided by the organisation. This is a subjective process. What one individual perceives as a satisfying incentive (for example, a good salary) may not be satisfying for another. This subjective element in motivation is critical, for individuals react to their jobs in terms of how they see them.

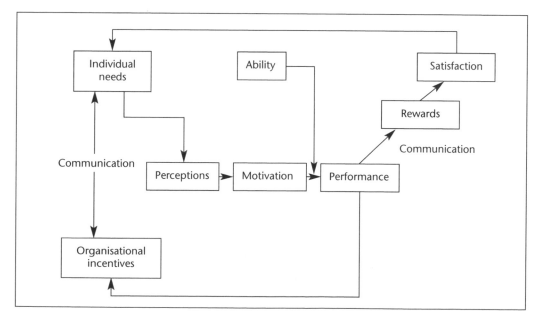

Figure 4.1 What determines an individual's motivation? (*Source: Working in Organisations*, First Edition, 1987)

For this reason, managing workgroups is a difficult process. Not only does the manager of the group have to consider the objectives to be achieved and the means and resources available, but they also have to raise the level of motivation of each individual in the group. A group that is poorly motivated is unlikely to make best use of the resources available or even attempt to acquire new resources. In these circumstances, the whole group will require the manager's attention. Poorly motivated individuals in a group are likely to function below their level of effective performance and could also demotivate the other, more positively motivated members. In such a case, the manager will need to attend to the poorly motivated members, not only to improve their performance but also to minimise their negative effect on the group.

The relationship between needs, incentives and perception is influenced by communication between the individual and the organisation. Organisations that inadequately inform their employees of opportunities for them at work are likely to demotivate them. These employees may have little respect for their employing organisation and hence do the minimum required. However, another form of communication exists, based on the views and beliefs of individuals. Poor performance can occur if individuals do not have the same views of their jobs as their supervisors. The supervisor may wish the individual to undertake tasks that he or she considers not to be part of the workload. Equally, the supervisor may apply criteria and standards of performance different from those of the subordinate. Lack of agreement on the basic principles of the subordinate's job may lead to the subordinate becoming demotivated.

Another complicating factor is the person's ability. Individuals' levels of ability influence their perceptions of their job as well as directly affecting their performance. Performance improves when both ability and motivation improve. Performance deteriorates when either of these deteriorates.

The three key variables of needs, incentives and perceptions form the basis of the three categories of theory to be reviewed here. These are:

- need theories,
- incentive theories and
- expectancy theories.

NEED THEORIES

What are needs?

If motivation is partly determined by people's needs then we must seek to understand what needs they have. The importance of needs as a factor in individual motivation is that needs initially arouse and energise behaviour; they are the prime causes of individual behaviour. Three important theorists, Douglas McGregor, Abraham Maslow and David McClelland, have investigated the needs that individuals experience.

The work of Douglas McGregor (1960) as described in his seminal book, *The human side of enterprise*, focused on the assumptions managers made about human nature and behaviour. His ideas can be distilled into the three postulates of Theory X and the six statements of Theory Y. The implications for motivation are obvious.

Theory X assumptions were:

1 Most people have an inherent dislike of work and will avoid it if they can.

2 Hence most people must be coerced, controlled, directed or threatened with punishment to get them to put forth adequate effort towards the achievement of organisational objectives.
3 The average person prefers to be directed, wishes to avoid responsibility, has relatively little ambition and wants security above all.

Theory Y assumptions were:

1 The expenditure of physical and mental effort in work is as natural as in play or rest.
2 External controls and the threat of punishment are not the only means for bringing about efforts towards organisational objectives. People will exercise self-direction and self-control in the service of objectives to which they are committed.
3 People can best achieve their own goals by aligning them with the goals of the organisation.
4 The average person learns, under proper conditions, not only to accept but to seek responsibility.
5 The capacity to exercise a relatively high degree of imagination, ingenuity and creativity in the solution of organisational problems is widely, not narrowly, distributed.
6 Under the conditions of modern industrial life, the intellectual potential of the average person is only partially utilised.

The assumptions about people made in Theory Y help to explain why we focus positively on the individual needs that people bring to their jobs.

Abraham Maslow (1954) proposed a hierarchy of five types of need (see Figure 4.2): physiological, security, social, self-esteem and self-actualisation. Physiological needs are those associated with basic biological requirements, such as hunger or thirst. Security needs are related to needs for protection from danger and threats, such as job security. Social needs are needs for expression of friendship or love or even working with a compatible group of people. Self-esteem needs are bound up with self-respect and personal autonomy. Self-actualisation needs are the needs for realising one's own potential, often through undertaking challenging work.

Maslow suggests, in relation to his hierarchy of needs, that:

• Each lower-order need must be satisfied before the next higher-order need assumes dominance.
• When an individual need becomes satisfied, it declines in importance and the need at the next level of the hierarchy increases in importance.
• When the individual moves up to the highest-level need, satisfaction of this need increases in importance (self-actualisation).
• The number and variety of needs increase as an individual's psychological development takes place.

Maslow believed in a 'needs ascendancy' process, sequential in nature, whereby one particular set of needs must reach a sufficient level of satisfaction before the next needs level becomes operational. The emphasis is on sufficiency, in that each successive level must be relatively satisfied before the next level of need becomes more important in motivating behaviour.

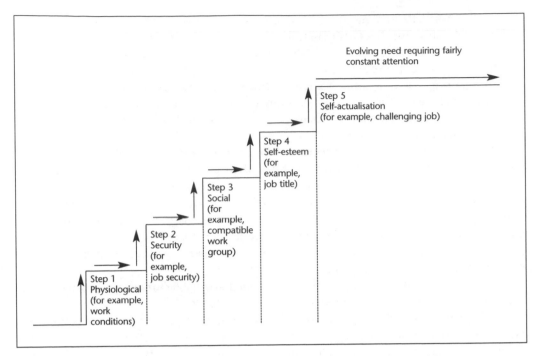

Figure 4.2 Maslow's hierarchy of needs (*Source: Working in Organisations*, First Edition, 1987)

An alternative view is that individual needs at work do not change in quite the systematic way Maslow envisaged.

Perhaps individual needs vary in relation to the incentive provided by the organisation. An individual could be involved in satisfying needs at levels 2 and 5 simultaneously. The attitude towards tenure in British universities and long-term employment in the public sector provides a good example. As a result of the changing psychological contract at work, job security is no longer guaranteed in such organisations. Hence, a university academic can be struggling to achieve tenure and security of employment and yet at the same time be involved in long-term, self-generated research. He or she may be satisfactorily managing both processes. Furthermore, needs can vary according to age and stages in an individual's life cycle.

What about Maslow's theory as applied to women managers? Women managers report lower basic needs and higher needs for self-actualisation. Female managers are more concerned than male managers with opportunities for growth, autonomy and challenge. Contrary to popular belief, females do not experience a greater need to belong than do males. Thus, there are sex differences in Maslow's hierarchy of needs and these differences favour the female manager.

David McClelland (1965) argues that not all needs are as universal as Maslow proposed. Many are socially acquired and vary from culture to culture. He defined three types of socially acquired needs: the need for achievement, the need for affiliation and the need for power. The need for achievement reflects the desire to meet task goals. The need for affiliation reflects the desire to develop good interpersonal relationships. The need for power reflects the desire to influence and control other people.

Further, McClelland argues that it is difficult for people to change their needs, once acquired. Pursuing this line of thought, it is important to diagnose needs at the selection stage. Managers can try to match individuals with particular needs to positions where these can best be satisfied. For example, an individual with a high achievement need should be in a job that offers high performance targets, like sales. A manager with a high power need should be in charge of the shop floor or a functional department – a position where he or she can exert control over others. A manager with a high affiliation need should be placed in a project team environment.

McClelland's original research focused on men. He found that female subjects did not respond to the instructions designed to arouse their achievement motivation and it was concluded that women were less achievement-motivated than men. The fact that females produced ample achievement imagery under relaxed (as opposed to experimental) conditions is particularly noteworthy. There are now data suggesting that the achievement motives of women are often experimentally suppressed in groups, especially mixed-sex groups, but are enhanced when women perform alone or are convinced that their achievements will not be noticed by men or offend them.

Additionally, Clayton Alderfer (1972) developed a three-factor theory of needs called 'ERG': Existence Relatedness and Growth.

ERG theory relates closely to Maslow's hierarchy of needs in that existence is similar to Maslow's physiological and safety needs, relatedness is similar to Maslow's social needs and growth is similar to Maslow's esteem and self-actualisation needs. Alderfer makes three important points, which are illustrated in Figure 4.3:

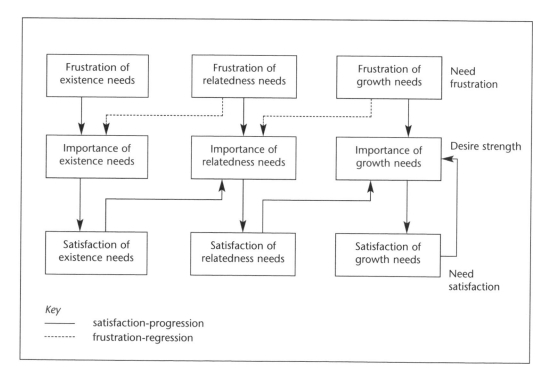

Figure 4.3 Satisfaction-progression, frustration-regression components of 'existence, relatedness and growth' theory (*Source*: *Working in Organisations*, First Edition, 1987)

- The less a need is satisfied, the more important it becomes.
- The more a lower-level need is satisfied, the greater the importance of the next higher-level need.
- The less the higher-level need is satisfied, the greater the importance the lower need assumes.

This last point, about need frustration, is particularly important. If individuals cannot get what they want from a job then they just demand more of what they can get. Hence employees may be disruptive at work, demanding more money, when what they really want is a more challenging job. If staff motivational problems are to be overcome it is important to recognise such 'displacement' behaviour.

INCENTIVE THEORIES

While need theories answer the question, 'What drives or stimuli cause individual behaviour?', incentive theories approach motivation from the other direction: 'What external factors influence human behaviour?' Managers exercise little conscious influence over the former, whereas they might have considerable influence on the latter. This is not to say that managers can afford to ignore theories of individuals' needs; such knowledge is important for several reasons. A manager has only a limited number of incentives to offer employees. It is therefore important to select staff with needs that can be satisfied within the job or organisation. An organisation has a diversity of jobs with different sets of incentives. Needs theories can help managers identify and differentiate between individuals' needs and allocate individuals to jobs where they can best become motivated. Lastly, although managers cannot directly alter individuals' needs, they can indirectly influence them by good management of the incentives through which they are satisfied.

Frederick Herzberg (1959) developed his theory of incentives by asking a sample of employees, 'When you are satisfied at work, what is making you happy?' and, 'When you are dissatisfied at work, what is making you unhappy?' The result was Herzberg's famous two-factor theory (see Figure 4.4). He named the dissatisfiers 'maintenance' or 'hygiene' factors, and the satisfiers 'motivators'. All the maintenance factors pertain to what are called the 'extrinsic' aspects of the job. Herzberg believed that if the maintenance factors were not provided to a sufficiently high standard then employees would be dissatisfied. If they were provided to an acceptable standard employees would only be 'not dissatisfied'; they would still not necessarily be motivated. High motivation can occur only when individuals experience both maintenance factors and motivators, which are of a different order.

The Herzberg theory is easy to appreciate and readily applicable in organisations. However, three points are not satisfactorily considered. First, certain factors, in particular money, can be both satisfiers and dissatisfiers. Second, not everyone is motivated by the intrinsic drives; someone's motivation can easily be influenced by their age and the stage of their life. Third, male and female managers do not respond in the same way. Women managers are more concerned with opportunities for growth, autonomy and challenge, and less concerned with the work environment and pay. Where this becomes a problem at work is where male managers have been found to underestimate the importance of intrinsic factors in motivating women. This can have important consequences for women managers' motivation and job satisfaction.

Hygiene/maintenance factors	Motivators
Company policy and administration	Achievement
Supervision	Recognition
Salary	Work itself
Interpersonal relations	Responsibility
Physical working conditions	Advancement

Figure 4.4 Herzberg's two-factor theory (*Source: Working in Organisations*, First Edition, 1987)

Money is a complicated motivator because it can be used to satisfy a number of different individual needs. For example, it can be used to purchase a house, thereby satisfying a basic physiological need; it can be used to give frequent cocktail parties, thereby satisfying a social need; or it can be used to buy expensive cars, thereby satisfying a need for self-esteem. Many individuals do not regard money as a high priority work incentive, but place high priorities on items that can be purchased with money.

Despite the conceptual problems surrounding it, money plays several important roles in relation to the individual and their attitude to work. At its most basic, money is used to compensate employees for their effort in the job. There is often a 'market rate' for the job, meaning some generally agreed range of payment. Sometimes money forms only one part of the reward package. (Today share options that provide ownership in the company are increasingly used to bind talented people to companies.)

Further, money allows individuals to compare their current job with jobs held in the past, with those of other individuals and with those in other organisations. Such comparisons can be highly motivating, for the individual can reasonably accurately attribute worth or merit to a job or organisation. Equally, money can give rise to feelings of inequity, since people can exaggerate their salaries when talking to colleagues. Secrecy surrounding pay policies in many companies aggravates this particular problem, especially in relation to inequality between male and female managers' salaries.

Whether money is viewed as a positive or negative motivator, it is a concrete means of measuring a job. Money is also used as a mechanism for indicating standards of individual performance. Merit rises, percentage increases or incentive bonuses all allow managers to reward their staff for competent performance. Whether or not the amount offered is significant, it may provide a psychological boost to the individuals concerned, and so exert a powerful influence on them.

The need and incentive theories can be compared (see Figure 4.5). Maslow's, Alderfer's and Herzberg's theories overlap considerably. Maslow suggests that there are five needs – physiological, safety, social, self-esteem and self-actualisation. Alderfer suggests that there are three – existence (Maslow's two basic needs), relatedness (Maslow's social need) and growth (Maslow's esteem and self-actualisation needs). Herzberg, more simply, implies that individuals have only two needs: one that equates to Maslow's esteem and self-actualisation needs and Alderfer's growth need, and the other that encompasses all the lower needs identified by Maslow and Alderfer. In fact, most job attitude questionnaires in common use today reflect the need structures of all three theories.

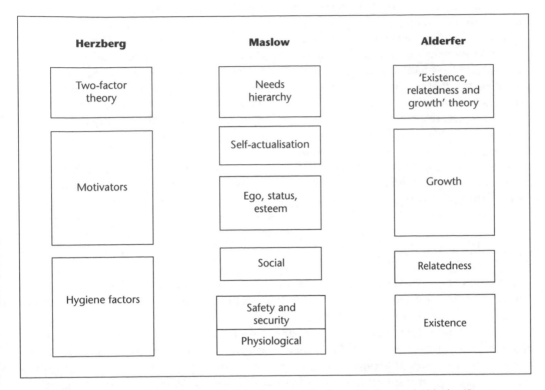

Figure 4.5 Theories of motivation: similarities between Herzberg, Maslow and Alderfer (*Source*: *Working in Organisations*, First Edition, 1987)

REALITY CHECK

BOSS TAKES HIS EMPLOYEES ON A SPANISH HOLIDAY

John Marshall decided to show his appreciation to his staff by paying £200 000 to take 119 staff and 173 of the partners, children and friends on a week's holiday to Majorca. Any member of staff, whether full-time or part-time, with a year's service, was entitled to enjoy the boss's generous offer of free flights and a free stay in self-catering accommodation. While they soaked up the sun in the Spanish Island resort in August or September 2003, they were paid as if they were at work. The time away did not go against their annual leave.

John Marshall, 46, is the owner of a furni-

ture company, Durham Pine, that posted a £2 million profit. His motivation for the extravagant gesture was simply a 'thank-you' to my staff. 'We have had a really good year. I was brought up in a council house and I know what it is to struggle. So doing something like this is perhaps a bit of pay-back.

'When I first started out working on farms I felt unloved and un-respected. Now that I am on the other side of things I don't want my employees to feel the same.

'There was nothing in particular that gave me the idea for the holiday but it just struck me and I thought "why not?" The other members of the board thought I was crazy when I told them my plan but I eventually won them round.

'It's been a long while since money was my motivation for working. So the thank-you letters I have had from some of the staff have made it that bit easier to get out of bed each morning.'

The employees went to Majorca in two waves, on the 28th August for those with children and on the 5th September for just couples. Maria Yohn, full-time receptionist at the company head office for five years, went with her husband and 2 year old

daughter. 'It was great meeting people and putting faces with names. We also met their families on a friendly basis.'

The self-made millionaire's career in retailing began in 1984 when he sold his car for £1500 to buy a second-hand shop. He formed Durham Pine two years later and he decided to specialise in pine furniture with one furniture store in Durham. He now has 75 shops across the country trading under the name DP Furniture Express.

Source: Mintowt-Czyz, L. (2003), 'Boss who's taking 119 of his staff on holiday', *Daily Mail*, (8 April), p 33.

EXPECTANCY THEORIES

The theories put forward by Herzberg, Maslow and Alderfer emphasise satisfaction of either extrinsic needs (provided for by the organisation) or intrinsic needs (inner drives within the person). One issue that is assumed and not explained is that of choice. There can be a limitless number of possible behaviours available to each individual that will partly or wholly achieve goals that in turn satisfy his or her needs. How do we choose between alternative behaviours or courses of action? Expectancy theory, sometimes known as instrumentality theory, deals with this question concerning the processes of 'decision-making'. According to expectancy theory, people choose between alternatives using rational, scientific, economic criteria. They examine the various rewards available according to their desirability in terms of satisfying personal motives. They will then choose the optimal reward according to their ability to perform given behaviours successfully. This choice, however, is influenced by how they think these behaviours are rewarded. In essence, we weigh up the probabilities of success in adopting alternative courses of action, and then choose the course of action likely to be most successful and at the same time achieve the greatest reward.

A strong proponent of expectancy theory is Victor Vroom (Vroom and Yetton, 1973). His theory is based on four premises:

- People have preferences (or 'valences') for various outcomes or incentives that are available to them.
- People hold expectations about the likelihood that an action or effort on their part will lead to the intended outcome or objective.
- People understand that certain behaviours will be followed by desirable outcomes or incentive rewards, for example, a pay rise or increased status.
- The action a person chooses to take is determined by the expectancies and preferences (valences) that the person has at the time.

Vroom argues that people will be highly motivated when they feel confident of achieving high performance, the attraction of the rewards is high, they feel that they are likely to receive the rewards if they perform highly and they feel fairly rewarded relative to others around them.

From this basis, Vroom developed a decision tree model, whereby individuals could attempt to quantify the degree of required effort by plotting out the results of their efforts (see Figure 4.6). Using the decision tree, they could assess their chances of meeting those task goals in relation to the amount of effort required, and equally consider whether the likely rewards for achieving task goals would be appropriate.

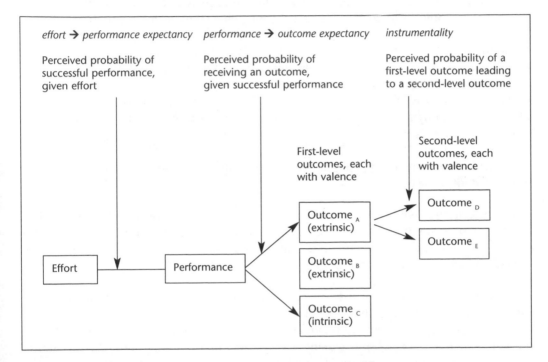

Figure 4.6 Major terms in expectancy theory (*Source*: Nadler, D.A. and Lawler, E.E. III (1997), 'Motivation: a diagnostic approach', in: Hackman, J.R., Lawler, E.E. III and Protek, L.W. *Perspectives on behaviour in organisations*, McGraw-Hill, p 23. Reproduced with permission from Ed Lawler III.)

Vroom's original model has been modified by a number of researchers. The following terms are now commonly used to describe expectancy theory:

- *Valence*: The strength of a person's preference for a particular outcome. It can be positive (desired) or negative (not desired).
- *Outcome*: A consequence or result of one's actions.
- *First-level outcome*: The immediate effect of one's action, for example, improved job performance. The first-level outcome is often the outcome of concern to the organisation.
- *Second-level outcome*: The personal consequences or outcomes that result from the first-level outcomes, for example, promotion.
- *Expectancy*: The probability that a behaviour (particular level of effort on the job) will result in a particular first-level outcome (improved job performance).
- *Instrumentality*: The strength of the causal relationship between the first-level outcomes and the second-level outcomes, for example, pay rise or increase in status and authority.

The two levels of outcome refer to the amount of effort an individual applies to doing a job and the results of that effort in terms of achievement (effort-outcome relationship). First-level outcome relates to expectancy 1 (see Figure 4.6), namely that the amount of effort applied influences the standard of work of the individual (effort-performance relationship). Second-level outcome relates to expectancy 2 (see Figure 4.6), namely that the standard of a person's work is influenced by the incentives offered by the organisation (performance-incentive relationship).

It can be appreciated, therefore, that people's performances and preferences influence their levels of motivation. Performance has been subdivided into the following characteristics:

- Productivity, that is, how efficient the person is in achieving tasks.
- Internal task goals, that is, those goals to be achieved in doing a task that the person is internally motivated to achieve.
- External task goals, that is, those goals to be achieved in doing tasks that are required of the individual by the organisation and which the individual may or may not be motivated to accomplish.

An individual's preferences, namely the expected result of application of effort, have been subdivided into:

- Intrinsic components, that is, outcomes that the individual is internally motivated to achieve, such as self-development or gaining valuable experience on the job.
- Extrinsic outcomes, that is, outcomes that the individual desires from the organisation, such as increased status or promotion.

Despite all these developments the basic elements of expectancy theory (expectancy, valence and instrumentality) have not changed.

Expectancy theorists do not maintain that people consciously and rationally go through this process of decision making. Expectancy theory simply highlights the rather complicated and subjective process of reaching a decision to act in a particular way, emphasising people's assessment of their ability to attain certain goals, the amount of effort required for specific outcomes and the probability of their being rewarded. All these are evaluated in relation to personal needs and wants. Expectancy theory does not necessarily provide a model to help individuals to make decisions, but examines the process by which they choose how to behave.

What determines motivation on the job?

So far we have explored the person-oriented components of motivation. We have explained:

- Behaviour, in terms of purposeful behaviour to attain desired goals.
- Rewards and satisfaction, in terms of those rewards and satisfaction that keep people working towards task goals.
- The relationship between task goals and human needs.

Needs, incentive and expectancy theories are covered by these components. The other key variable in any discussion of motivation are the jobs that people hold.

Understanding the requirement of the job is vital and an equally complex factor in trying to improve employees' performance at work. How many of us truly understand what is required or expected of us in our job? Moreover, most jobs alter in terms of tasks to be undertaken, as do people's performance expectations. At times, the individual and the boss may not be aware of the implications of such changes and only understand what is happening in retrospect. This has implications for the performance, rewards and satisfaction of the individual. While in some cases the individual does not know what is expected, in other cases the problem is that the employee reports to more than one boss and they have differing views of what is required. Thus, the way work is designed is one consideration.

Rewards can also affect motivation. The environment and culture of the organisation influence the individual and their performance in their jobs. Certain basic conditions – such as computer failure – will always impair performance. Hence, the action levers that can be 'pulled' are the second consideration in promoting a more motivational work environment.

WORK DESIGN

The structure of a job creates different expectations and behaviour patterns in each job-holder. For one sort of job, the expectation could be that, 'The harder I work, the more bored, fatigued, tired, depressed, I will become.' For another job, the expectation could be the reverse – self-satisfaction, a feeling of greater professionalism, accomplishment and possibly greater extrinsic rewards (pay, status, promotion). Irrespective of extrinsic rewards, the first job is unlikely to stimulate greater effort in the individual, while the second is likely to induce a higher level of performance.

Thus the job itself is a vital source of expectancy, and hence motivation, among people working in organisations. We constantly experience the consequences of our work-related performance. The job itself is the point in the organisation where individuals are likely to see the most direct connection between how they do their work and what outcomes they receive. Hence it is important to understand how the nature of jobs and the design of work affect individual behaviour.

J. Richard Hackman and Greg Oldham focused on the concept of job enrichment, which is essentially a combination of scientific management principles (see Chapter 2) and behavioural theories of motivation. From their original study of job characteristics, three psychological states emerged as crucial to both motivation and satisfaction on the job:

- The person must *experience the work as meaningful*, as far as his or her own values are concerned. If the job appears to be trivial or insignificant, then they are unlikely to be internally motivated.
- The person must *experience responsibility* for the results of their work, and must be aware of their accountability for work outcomes. If they view the quality of the work done as depending more on external factors than on their own efforts, they have less reason to feel personally proud when they do well or disheartened when they do not.
- The person must have *knowledge of the results of their work*. If they rarely find out whether they are doing well or badly, they have no basis for feeling good about doing well, or unhappy about doing badly.

The more an individual experiences these three psychological states, the more they will experience intrinsic motivation, namely motivation based on doing the job, rather than on external rewards. Hence they are likely to have positive feelings when they consider their work as meaningful. They are likely to have a high sense of self-regard, for they can measure their own effectiveness and in turn need to be held accountable for the results of their efforts.

Hackman and Oldham (1980) identified a number of job design characteristics that, if competently managed, will stimulate these psychological states.

Experienced meaningfulness is composed of three elements:

- Skill variety – a job that requires a person to use a number of different skills and talents to carry out a variety of different activities. A person with a job that stretches their talents, skills and abilities is likely to feel that the job is worthwhile.
- Task identity – a job that requires completion of a whole and identifiable piece of work, with a visible outcome. Doing a whole job, putting together an entire product, being able to point to an item in a shop window and say 'I made that', is more satisfying than being responsible for only a small part of the job.
- Task significance – a job that has a significant effect on the lives of other people. Putting drawing pins into boxes is likely to be experienced as less worthwhile than putting medical prescriptions into bottles, even though the skill levels required may be the same; in the second case, lives may be at stake.

Experienced responsibility for work outcomes comprises one element, namely autonomy. This relates to freedom, independence and discretion in scheduling one's own work and determining the procedures to be used in carrying it out. As autonomy increases, so people seem to feel more personal responsibility and involvement in the successes and failures that occur on the job, and are more willing to accept accountability for the outcomes of the work.

Knowledge of the results of work activities is composed of two elements:

- Feedback from the job; actually carrying out the work activities gives some direct information about the effectiveness of the worker's performance.
- Feedback from others; other people, supervisors, co-workers, and so on, give the worker information about how well or badly they are doing.

Feedback from the job is more immediate and more potent on the employee than feedback from other people. The individual is able to look at the work being done and gauge their performance directly, based on sound data which can be used for job behaviour change.

These core dimensions – skill variety, task identity, task significance, autonomy and feedback – influence the level of the critical psychological states (see Figure 4.7) experienced by the job holder in terms of experienced meaningfulness of the work, experienced responsibility for work outcomes, and knowledge of results of work activities. High levels of the critical psychological states are likely to lead to favourable personal and work outcomes, such as high internal motivation, high work performance, high satisfaction, low absenteeism and reduced staff turnover.

However, there are moderating factors related to individual differences between people. Employees have differing growth need strengths which affect the influence of the job dimensions on internal motivation and performance. People with high needs for personal growth and development will respond positively to jobs which are high on the core job dimensions; people with low growth needs will feel 'overstretched' and unable to cope with jobs which are high in these dimensions (see Figure 4.7).

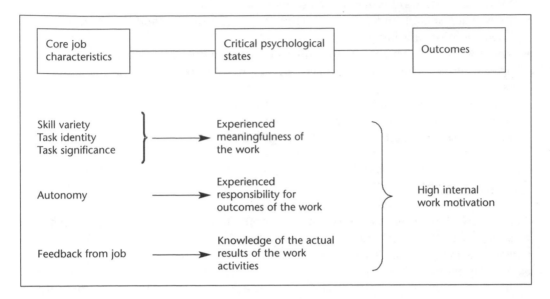

Figure 4.7 Job characteristics that foster high internal work motivation (*Source*: Hackman, J.R. and Oldham, G.R., (1980), *Work redesign* © Addison-Wesley, Reading, Massachusetts, p 77, Figure 4.2. Reprinted with kind permission from Addison-Wesley.)

The motivating potential of a job does not directly cause employees to be internally work motivated. A job high in motivating potential creates conditions where, if the job holder performs well, that behaviour is likely to be reinforced. Job characteristics, then, provide the framework for internal motivation. Whether individuals do experience their jobs as highly motivating depends upon the characteristics of the individual.

Hackman and Oldham argue that not all jobs should be enriched or designed to be high on the core motivation dimensions. The nature of the work, the job as envisaged by management and the individual job-holder all need to be taken into account in determining how the job should be designed.

ACTION LEVERS

In applying motivational concepts to work, a number of 'action levers' are available to managers:

- Identify needs, abilities and preferences for rewards at the recruitment stage. Hire not the 'best' candidate, but rather the one who most closely matches the job and the organisation.
- Once individuals are in the job do not assume that their needs will stay the same. They need monitoring, probably annually. Such monitoring can be conducted through an unstructured interview or by using a structured questionnaire.

- Understand what rewards you can give for high performance. Money is only one form of reward. Personal resources are as important (for example, personal recognition for performance) to subordinates, performing for the good of the department, working on the intrinsic aspects of the job.
- Make sure the reward system is applied fairly.
- Individuals should understand the requirements of the job and the reward system. Effective communication is vital.
- Those individuals capable of stretching themselves more in the job should be encouraged to do so. This may be achieved by emphasising the rewards available for high performance.
- Individuals should be shown how to become better performers. Again, effective communication is the key to providing supportive feedback and guidance.
- Reinforce superior performance with the appropriate rewards.

Commitment

So far motivation has been discussed in terms of the fit between an individual's needs and what is provided in the job. However, there is a broader explanation of what keeps an individual in a job and that is commitment. Commitment is the will to work. It has been extensively researched over the past 30 years. High levels of commitment are associated with reduced turnover and absenteeism in particular. As organisations seek improved performance and more involvement from their employees, the issue of commitment becomes increasingly important for managers.

Morrow (1993) defines commitment as 'a state in which an individual identifies with a particular organisation and its goals and wishes to maintain membership in order to facilitate these goals.' Morrow felt that the idea of organisational commitment should be re-evaluated and in 1993 developed a concentrically layered model reflecting the composite nature of commitment at work (see Figure 4.8).

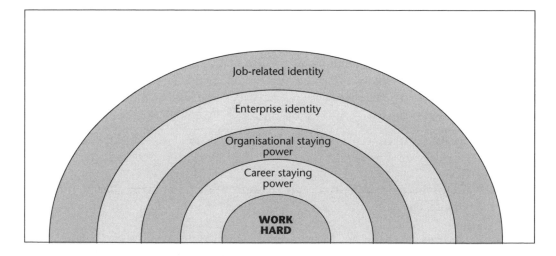

Figure 4.8 Capturing Morrow's (1993) inter-relationships of work-related commitment

Morrow related this order to the permeability of outside influences which could be exerted on these component parts. For example, job involvement might be temporarily affected by a problem with a manager at work, yet the individual might continue to feel committed to their career and to staying with the company. Morrow's five constructs are defined as follows:

- Work ethic endorsement is an internal attribute, the 'natural' inclination to work hard.
- Career commitment is the strength of motivation to work in a chosen career role, including a profession, namely, career-oriented staying power.
- Continuance organisational commitment is the desire to stay in the company, namely, organisational staying power.
- Affective organisational commitment is the degree to which individuals feel that they are part of the company through shared goals and values, namely, the identity people share in the enterprise.
- Job involvement or identity with the job, is the degree to which the individual identifies with the job. Job involvement can be influenced more easily than the internal layers. Job involvement most closely links with motivation.

The links between these five elements of work commitment are still under investigation.

Another researcher, Cohen (1999), through his work with Canadian nurses, showed that working hard led to job involvement which led to career commitment. Both job involvement and career commitment led to a desire to stay in the company and positively feel part of the company through shared goals and values. Motivation (as expressed by job involvement) is thus closely related to commitment.

Summary

Motivation answers the fundamental question, 'What stimulates people at work?' Motivation is derived from its Latin root *'movere'* to move. The level of individual motivation is determined by the amount of energy people invest in their work. It is the fit between person and job that determines an individual's level of motivation. This is a subjective process and what one individual perceives as satisfying may not be satisfying for another. The relationship between needs, incentives and perception is influenced by communication between the individual and the organisation. Another complicating factor is ability – individuals' levels of ability influence their perceptions of their job as well as directly affecting their performance. Performance improves when both ability and motivation improve.

NEED THEORIES

If motivation is partly determined by people's needs then we must understand what needs they have. McGregor's work on Theory X and Theory Y highlighted the importance of the needs that individuals bring to work.

Maslow proposed a hierarchy of five types of needs – physiological, security, social, self-esteem and self-actualisation. Maslow believed in a needs ascendancy process, whereby one set of needs must reach a sufficient level of satisfaction before the next level becomes operational. McClelland argued that not all needs are as universal as Maslow stated. He defined three types of socially acquired needs – the need for achievement, the need for affiliation and the need for power. McClelland argued that it is difficult for people to change their needs, once acquired. Clayton Alderfer developed a three-factor theory of needs – existence, relatedness and growth. He said that the less a higher level need is satisfied, the greater the importance of the lower need.

INCENTIVE THEORIES

Incentive theories look at how external factors influence human behaviour. Herzberg differentiated between hygiene factors, which at best could only hold people in their jobs, and motivators, which really motivated individuals. There are similarities between Herzberg's, Maslow's and Alderfer's theories. However, an incentive for one person may not encourage the other. Recent research has shown that female managers are more concerned with opportunities for growth, autonomy and challenge than male managers. Contrary to McClelland's original results, women managers do express a high need for achievement but this is often controlled in front of men.

EXPECTANCY THEORIES

Expectancy theory deals with the process of choice. Vroom argued that people will be highly motivated when they feel confident of achieving high performance, the attraction of the rewards is high, they feel that they are likely to receive the rewards if they perform highly and they feel fairly rewarded relative to others round them.

MOTIVATION ON THE JOB

Two factors influence the way people feel about their jobs, namely the way work is designed and the levers managers can utilise to improve the levels of motivation at work.

WORK DESIGN

The structure of a job creates different expectations and behaviour patterns in each jobholder. Hackman and Oldham in their job characteristics model identified three psychological states as crucial to both motivation and satisfaction on the job:

- The person must experience the work as meaningful.
- The person must experience responsibility for the results of the work.
- The person must have knowledge of the results of the work.

ACTION LEVERS

Eight action levers are identified that managers can call upon to make people feel more positive about their roles and work. These are: matching the person and the job, monitoring, rewarding, applying rewards equitably, communicating, stretching people, providing feedback and reinforcement.

COMMITMENT

There is a broader explanation of what keeps an individual in the job, and that is commitment. Morrow defines commitment as 'a state in which an individual identifies with a particular organisation and its goals and wishes to maintain membership in order to facilitate these goals'. Job involvement (close to our definition of motivation) leads to career commitment, a desire to stay with a company and positively feel part of the company – the three aspects of commitment.

5 *Teamworking*

Synergy is the aim of all teamworking – to produce an output where the whole is greater than the sum of its parts. The team's outputs are synergetic when they exceed the sum total of capabilities of the individual members. When a quality improvement team, for example, is well directed, well structured and well supported, its potential for synergetic outcomes can be boundless.

In this chapter we first look at some colourful examples of teamworking, then at the definition and purposes of teams. We explore some ways of building better teams through experimental learning activities. We cite some of the conclusions from J. Richard Hackman's research on effective and ineffective teamwork. We look at virtual teams and how they differ from face-to-face ones. We then examine team development and Belbin's team roles in detail. This is followed by a description of 'hot groups'. Then we explore an alternative frame of analysis to Belbin's team roles, that of team competencies developed by our Cranfield colleague, Tim Mills. Finally we look at failed teamwork, commonly referred to as 'group think'.

Impact of teamwork

Teamwork is essential to managing in organisations, to increase productivity, efficiency, motivation, job satisfaction, creativity and customer-responsiveness. It has been for many decades. The scientific use of modern work teams began in the 1960s when some of the best elements of Japanese teamworking were taken up in the West. Their widespread deployment came with the Quality Circle and Total Quality Management movement in the 1980s. By the late 1980s and early 1990s, self-managing teams or empowered work teams dominated. By the mid 1990s teamworking took on a global dimension as multinational and global companies such as General Electric, Motorola, Texas Instruments, Ford and Goodyear set up teams in their international subsidiaries in Europe, Latin America and the Pacific Rim. The relevance of teamwork has escalated as global organisations are under pressure to find new ways of operating to increase their competitive edge while providing a better quality of working life and increased flexibility for employees. Virtual teams – groups of people working in an interdependent way with shared purpose across space, time and organisational boundaries using technology to communicate and collaborate – have emerged on a vast scale worldwide (Lipnack and Stamps, 2000).

The achievements of traditional teamwork can be astonishing, as illustrated by the following examples:

* The Building Industry Association of San Diego County organised a competition to see if two teams could break the world record for building a house. The record then stood at

4 hours 20 minutes. The house was a three bedroom, two baths, nine room house (not a prefabricated one), with attached garage (1500 square feet of space) and fully landscaped. The Building Industry Association was interested in promoting teamworking and new ways of doing things. The winning team shattered the world record with a new time of 2 hours and 45 minutes. To do so they meticulously planned and practised each aspect of the operation. Concrete for the house's foundations, for example, was preheated so that it would harden within an hour of pouring. In the competition, the two 350 member teams had to rethink the house-building process completely, as it would normally take 90 days to build the house. There was a focus on safety, rigorous building code requirements and teamwork among architects, builders and suppliers. Each builder knew that his or her assignments would affect the next person's ability to complete their part of the job so everyone had to work as a well-coordinated team. Referees wearing the black and white striped shirts of football referees roamed the building sites ready to blow the whistle on safety or building code violations ('The Four Hour House', video, Building Industry Association, San Diego, California, 1983).

- On a much smaller scale a similar co-ordination is required of Grand Prix Formula 1 pit stop teams. They have 15 members and can change all four tyres of the racing car in a target time of under 6 seconds. They have done it in less time – 4.3 seconds. The 16th member of the team is the driver who must position the car within 6 to 12 inches from where the mechanics are poised waiting to pounce on the car. Three men stand at each of the four corners of the racing car. One has the wheel gun, another takes the wheel off and the third puts on the new wheel with the fresh tyre. There is a mechanic at the front of the racing car to operate the front jack and another at the rear to operate the rear jack. The 15th man stands behind the driver's head to steady the crash hoop while the car is on the jacks. Naturally each person's work impacts on that of the others. Military precision is required in the teamwork to avoid delays of seconds that could lose the race.
- Teamwork is essential in the world of music. When jazz groups perform a number poorly, they call it a 'train wreck'. In classical music, the orchestra conductor Roger Nierenberg (1999) uses the metaphor of a concert orchestra to demonstrate to managers the dynamics of leadership, teamwork and communications within organisations. To get managers to stand in his shoes as the conductor of the orchestra and to hear and direct the orchestra from his perspective became an unforgettable learning experience in teamwork for them (Nierenberg, R. (1999), 'The Music Paradigm', Money Programme Lecture London: BBC Videos for Education and Training).
- The teamworking of a cabin crew in a long haul flight is crucial to the safety of the passengers. Seventy per cent of airplane crashes are caused by failures in teamwork rather than by individual human error or mechanical malfunction.
- Teamwork among the RAF Red Arrows includes debriefing sessions when the pilots frankly critique each other's performance and openly discuss mistakes they have made, including the team leader's in their flight displays. This open process is essential to limit the danger of flying formation aerobatics wingtip to wingtip at over 600 mph. Squadron Leader Les Garside-Beattie described the Red Arrow experience with a simile: 'Imagine driving down the outside lane of the motorway with eight other cars, all doing 200 miles an hour, bumper to bumper, knowing that no one would do anything silly, each relying on the other to do their job.' (Owen, H. (1996),'Creating top flight teams: the unique teambuilding techniques of the RAF Red Arrows', in *The hungry spirit: beyond capitalism a quest for purpose in the modern world*, London: Kogan Page, p 10).

As Thomas S. Kuhn says: 'You don't see something until you have the right metaphor to let you perceive it.' The idea of 'team' at work must be one of the most widely used metaphors in organisational life. A group of workers or managers is generally described as a 'team', in much the same way that a company or department is so often described as 'one big family'. But often, the new employee receiving these assertions quickly discovers that what was described as a 'team' is actually anything but. The mental image of cohesion, co-ordination and common goals that was conjured up by the metaphor of the team was entirely different from the everyday reality of working life. (Kuhn, T.S. (1970), *The structure of scientific revolutions* (2nd edition) Chicago: The University of Chicago Press, p 48).

Teams, as a sporting metaphor, are universally used by managers, consultants and management educators. When a top flight football team such as Arsenal or Manchester United is playing well, it is a joy to watch as passes are made swiftly with pinpoint accuracy and plays are executed with creativity and style that create opportunities and, eventually, goals. When the teamwork is missing, the team loses possession and makes many mistakes; nothing seems to work and watching the game can be an embarrassment for everyone.

In the build up to the Rugby World Cup 2003, England's star fly-half, Jonny Wilkinson, scored his 700th point for his country. His reply to the journalist, who reminded him of his personal milestone in scoring the 700th point, was characteristically modest and shifted the credit for his achievement to the entire team. 'Seven hundred points? Really? Well, that's very satisfying.' Wilkinson said. 'What you have to understand is that I am in a highly privileged position in this England side,' he continued. 'I may be the person who puts the points on the board, but all those points are the product of hard work by others. You wouldn't believe the amount of effort some people put in to win a simple penalty in front of the posts. The fact that I'm the bloke who propels the ball between the sticks doesn't tell anything like the whole story.' (Hewett, C. (2003), 'Wilkinson refuses to rest in quest to be perfect ten', *The Independent Rugby World Cup*, (4 October), p 13).

But teams are more than metaphors; they are the building blocks of work organisations.

What is a team (or group) at work?

Above all, a group is any collection of people who actually think of themselves as a group. This distinguishes them from a random crowd of individuals as in a bus queue, pub or supermarket. In addition to thinking of themselves as a group, they have a common purpose for being together and usually some collective identity, defined membership criteria and different roles to play. Groups at work are called work groups, committees or teams.

They have many different purposes that define them:

- They are used to help distribute work. 'Work groups' are organised around certain competencies, skills, talents or responsibilities required to do the work, as in the design team, or the information technology group.
- They help with the management and control of work, as when certain groups are assigned to particular managers who direct their efforts for a specific range of activities or duties.
- They are used for problem-solving, as with quality improvement teams or groups to develop new products.
- They can be used for fact-finding and decision-making, as with certain task forces.

- They are used for negotiations and conflict resolution, as with staff associations and trade unions or joint negotiating committees.
- They serve a co-ordination function between levels of the organisation, as in a liaison committee.
- They are used to sample something or to test products or ideas, as in focus groups used in market research.
- They are used for inquiries and investigations to establish facts, as an inquiry group investigating an accident.
- They are used to deepen commitment, or bring about employee involvement, as in a consultative committee looking at changes such as a new work organisation.

Do people need to be taught how to work in teams?

The manager or team leader must certainly understand how teams work and be able to make use of group dynamics in setting out to achieve the goals and objectives of the organisation. Team members, as well, benefit from understanding how teams work.

Experiential learning is useful. Many teambuilding events are set in the outdoors where people, through experiencing activities, grow to understand more about team roles in real situations. The outdoor experience might be orienteering, rock climbing, abseiling, sailing, rafting or canoeing, or simulated survival or mountain rescue activities. In a challenging environment that heightens the experience, members of a team learn more about the importance of leading and communicating, sharing information and making good decisions, fulfilling the various roles required for effective teamworking. In the harsh outdoor environment there can be real consequences when they fail or fall short.

Often teams take an away-day together where they withdraw from the work environment to reflect on their teamworking or simply to get to know each other better in a relaxed setting, at times with recreation on the agenda. For high-energy teams there are challenging competitive events or charity activities. As a team event each year, members of the Cranfield School of Management Master of Business Administration class enter the London Marathon and run the 26 mile course in a fibreglass centipede costume to benefit charity. British Telecom's Global Challenge – a sailing race, the wrong way around the world (against prevailing winds) – is an ultimate test of team-work.

Teambuilding events can also be fun. In the US, a teambuilding fad places a management team in a top chef's kitchen and gives the team a fine meal to prepare under the watchful eyes of trained cooks and process consultants. Such cooking experiences at the Viking Culinary Arts Center are aimed at fostering trust and communications skills.

The thinking developed by David Kolb (1984) and colleagues shows the cyclic nature of experiential learning, namely that:

- concrete experience leads to
- observations and reflections, which, in turn, enhance the
- formation of concepts and generalisations, which ultimately lead to
- testing of implications of concepts in new situations.

In addition to learning about teamwork from experiential learning, there is a growing body of research on effective teamworking. *Groups that work (and those that don't)* is an edited book by J. Richard Hackman (1989) based on research by doctoral students from the University of Michigan and Yale University on teamwork. The book links detailed descriptive accounts of specific work of 27 task-performing teams with theoretical ideas on team-working to generate action points for practical application and further research.

Among its major findings are:

- Temporal features such as time limits, deadlines, cycles and rhythms had a significant impact on group working. They also created the group climate and contributed greatly to the quality of group experience.
- Groups experience self-fuelling downward (unsuccessful and negative) spirals or upward (successful and positive) spirals. Those groups that found themselves performing badly got worse over time, while those groups that got themselves into a high performance groove got better. A lot had to do with how the groups were structured and how they were perceived by those outside the group whose praise (or negative comments) labelled the group and contributed to its confidence and success or its negative self-image.
- Dealing with the dynamics of authority held great consequences for effective teamwork. Four authority issues were salient to how the teams handled their tasks:

  - amount of authority the group had to manage itself,
  - stability of the authority structure,
  - timing of intervention by those in authority, the best time for intervention being at the group's start-up, and
  - substantive focus of those interventions. A poorly focused intervention directly into a group's processes, for example, can destroy the group's sense of responsibility for the outcome of the work.

- The context of the group's work – the stuff they work with – shapes the emotional lives of the members and their interactions in teams. For example, top management teams dealt with issues of strategy, power and influence, while production teams focused on technology in their work context and human service teams dealt with people's needs.
- Teams have specific risks and special opportunities open to them. For example, a top management team has the risk of the absence of supportive organisational context, but the opportunity of designing themselves as they see fit and having influence over their own conditions required for team effectiveness. (They control the resources needed and 'call the shots'.) The main risk for customer service teams is to get so involved with the client's needs that they neglect those of the parent company. Their opportunities include being a bridge between the company and its customers, the primary link between the organisation and its environment.

In a discussion of 'trip wires' that cause teams to fail, the research illustrated one such 'trip wire' that is frequently set off in quality programmes: 'specify challenging team objectives, but skimp on organisational supports'. Main supports include:

- a reward and recognition system that recognises and reinforces superior team performance and achievements,
- an educational system that supplements the members' own knowledge and expertise with whatever training or consultancy inputs they feel they require,

- an information system that provides the team with data forecasts and research they feel they need to achieve their objectives, and
- the material resources – staff, money, working space and meeting room, tools, technology, equipment, travel budgets, and so on needed to attain their aim.

REALITY CHECK

HOW DO VIRTUAL TEAMS DIFFER FROM FACE-TO-FACE TEAMS?

'Virtual teams have become possible since the advent of the Net and other advanced forms of electronic communication. A virtual team is a group composed of members who work at a physical distance from each other with common goals. They use new technology to communicate and collaborate across constraints of time and space and organisational boundaries. The members rarely meet face-to-face and are often from different national cultures. The teams are often cross-functional and deal with customers' problems or the design of new work processes. The members of virtual teams are highly skilled people with technical expertise, rather than interpersonal skills.' (Kirkman et al, 2002)

Kirkman goes on to highlight how little is known of virtual teams, partly because of the absence of research and partly because they are simply new.

Source: Kirkman, B.L., Rosen, B., Gibson, C.B., Tesluk, P.E. and McPherson, S.O. (2002), 'Five challenges to virtual team success: Lessons from Sabre, Inc.' *The Academy of Management Executive,* **16**(3), p 70.

Trust is at the top of their list. As one of the managers we interviewed put it: 'You trust people when they deliver what they promise! In a virtual team you start trusting each other when you meet your commitments. Everybody has their role, knows what is their responsibility and is committed to achieving results.'

Table 5.1 below summarises their major findings:

Table 5.1 The 16 team competencies (*Source*: Mills, T. and Tyson S. (2001), 'Organisational renewal: challenging human resource management', presented on 15 November 2001 at the HRM Network Conference, Nijmegen School of Management, The Netherlands (With permission to publish by Professor Shaun Tyson).)

	Enabling (task competencies)
Communicating	How well does the team facilitate effective communication? This includes effective use of formal communication channels, how well team members access and share information, and how effectively information is absorbed by the team.
Integrating	This competency is dependent upon those process elements that enable the team to become integrated to an appropriate level to ensure effective task actions. It includes effective task planning, working to team member strengths and successfully co-ordinating actions.

Adapting	How competent is the team at enabling flexibility in the face of changing task demands? This includes such aspects as role substitution, finding effective solutions to problems and being able to make radical changes to plans in new demands required.
Situational sensing	How well does the team manage the collective ability to understand the task environment and monitor changes? This competency includes the ability to see the broad picture, monitoring the team's performance and develop a shared understanding of important issues.
Evolving expertise	This competency describes the team's ability to achieve and exhibit domain expertise within the team. How well do team members share expertise, and how effective is the team at ensuring development?
Creating	This competency describes the way the team facilitates creativity. This includes how well the team generates and develops new ideas, how much team members are encouraged to work together to solve problems and how willing the team is to implement new ideas and ways of working.

Resourcing (knowledge competencies)

Knowing	This is a resource competency that encompasses the shared understanding of that knowledge required by the team to achieve a successful task outcome.
Contextualising	How well does the team achieve a collective understanding of environmental and organisational factors that constrain team processes? How well are organisational goals understood? Is a common understanding of the structure of the organisation shared? Does the team access resources from outside itself if required?
Team wisdom	This describes the level of collective knowledge pertaining to aspects of the team itself. This includes knowledge of the strengths and weaknesses of team members, knowing what team colleagues have knowledge of and sharing an understanding of the team's structure.

Fusing (team climate competencies)

Emotional maturation	This competency requires processes within the team that enable emotional understanding to develop between members. Such empathy is represented by sensitivity to team member feelings, ability to share emotional concerns and a willingness to challenge inappropriate behaviour.
Bonding	How well does the team manage to achieve social integration between team members? This is assisted by such things as a shared sense of humour, feeling a sense of fun from team interaction and having some social contact outside the work environment.
Openness	This competency enables the creation of an environment within the team where members are free to express themselves in a valued way. This requires honesty between team members, assured confidentiality and a willingness to admit personal shortcomings within the team.

Affiliating	The outcome of this competency is a high level cohesion. Team members express a sense of belonging to, and ownership of, the team. Aspects of this include loyalty to the team, a feeling of being involved with the team activity and respecting members' contribution.
Committing	How does the team achieve a collective commitment to the task? Important aspects are likely to include how effective team members feel rewarded for their efforts, how much responsibility the team takes for achieving task outcomes and ensuring equal efforts from all team members.
Inspiring	How does the team achieve a sense of 'wanting to perform' to bring about the team success? This is likely to be aided by ensuring interest is taken in the task, ensuring the team feels appreciated for its contribution and generating a sense of fulfilment on task completion.
Believing	This competency describes those factors that facilitate a sense of team efficacy within the team. This is a type of team belief and team confidence. Included is celebration of success, taking trouble to maintain morale and dealing with criticism in a positive manner.

Early research into group behaviour

Elton Mayo in 1924 was the first management researcher to study group norms systematically and the use of sanction to enforce them. His studies at the Western Electricity Company's bank wiring room at the Hawthorne works outside Chicago became an early classic in managing. He found that by improving the quality of the light in the wiring room, productivity markedly improved in the group he was observing as compared with the control group where the lighting was kept the same. Yet when the lighting in the observed group was returned to its original state, productivity still continued to improve, leading Mayo to the conclusion that the productivity increase had nothing to do the lighting improvements, but with the social interaction and attention the employees in the experimental group received from his team of researchers.

His major findings from the Hawthorne studies and subsequent work were that:

- People at work were motivated mainly by their social needs.
- People sought meaning at work in their social relationships because scientific management (Taylor and others) had driven meaning out of work itself.
- Work groups did more to shape people's behaviour than management incentives and controls.
- A supervisor will only be as effective as he is able to satisfy his subordinates' social needs.

Mayo established the behavioural school that emphasised the social role of a manager. Rather than be ruthless, rational organisers of work tasks, managers needed to be people-centred and to act as facilitators to maintain group morale which was the key to effective performance.

Team development

Teams are not static. They grow and develop into more effective groups or decline from peak effectiveness. They need attention and maintenance. Some social scientists have identified stages in a team's development (Tuckman, B.C. (1965), 'Development sequence in small groups', *Psychological Bulletin*, **63**(6), pp 384–99; Tuckman, B.C. and Jensen, M.C. (1977), 'Stages of small group development revisited', *Group and Organization Studies*, **2**(4), pp 419–27). Tuckman was among the first to chart a team's progression (see Figure 5.1). He identified four stages in a teams' development: *forming*, *storming*, *norming* and *performing*.

In the *forming* stage team members got to know each other and to establish more personable relationships. They learned to confirm to the organisation's traditions and standards. They tested boundaries in their interpersonal relationships and task behaviours.

During the *storming* stage conflicts happen. They could occur over rival leadership challenges or simply because of interpersonal behaviours. The source of the conflict could be resistance to group influences or task requirements. The group could split at this stage.

Emerging with a single leader, the team moves into the *norming* stage of development. Here norms of behaviour and group cohesiveness are established. New group standards are set for the group members and roles are determined.

The *performing* stage occurs when the team members start performing tasks together. Role clarity has been established and genuine teamworking is actually taking place.

A further stage of restoring or declining may follow as the team loses energy and effort.

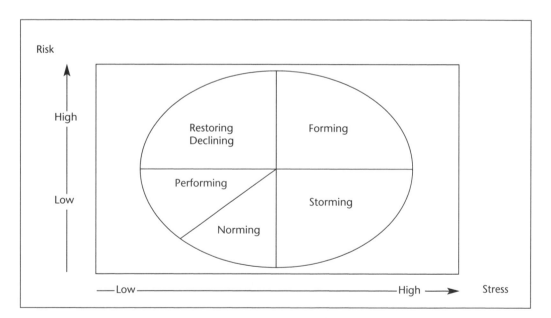

Figure 5.1 Building a team (*Source*: Adapted from Tuckman, B.C. (1965), by John Bank)

Team roles

The roles that individual members perform in groups have an important effect on team performance. Roles are patterns of actions associated with individual members, and their positions, in particular settings. They may be, in a group situation:

- *Formal* – the chairman, the secretary, the treasurer; or
- *Informal* – the expert, the comedian; or
- *Task-oriented* – the proposer, the analyst; or
- *Maintenance-oriented* – the encourager, the harmoniser.

Meredith Belbin (1981) conducted a research project at the Henley Management Centre, UK, over a period of eight years, examining the patterns of behaviour displayed by team members participating in a management game. He started his observations without preconceived ideas about teams.

Some companies use the theory to build teams for special projects like the launch of a new product or service. Belbin tried to determine whether there were any common characteristics among groups which could be classified as either high or low performing. He used psychometric measures to analyse the sorts of people who made up successful teams. From this evidence, he established that successfully performing teams were composed of people who collectively showed a capacity to work in eight different roles (see Table 5.2). When these eight roles were truly represented, the team appeared to be balanced, for it made the best use of its resources; it was flexible and resilient and had a few creative members, a lot of team players and was less dependent on key people than the unsuccessful teams. Eventually, Belbin considered he was able to predict success on the basis of testing and allocating individuals prior to team formation, although he does show that it is easier to predict teams that will fail than those which will succeed. It was not the team with the highest IQs that won the business game, but rather the team with the best mix of roles.

THE EXPERT ROLE

Belbin later added this role, but it is not a managerial role. The expert role is the one that derives from the managers' technical expertise, whether that is in architecture or engineering or computer technology. (It is usually this superior expertise that gets the person promoted into management in the first place.) This role is usually occupied by the 'boffin', whose contribution comes from outstanding, state-of-the-art technical knowledge and skill. Experts are dedicated self-starters. The strength of the role lies in the fact that the technical view is current, free of errors and single-minded but when this strength is overdone it can turn into the weakness of over-reliance on narrow, technical solutions to problems, while overlooking the 'big picture'.

Hot groups

Like the name implies, hot groups are highly-charged groups that come together to achieve a dedicated task. They are usually small groups that get totally caught up in the work and share the same characteristics of vitality, being absorbed with their work and each other, enjoy debating, laughter, creativity and very hard work.

'When hot groups are allowed to grow unfettered by the usual organisational constraints, their inventiveness and energy can benefit organisations enormously.' (Leavitt and Lipman-Blumen, 1995, p 109).

Table 5.2 Belbin team roles

	Chairperson	Shaper	Implementor (company worker)	Critic (monitor evaluator)	Networker (resource investigator)	Plant	Team-player	Finisher
Distinctive contribution to the team	Bonds and energises the team at stage one when it is forming. Establishes and maintains a sense of purpose. Promotes progress and involvement by all members of the team.	Unites the group's effort and pushes them forward to decisions and actions. Brings dynamism and sense of purpose to the team. Performance orientated.	A practical organiser who turns ideas into manageable tasks. Brings self-discipline, reliability and efficiency to the team. Sets the pace for getting on with the job by establishing/adopting systems and procedures at stage three when norms are established.	Prevents the team from committing itself to misguided projects or bad decisions. Brings a dispassionate, analytical logic to situations. Critical attitude can fuel the infighting stage two when the group is 'storming'.	Keeps the team in touch with the 'outside world' through an extensive network of personal contacts and a lively interest in anything that is happening anywhere. Brings a sense of 'fun' as well as numerous workable ideas. Helps stimulate activity and encourage innovation in the norming stage.	Contributes original and creative ideas and solves difficult problems. Brings breadth of vision and stimulating presence to the team. Is responsible for some of the friction in stage two when the group is struggling with roles.	Promotes unity and harmony in the team. Brings friendliness, sensitivity and caring to the team. Makes everyone feel an important and valued member at stage one when the team is forming and when people are feeling uncertain and apprehensive about their involvement.	Progress chasers. Concentrates on and keeps others to schedules and targets. Brings a conscientious approach to quality and standards of performance. Ensures that final outputs of the team are unspoilt by carelessness, sloppiness or error.
Characteristic behaviours	Clarifies goals and objectives. Sets priorities. Promotes decision-making.	Driving force. Competitive. Quick to challenge and respond to challenge.	Methodical and systematic, logical and orderly.	Assimilates and evaluates large quantities of complex information.	Always knows someone, somewhere, who can help out.	Good ideas, poor at following through. Concerned with fundamentals, bored with detail.	Listening to others and building on their ideas.	Searches for errors, omissions and oversights. Maintains permanent sense of urgency.

	Focuses people on what they do best. Brings out the best in others. Assertive but not domineering. Good communicator: ask questions, challenges assumptions, listens, clarifies, summarises. Motivates the team.	Often rows, but they are quickly over and equally quickly forgotten. Does not hold grudges. Exudes self-confidence which often belies self-doubts. Only reassured by results.	Reliable, responsible and hard working. Doesn't like speculation or 'airyfairy' ideas. Always knows what's going on.	Mulls things over before deciding. Objective approach to problems. Readily finds faults in the behaviour of others. Not ambitious but competitive, especially with Plant and Chairman.	Often radical and unorthodox in approach to problems. Gets on best with the chairperson; tends to ignore or dismiss other team members. Wants to spend all the team's time on his or her ideas.	Rarely in the office, and if is, probably on the phone. Positive and enthusiastic but drops things quickly. Relaxed, sociable, gregarious. Active under pressure and a good improviser. Undertakes the role of salesperson, diplomat and liaison officer for the team.	Smoothing over friction between team members. Bringing people into discussion. Counselling team members on their concerns. Organising social events.	Conscientious about order and deadlines. Needs to check every detail, personally.
Forgivable faults	Intelligent but not brilliant. Can lack creativity.	Prone to provocation and short-lived burst of temper. Can be arrogant and abrasive. Impulsive, impatient and easily frustrated. Most prone to paranoia.	Can be somewhat inflexible. Slow to respond to new possibilities (sudden change may throw them). Status conscious – can lead to competitiveness.	Can lack spontaneity. Can dampen a group's enthusiasm with their criticisms. Can lack imagination.	Poor at taking criticism of own ideas – gets prickly and often sulks. Can be careless with detail. Can fail to communicate with ordinary people.	Quickly loses interest. Can be easily bored or demoralised. Can spend time on irrelevancies to the team.	Can be indecisive in 'crunch' situations. Can show little sense of urgency. Avoids confrontation.	Inclined to worry unduly. Reluctant to delegate. Impatient with more 'casual' members of the team.

Hot groups are not usually planned. They spring up spontaneously, when the conditions are right, in many different settings from social and organisational to academic, scientific or political. They labour intensely at their task – with their members living, eating and sleeping their work because they share a belief that they are on to something significant, full of collective, extrinsic meaning. Older members rediscover the energy and excitement and joy of the youth in their involvement with hot groups. The preoccupation the members have with the task at hand for a hot group resembles obsession. Creativity knows no bounds as the intellects and the imaginations of the members are in top gear. The members live on the edge sustained by the challenge of what they have undertaken.

It was a hot group that invented the Apple Macintosh computer. That hot team thrived for two major reasons. Firstly each team member had the state of the art knowledge of the computer they were trying to invent in their fingertips and were intensely committed to the task. To become a member of the team, a person had to share a passion for making computers and be vetted by the entire team to see if they were 'one of us'. They enjoyed their work immensely and found it meaningful for themselves. To make computers beautiful and fun to use was their mission. Secondly, they were sheltered from the rest of the organisation, given their independence and distinctive identity. (Steve Jobs was an energetic member of the hot group and had the power to protect them and win the resources they required.) They even hoisted a pirate's flag over their designated building to celebrate their autonomy and rebel spirit. The end product had a hidden tribute to the hot team that created it. The metal plate inside each Apple Mac was inscribed with the names of each member of this hot group. The Apple Mac became a breakthrough product that for millions established Apple as the computer company of choice for the connoisseur.

Hot groups are often associated with the arts. The hot group that created *One flew over the cuckoo's nest* was a most unlikely one to win five Oscars and six Golden Globe Awards for their film. It included Milos Forman, a Czech director with only one previous American film on his CV. (The description of the team as a hot group is based on John Bank's interview with Milos Forman on tour with Jack Nicholson and the production team to promote the film in London in February 1976.) The producers were Saul Zaentz, a man with no experience in film-making at the time, and Michael Douglas, an actor who had been given the film rights to the novel by Ken Kesey by his father, Kirk. There were two scriptwriters, Lawrence Hauben and Bo Goldman. Star actor, Jack Nicholson took the lead role of R.P. McMurphy. Louise Fletcher, who was living in England then, came out of retirement to take the part of Nurse Ratched after five well-known actresses had turned it down. Will Sampson, who played Chief Bromden in the film, had never acted before. Set in a mental hospital, the film is an allegory for modern society. The film collected academy awards for best actor, best actress, best director, best adapted screenplay, and best picture.

Forman had been a scriptwriter himself at the Prague Film Academy before becoming a prize-winning Czech director with an international reputation for black comedy. He insisted that the key to a good film had to be in the script. Together with the script writers Hauben and Goldman, he spent several weeks in residence at the Oregon State Hospital in Salem, getting to know the patients and working closely with the hospital's superintendent, Dr Dean Brooks.

As Forman recalled: 'We were in the nurses' quarters and had total access to every part of the hospital; the key to each section and to each ward was at our disposal day and night. It was important to watch behaviours because I did not want to be accused of being phoney, but it was equally vital not to become too involved. I didn't want to end up as an expert on lunacy.'

'We finished by working in close co-operation with the hospital. Its director, Dr Brooks (who plays the head of the asylum in the film), felt that it would help many of his patients to be involved in some way with a Hollywood movie. He wanted to use us for therapeutic purposes and in some cases it worked. And we in turn used his facilities. I picked a model patient for every character in the movie and told each actor to track his model, to watch how he walked, talked, moved. It must have succeeded to some extent because the film was requested for a psychiatric conference in Paris.' (Quote from the author's interview with Milos Forman on tour with Jack Nicholson and the production team to promote the film in London in February 1976.)

The hot group not only decided to mix actors and real patients in the filming, but also involved members of the local community in every aspect of the project. (For the 35 professional acting roles in the film, the team auditioned 900 actors to get the casting right.) Forman explained that although he had searched America for an actor to play the part of Indian Chief Bromden in the film, he could find no one. Then one day Mel Lambert, an actor, met a 6' 5" Indian – Will Sampson – and took him to an airport lounge in Portland, Oregon while both Forman and Nicholson flew in to interview the man for the part. The Indian was unknown and not an actor, but a rodeo rider.

'Suddenly the door opened and this huge man came in. I really got excited, but there was still a question as to whether or not this guy could do it. The first thing I learned was that he was very intelligent, which was encouraging because that's a big help in acting. Then I did a short reading with him and found him very responsive,' Forman recalled. His role was pivotal, his image impactful. Mel Lambert remained a member of the hot team and became the Harbour Master in the film.

Forman admitted that there is an indescribable aspect to the creative intuition that came out of their unique teamworking in producing the film. 'You soon find that there is something in your work that is uncontrollable. You don't know where it came from and how it works and you're afraid that it will go. It's the same for all artists and it makes you insecure and very vulnerable. Luck and timing are important. Genius in your work is decided by others,' Forman said.

No doubt, Milos Forman and the band of people that gathered together to form the hot group that produced one of the best films of the last century did not consciously set out to do so. But they have demonstrated how a hot group works best in a temporary organisation. They could have been just a group of specialists doing their specialities. But each of the team members was chosen carefully and the entire team got embedded in a hospital in a local community. They added professionals and non-professionals to the team, hospital staff and patients and local people from the community. Together they shared a passionate vision of producing a film of great importance, something meaningful that would deeply touch the lives of the production team and the worldwide viewing public.

Hot group members feel that they are stretching themselves, surpassing themselves, creating 'personal best' timings as sprinters in athletics, breaking through barriers. They thrive in organisations that are deeply seeking the truth. Forman was aware of that in his remarkable film-making effort. He summoned up a proverb to explain it: 'Follow those who are seeking the truth, but run away from those who have found it.'

Team competencies

Belbin's work on team composition highlights the importance of having particular team roles filled by suitable individuals in order to produce high performance in teamwork in an ideal team. Belbin's insight into teamwork is from the perspective of the team as an entity made up of individuals where effectiveness depended on each individual carrying out key roles successfully. The popularity of Belbin's roles derived from its usefulness in team development through determining the set of team roles that existed in a particular team and then focusing on the strengths and weaknesses of the individuals in their team roles and their preferred ways of working together. Hence competence exists at the level of the individual.

From another totally different perspective Tim Mills and his researchers at Cranfield, in the fifth year of their project, have focused on team competency by taking the team as the unit of analysis (rather than a collection of the individual roles). The Cranfield approach is in line with other more recent approaches at examining team effectiveness (Cannon-Bowers and Salas, 1997). Cranfield researchers began their work looking at the Arsenal ladies' football team and musicians playing at Ronnie Scott's jazz club in London to see what they could learn that was applicable to business. For one thing, we expect sports teams and music groups to practice together and rehearse to improve their effectiveness investing time, energy and money in the process; whereas in business we generally expect work teams to excel immediately without much attention to teambuilding or practice. The Cranfield research spelled out: 'The question then becomes one of collective competence. More specifically, what are the collective skills, attitudes, and behaviours, and what is the collective knowledge required for teams to operate effectively? This approach does not denigrate the importance of individual competency; it simply shifts the level of consideration to the team or the group processes that enable effective performance' (Mills, T. and Tyson S. (2001), 'Organisational renewal: challenging human resource management', presented on 15 November 2001 at the HRM Network Conference, Nijmegen School of Management, The Netherlands, p 1).

To develop the team competency model Tim Mills and his researchers first selected a range of different teams to observe, film and interview. They used a variety of methods to generate qualitative data, including focus groups, one-to-one interviews, telephone interviews, virtual interviews, surveys, critical incident analyses and direct observation. Besides football teams and jazz groups, they included call centres, firms with sales teams, health care providers and even a project team at Warwick castle, the Midlands tourist attraction near Stratford-upon-Avon. They also selected virtual teams working physically far away from each other.

The diverse sample of teams created a problem of its own; how much could one generalise from one team to another? Are the things that contribute to the success of one team, applicable to the success of another? Does the teamwork underpinning a particular Premier League Football Champion team have any relevance for the London Symphony Orchestra? An analytical framework was first constructed to enable comparisons to be made between the teams chosen for the study. A two-by-two matrix that delineated four quadrants of team operation was designed. This enabled the researchers to select a sample of teams from each quadrant to ensure the broadest range of teams (see Figure 5.2).

The researchers produced a model (see Figure 5.3; The team competency model) identifying 16 competencies that are important to team performance (see Table 5.1; The 16 team competencies).

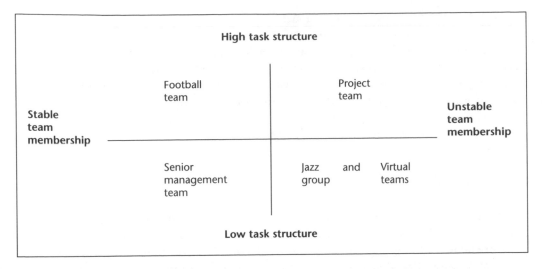

Figure 5.2 The study teams fitted to the stability/structure matrix (*Source*: Mills, T. and Tyson S. (2001), 'Organisational renewal: challenging human resource management', presented on 15 November 2001 at the HRM Network Conference, Nijmegen School of Management, The Netherlands (With permission to publish by Professor Shaun Tyson))

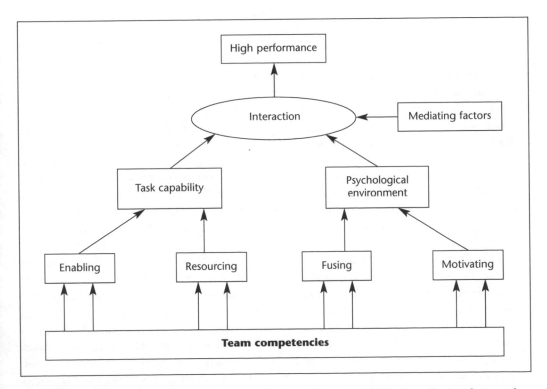

Figure 5.3 Team competency model (*Source*: Mills, T. and Tyson S. (2001), 'Organisational renewal: challenging human resource management', presented on 15 November 2001 at the HRM Network Conference, Nijmegen School of Management, The Netherlands (With permission to publish by Professor Shaun Tyson))

In stage one of the research, the model was created; in stage two a survey instrument was developed that was used to gather quantitative data from about 100 teams with over 500 team-members to enable statistical analyses, to explore the competency model further. From the surveys, an assessment instrument was designed to help teams determine their team competencies profiles. Although it is early days for the implementation of the instrument, already it is proving valuable to organisations that want to learn about their team competencies, improve their profiles and function better as a unit. The instrument also can set off warning signs if a team is dysfunctional.

Group think

'Group think' is the outcome of a group that is poor. It is the opposite of synergy. It is the product of a dysfunctional group. We have all been in groups that achieved so little that most members of the group felt that they could do better on their own. The launch of America's Space Shuttle Challenger is a classic case of group think. The launch decision was taken by NASA managers, who did not want to listen to outside experts warning them of the risk of the launch due to cold temperatures and the design of the rubber O-rings on the shuttle's booster rockets. The NASA decision-makers ignored existing data on the poor performance of the booster rockets due to a faulty design.

I.L. Janis (1973) identifies eight early warning signs of group think, nearly all of which were present in the launch of Challenger. (Report to the Presidential Commission on the Space Shuttle Challenger Accident, 6 June, 1986, Washington, DC, pp 40–72.)

- *Invulnerability*. 'Groups that have great cohesiveness are overly optimistic and take risks outside the normal envelope of safety. They do not see the added risk. Within their ranks, there either are no dissenting voices or they suppress them.' NASA managers were a cohesive group of white, male, engineers or engineers-turned-managers, with a 'can do' mentality or a 'macho-techno' risk-taking attitude and a fixation on achieving difficult targets. They inhabited and helped create a company culture where added risks were taken as commonplace and hardly noticed. As Diane Vaughan explained: 'When signals of potential danger occurred on the eve of the Challenger launch, the patterns that shaped decision making in the past – the production of culture (that shows how the work group normalised the joint's technical deviation), the culture of production and structural secrecy – were reproduced in interaction, to devastating effect. The norms, beliefs and procedures that affirmed risk acceptability in the work group were a part of the worldview that many brought to the teleconference discussion . . . What had previously been an acceptable risk was no longer acceptable to many Thiokol engineers. That night, the five-step decision sequence was initiated, a final – and fatal – time, with one alteration. It was followed not by a successful launch, but by a failure: that piece of evidence too fascinating to ignore, too clear to misperceive, too painful to deny, that makes vivid still other signals they do not want to see, forcing them to alter and surrender the worldview they have so meticulously constructed' (Vaughan, D. (1996), *The Challenger launch decision: risky technology, culture and deviance at NASA*, Chicago: The University of Chicago Press, p 67).
- *Rationale*. 'Cohesive groups have a facility for using logic to dismiss data that does not agree with their rational arguments.' In the Challenger launch case, the engineers at

Morton Thiokol, the company that built the booster rockets, argued that to launch the space shuttle in temperatures far below the established norm of 53°F posed a serious risk of O-ring failure. They pointed to erosion on both the primary and secondary O-rings from previous launches (15 out of 16 times). Yet both arguments were dismissed as 'unproven'. (BBC *Panorama* Broadcast, 'The dream that fell out of the sky', 28 April 1986.)

- *Morality*. 'Moral or ethical arguments against actions or policies fail to convince the group.' In the Challenger launch decision the question of how could NASA, famous for its care of the astronauts, not involve them in the decision to take an added risk in the cold weather when it was their lives at risk, did not come up among the decision-makers. They chose to not even tell them about the added risk. (BBC *Panorama* Broadcast, 'The dream that fell out of the sky', 28 April 1986.)

- *Stereotypes*. 'People who practice group think very often use stereotypes of those who oppose them and take no notice of evidence to the contrary.' In the Challenger case, engineers within NASA (with one exception) did not speak up to agree with the outspoken opposition to the launch from the engineers at Morton Thiokol for fear of being branded poor team players or nay-sayers or worse. One of the reasons cited for not telling the seven astronauts of the extra danger of the launch of Challenger was that 'they would have gone anyway', implying they were stereotyped, gung-ho risk-takers. In reality most astronauts are former fighter pilots and test pilots or scientists, people who define 'the right stuff' as the ability to push at the outer edge of the envelop of safety without punching through it. (Wolfe, T. (1979), *The right stuff*, London: Cape.)

- *Pressure*. 'Anyone in the group who expresses doubts about the rightness of an action is pressured to keep quiet or at least not to be able to unduly influence the group or to sway the groups' decision.' When the senior managers at Morton Thiokol first raised their opposition to the launch of Challenger, they were met with fierce opposition from the NASA managers at the Marshall Space Flight Center in charge of rocketry. They were told to prove that it was unsafe to launch the shuttle – that it would fail; reversing the normal procedure where it was NASA's obligation to demonstrate that it was safe to launch. Within the Marshall team, the pressure to conform to the decision to go was so great that only one engineer, Ben Powers, opposed the launch. He had 14 years experience with rockets. (BBC *Panorama* Broadcast, 'The dream that fell out of the sky', 28 April 1986.)

- *Self-censorship*. 'Feeling or doubts about the group's behaviour are not taken outside the group because that would damage its cohesiveness.' No one in the Marshall team referred their problem with Morton Thiokol opposition to the launch of Challenger to other NASA managers. Mission control and Launch control heard about the several hours of debate over the decision only after the shuttle was lost in the launch. (BBC *Panorama* Broadcast, 'The dream that fell out of the sky', 28 April 1986.)

- *Unanimity*. 'It is important to achieve unanimity in decision-making – so important that dissenting views are erased from the group's consciousness.' In retrospect the Presidential Inquiry into the Space Shuttle Challenger Accident said that NASA's decision to launch was flawed because the decision-makers had ignored data at hand and the warnings from Morton Thiokol and Rockwell that it was not safe to launch for two separate reasons – the cold temperatures affecting the O-rings and the ice on the launch pad that could damage the vehicle on blast-off. Even after their senior managers at Morton Thiokol reversed their opposition to the launch, the engineers put their objections to the launch in writing. In an effort to achieve unanimity, the senior managers at Morton Thiokol urged one of their members to 'take off his engineer's hat and put on his management hat' (Report to the Presidential Commission on the Space Shuttle Challenger Accident, June 6, 1986, Washington, DC, pp 82 and 94). They were obviously worried about losing a NASA contract worth over one billion dollars.

* **Mindguards.** 'Teams involved in group think close ranks and protect each other in their decision-making. They collectively defend the group against outside criticism as though by supporting the group they can nullify dissent from others.' Even in the glare of national TV coverage and under the harsh questioning of knowledgeable members of three inquiries from the White House and Congress, the decision-makers in the Challenger launch decision, defended themselves and admitted to no wrongdoing or errors of judgement. For them it was an accident (US House Committee on Science and Technology (1986), Investigation on the Challenger Accident Report, Washington, DC: Government Printing Office).

ANOTHER SPACE SHUTTLE – COLUMBIA – LOST FOR SIMILAR REASONS

According to the Columbia Accident Investigation Board's Report on the loss of the space shuttle Columbia on 1 February 2003, NASA has found itself again a victim of group think. The report criticises NASA management for not learning from the Challenger accident. Flawed management procedures were 'as much a cause' of the Columbia, the report states, as were technical faults. NASA managers had at least eight opportunities to evaluate damage to Columbia after a piece of foam, the size of a suitcase, broke off from Columbia's fuel tanks and struck a wing on blast-off. NASA's management team had failed to heed the earlier warnings to radically change its culture and its attitude to flight safety (Columbia Accident Investigation Board Report, Vol 1, August 2003, Limited first printing by the Columbia Accident Investigation Board. Subsequent printing and distribution by the National Aeronautics Administration and the Government Printing Office, Washington, DC).

Diane Vaughan, a risk specialist and sociology professor at Boston College, remarked that some of the same organisational flaws at the US space agency that contributed to the Challenger explosion were again evident in the loss of the Columbia. 'Again there were plenty of signs that technical standards weren't being met. That's the parallel,' she said (Calaman, P. (2003), 'Eerie echoes of challenger disaster', *Toronto Star*, (2 February), p B04).

In an interview with the Toronto Star, Vaughan pointed to the continuing problem with heat tiles breaking off the space shuttle on re-entry. She said this was eerily similar to the repeated problems that NASA experienced with damage to the rubber O-rings separating sections of the solid rocket boosters, ultimately identified as the cause of the Challenger disaster. 'Something that is initially interpreted as a danger becomes routine and acceptable with experience,' Vaughan said, critical of the culture in NASA that grew accustomed to accepting great risk. 'It's an incremental descent into poor judgement. They do things exactly according to the rules – but they reinterpret the rules.'

Summary

All teamworking aims at achieving synergy, where the output is greater than the sum of its parts. Teamworking, done properly, increases productivity, efficiency, motivation, job satisfaction, creativity and customer service.

ESSENCE OF A TEAM

A team must think of itself as a group, have a common purpose from banding together and (usually) have some collective identity, a defined membership criteria and different roles to play, otherwise it is a random crowd.

Teams have many different purposes, from helping to distribute work to problem-solving to fact-finding or for inquiries. Sometimes they are used to bring about employee involvement or for consultation.

Understanding group dynamics can be helpful in improving one's teamworking skills. Experiential learning, as in teambuilding events in the out-of-doors can improve teambuilding.

Kolb's learning cycle is useful for understanding experiential learning. The learner moves from the (a) concrete experience, to (b) observations and reflections, to (c) formation of concepts and generalisations, to (d) testing the implications of concepts in new situations.

RESEARCH INTO TEAMWORKING

Two excellent empirical studies of teamworking were reported on:

- Groups that work (and those that don't).
- How virtual teams differ from face-to-face ones.

A virtual team is a group composed of members who work at a physical distance from each other with common goals. They use new technology to communicate and collaborate across constraints of time and space and organisational boundaries. The team members rarely meet face-to-face, are often from different nations, and are usually highly skilled people with technical rather than interpersonal skills.

EARLY RESEARCH

Elton Mayo was the first management researcher to study group norms systematically and the use of sanctions to enforce them in the 1920's. His research emphasised a manager's duty to understand and satisfy the social needs of the workforce.

TEAM DEVELOPMENT

Tuckman's team development wheel shows five stages of team maturity from (a) focusing, to (b) storming, to (c) norming, (d) performing and (e) restoring and declining.

The eight Belbin team roles are useful for role analysis of what happens in teamworking. The eight roles are chairperson, shaper, company worker, critic, networker, plant, teamplayer, and finisher. At a later date Belbin added the 'expert' role but whilst many managers are indeed experts, it is not a management team role.

HOT GROUPS

Highly charged groups that come together to achieve a dedicated task are called hot groups. They tend to be small and intense in the way they go about things, filled with absorbing action, debating, laughter and creativity, and very hard demanding work. Steve Jobs organised a hot group to produce the Apple Macintosh computer. Milos Forman built a hot group to produce 'One flew over the cuckoo's nest.'

TEAM COMPETENCIES

Whereas Belbin's work on team composition argues for the importance of having specific team roles filled by suitable people to produce high performance, Tim Mills and others at Cranfield focus on team competencies by taking the team as a unit of analysis instead of a collection of roles. After extensive research the Cranfield team designed an instrument that helps teams determine their competencies profile.

GROUP THINK

'Group Think' is the outcome of a group that is working poorly together. It is the opposite of synergy. The launch of the space shuttle Challenger was used to illustrate all eight aspects of group think as identified by Janis, for example, 'invulnerability', where the group have great cohesiveness, are overly optimistic and take risks outside the normal envelope of safety. According to the Columbia Accident Investigation Board's Report, NASA allowed 'group think' dynamics to continue, and these dynamics were 'as much a cause' of the loss of Columbia in February 2003, as were the technical faults.

6 *Diversity and Individual Differences*

Valuing diversity and individual differences is one of the most challenging issues facing managers. Differences between colleagues when poorly valued can give rise to conflict and demotivation. Differences managed positively can foster creativity, better decision-making, greater commitment, higher performance and competitive advantage. At the start of the chapter we examine the importance of valuing diversity in organisations. We then explain individual differences, examining the nature of perception and the attributes others display and why they are critical to understand other people. Finally we look at how such insightful understanding can be utilised to influence others positively.

The meaning of diversity

Diversity means, 'being diverse, unlikeness, different kind, variety' according to the Oxford Dictionary. Diversity is used to describe the different kinds of employees in organisations. Whilst some diversity definitions focus on visible difference (different from what norm?), more general definitions imply that everyone is different. Diversity, then is simply 'otherness' or those human qualities present in other individuals and groups that are different from our own and outside the groups to which we belong. For employers, the way diversity is understood in their organisation will influence how they manage it. For example, AstraZeneca's website says:

We want to draw upon the widest possible pool of talent, and to be the <u>*employer of choice*</u> *for people already employed within the company, as well as for potential recruits. We will widen the range of people AstraZeneca employs and ensure that the diversity of their backgrounds, experiences and abilities is fully recognised and developed.*

www.astrazeneca.com

Such a public statement sets out the rationale for valuing diversity and goals for its achievement, as well as the means whereby it will be done. It reveals an intention to recruit on talent and merit without discrimination and to celebrate diversity. Differences will not be assimilated into some norm. There is also a promise of recognition and development.
Opportunity Now state that:

Being an employer of choice requires respect for the talents of all individuals regardless of sex, race, disability, age or sexual orientation. It means being fair to all in recruitment, promotion and development of people and capitalising on the added value that diversity brings.

www.opportunitynow.org.uk

Both statements call for equal opportunities, something that has been advocated for decades.

The most general categories of diversity in employment terms are demographic categories like sex or other primary dimensions such as ethnicity, race, age, sexual orientation and disability. These tend to be immutable characteristics that we are born with.

Informational categories of diversity as secondary dimensions are more mutable characteristics. They include religion, personal values, education, military service, work experience and language to name a few. Many people do not change their religion, but attitudes towards such aspects of diversity can alter substantially.

There are other diverse groups, for example, those with different employee status or conditions, like part-time workers or youth trainees. Some differences are visible, such as sex and race; other differences may be invisible, such as religion, or sexual preference. Some diversity categories such as sex and age are straightforward in employment terms, as it is a requirement for these categories to be recorded by employers. (Ethnicity is more complex, because of the various population compositions across Britain, and variations in labelling ethnic groups.) Disability can also be complex, as many individuals who are eligible for classification as disabled, for example people with dyslexia, choose not to disclose their disability to employers. Many individuals are different on more than one dimension. The 'black' category is diverse in itself: 'black' has many meanings, for example, Afro-Caribbean, Afro-American and African, and may also include Asian.

Diversity is inherently linked with social and group identity, because it is not just how we see ourselves, but also how we locate other people within a system of categorisations, and how important we perceive those categories to be at any given time or place. The fact that we may not identify strongly with our particular sex or ethnic group does not change the fact that others may very well change their behaviour towards us on the basis of those categories. So the concept of 'diversity' is complex, and has different meanings for different people in different contexts, including organisations.

Why diversity matters at work

There are many reasons why diversity is a critically important issue in the workplace. Women now make up nearly half of the workforce in the UK, and they are at least as well qualified as men. Ethnic minorities comprise over 6 per cent of the workforce across the country, but in some London communities, the proportion can be somewhere between 30 and 50 per cent. Demographic trends show that the working population is ageing, and there is a reduction in the number of young people entering the workforce due to lower birth rates and negative population growth.

Companies make great efforts to offer equal opportunities and to treat all individuals without prejudice. They are motivated to do so by social justice considerations. They also want to be good corporate citizens. Establishing a level playing field for all is the aim.

Today, however, in addition to continuing these efforts for increasing employee diversity for social and ethical reasons, organisations are developing the business case for diversity. These organisations believe that increasing employee diversity is good for their businesses. They claim that greater workforce diversity offers them competitive advantage in recruitment, especially when there is a shortage of skilled workers and managers due to demographic trends. The business benefits of having a more diverse workforce include:

becoming an 'employer of choice' for diverse people in a wider pool of talent; improving creativity and obtaining better decision-making due to diverse perspectives and contributions; basing promotion on merit and developing individuals to the best of their abilities, and enjoying increased commitment from diverse employees. In short, the business case for diversity argues that increased diversity equals better bottom-line results.

The present British work system (which was designed in patriarchal mode for males in family structures of previous generations that were mostly white) tends to work against those who are different. Yet legislation to deal with this issue, such as the Sex Discrimination Act of 1975, has led to little change in the last 30 years. The good intentions of the Equal Pay Act and the Racial Discrimination Act have also eluded women, never mind the more subtle discriminations they experience.

Research consistently shows that those in power in organisations tend to recruit in their own image, prolonging stereotyping of the managerial role. An apt phrase is 'Think manager, think male,' but many would say, 'Think manager, think white male,' or even 'Think power, think white male.' Hence, many of those who are non white, female and visibly different do not reach the levels that their talents could be expected to attain, causing them to feel excluded on ground of difference rather than on merit. Many in the dominant group, the white males, appear to be unaware of the inherent disadvantages others experience, particularly affecting career progression, faced at work by those who feel they do not fit or who are perceived not to fit the organisational norms for management and leadership. As the *New Yorker* cartoonist Warren Miller so aptly illustrated in January 1992, career success in the past gave educated white males unfair advantage. Legislation alone has been shown to be insufficient. Further action is needed to increase awareness to change attitudes and practices to effect real progress. Developing the under-utilised talent pool of female, ethnic minority and other 'diverse' workers have become an imperative for progressive organisations.

REALITY CHECK

TROUBLE AT TEXACO

According to Jack White, while Texaco was pushing out its employee diversity policy in the UK in November 1996, something else was happening in the background.

'Texaco's top executives openly discussed shredding minutes of meetings and other documents that were sought by black employees in order to bolster their charges that Texaco discriminated against minorities in promotion and fosters a racially hostile company culture. What is more, the tone and substance of the discussion were racially offensive.'

The politician and civil rights activist, Jesse Jackson, became involved with the result that Texaco Chairman, Peter I. Bijur agreed the following settlements:

- US$115 million in cash to approximately 1400 current and former Afro-American workers.
- US$26.1 million increase in pay for Afro-American employees.
- US$45 million for diversity training.
- The creation of an equality and tolerance task force composed of three members selected by the company, three members named by plaintiffs in the lawsuits and the chairperson to make:
  - Changes in employment policy,

– Reports twice yearly to the Board, – Judgements from information available from company records.	*Source:* White, J.E. (1996), 'Texaco's high-octane racism problems', *Time Magazine*, (25 November).

What are the management implications?

There are two issues confronting managers. First is the lack of diversity amongst current business managers and leaders. (How has this situation arisen? and how can it be changed?) Second is the key issue of managing diversity. (How can meaningful diversity policies be developed and implemented?)

There has been significant change in the employee profile over the last half century, with women staying in the workforce for all of their adult lives, increasingly in full-time jobs, as well as ethnic minority employees joining the workforce. There has been much social change during this period, particularly the breakdown of traditional family structures. This has often been linked with a change in women's expectations for their careers and their lives.

Girls are now outperforming boys at all stages of education, and yet somehow, their early promise of excellence has not translated into promotion in their careers at the same rate as their male peers. In addition, technological change has impacted upon the nature of work itself as well as the way in which work is managed. Yet management and leadership structures have generally remained static, with organisations still recruiting new leaders and managers similar to the existing cadre – white, middle-class, middle-aged heterosexual males, the so-called business mainstream (see Cartoon 1).

Cartoon 1 Reproduced with permission of Brian Bagnall

Progress for women and ethnic minority members has come at junior and middle management levels, especially in the public sector. This has not happened at senior levels. Women have not achieved equivalent representation in management and leadership positions, especially in larger organisations. The Equal Opportunities Commission (2002) recently reported on the status of women and men in management in Britain, stating that the glass ceiling is still much in evidence.

Some very different employment patterns exist for women:

- One in four women is now likely to remain childless.
- More women return to work straight after having a maternity break.
- More women work full-time for much of their careers.

Women are still not getting a fair deal in terms of management opportunities, compared with men. Whereas previously women were said by men to be disadvantaged with so-called good reason, that they were not as committed to their careers and that they would have long periods away from work, now that many of these perceived obstacles have been removed, women appear to be continuing to be disadvantaged simply by being female.

Often feeling undervalued, uncomfortable with the organisational values of their employer, or seeing their aspired career paths blocked, many women and ethnic minority individuals turn to employment in smaller firms, or move to self-employment to set up the kinds of organisations that reflect their own values. These departures represent a loss of valuable resources to the organisation in terms of skills and knowledge, as well as expensive recruitment costs to replace the leavers.

In *Fortune* magazine's list of the 'Most powerful women in business', Patricia Sellers asks the question of women when they ponder top jobs in business, academia and government: 'Power: do women really want it?' For the article Sellers interviewed Ann Fudge, a graduate from Harvard Business School, who has a list of top positions on her curriculum vitae including: General Electric board member, current Chairman and chief executive officer of ad conglomerate Young & Rubicam. The former outstanding executive at Kraft Foods has combined the roles of chief executive and wife, mother, grandmother, world traveller and public service advocate. She earned her present top job at the ad agency after a two-year sabbatical that some people predicted would kill her career.

'We need to redefine power!' she (Fudge) said. She wants to get rid of the traditional definition of the word. 'Do we have to follow the boys' scorecard?' she asks.

'No we don't,' say more and more women – and that's just the point. Like Fudge, they say they view power differently from the way men do: they see it in terms of influence, not rank . . . Dozens of powerful women we interviewed tell us that they don't want to be Carly Fiorina, the chief executive officer of Hewlett-Packard (and No 1 on our list of most powerful women for the sixth year in a row); many don't want to run a huge company. But there is a fundamental disconnect here. Those very same women also tell us that they foresee the day in which there is parity in terms of sex representation at the top of corporate America. (Sellers, P. (2003), 'Most powerful women in business, power: do women really want it?' *Fortune*, (13 October), pp 1–2, www.fortune.com/fortune/articles/0,15114,490359,00.html)

Fudge concludes from her interviews that women do not like the term 'power'. It is too macho, 'in your face and aggressive'. Even Hilary Clinton dislikes the word power and, although she understands power, does not think about it in relationship to herself. But substitute the word 'leadership' for 'power' and women feel differently.

'When it comes to professional modesty, "women overdo it," says Citigroup's Magner, herself a model of self-effacement. When she interviews candidates for stretch assignments, she says, women often tell her they're not ready. Men almost never do. Says Magner: 'One of the things I tell women is, "Listen, next time someone offers you a job, don't tell them why you're not capable. Keep it to yourself!"' (p 3).

Diversity is still often seen as a compliance issue by managers, who reactively ensure that their organisational practices are in line with current equal opportunities legislation. Instead of doing the minimum in terms of compliance, managers can play a key role in ensuring that diversity is managed well, and that changes and initiatives lead to sustainable progress. Leaders can ensure that the corporate values, culture and practices do not isolate 'diverse' individuals. Moreover, managers need to articulate both the ethical case and the business case for increasing employee diversity.

REALITY CHECK

DISCOVERING COMPLEXITY AND VALUE IN PROCTER AND GAMBLE'S DIVERSITY

R. Thomas Roosevelt Jr reports that Procter and Gamble traditionally recruited individuals to upper management positions from within the organisation. Thus, considerable emphasis was placed on attracting the very best for the recruitment of younger people, including 'talented minorities and women'. It was also recognised that diversity management had to be spread beyond recruitment and so Procter and Gamble, in May 1988, formed the corporate diversity strategic task force, to clarify the concept of diversity, define its importance for the company, and identify strategies for making progress toward successfully managing a diverse workforce.

The task force, composed of men and women from every corner of the company, made two discoveries. First, diversity at Procter and Gamble was far more complex than most people had supposed. In addition to race and sex, it included factors such as cultural heritage, personal background, and functional experience. Second, the company needed to expand its views of the value of differences.

The task force helped the company to see that learning to manage diversity would be a long-term process of organisational change. For example, Procter and Gamble has offered voluntary diversity training at all levels since the 1970s, but the programme has gradually broadened its emphasis on race and sex awareness to include the value of self-realisation in a diverse environment. As retiring board Chairman John Smale put it, 'If we can tap the total contribution that everybody in our company has to offer, we will be better and more competitive in everything we do.'

Source: Roosevelt, R.T. Jr. (1990), 'From affirmative action to affirming diversity', *Harvard Business Review,* **68**(2), p 113.

Gardenswartz and Rowe (1998) suggest that employers ask the following questions about diversity in their organisation:

• In how many countries does your organisation operate?
• How many languages are spoken by your customers?

- How much does employee turnover cost your organisation?
- How much does your organisation spend annually on recruitment?
- How much have discrimination suits cost your organisation in the past year, in legal fees and settlements?
- What are the demographics of your customer/client base (for example, age, income, sex, education, ethnicity)?
- How frequently does inter-group conflict sap productivity?
- Is there a higher level of turnover among certain employee groups?
- Are policies and benefits attractive to potential recruits?
- Is your organisation losing top talent because people do not feel heard, included or valued?
- Do employees feel that their skills and talents are well rewarded?
- Is there some career advancement possibility for employees and a focus on developing people internally?

REALITY CHECK

THE DIVIDENDS OF DIVERSITY

At these 50 best companies, the CEO leads the diversity mantra and he does more than merely encourage his executives to build a diverse workforce: he makes part of their bonuses depend on it. 'What gets measured gets done,' explained Jim Adamson, chief executive officer of Advantico, which came second from the top of the list. Employees at these companies are encouraged to discuss and debate sensitive race issues in the workplace without fear of damaging their careers. Lucent Technologies, ranked number 16, goes as far as giving financial support to groups representing Asian, black and Hispanic workers as well as to gay, lesbian and disabled groups. These employee groups have national conventions and each has its own website.

How well do these companies with proven track records in employee diversity deliver to their shareholders? 'The average return to

investors for the publicly traded companies on our list walloped the S & P 500 index over the past three and five year periods: 125.4 per cent to 112.2 per cent and 200.8 per cent to 171.2 per cent respectively,' Fortune *reported. 'No one can say that companies striving for and in most cases investing heavily in ethnic inclusion at every level are doing so at the expense of profits.' It should be noted that most of these companies have supported their diversity policies in the downturn period of 2000–2003, emphasising their commitment to equality of opportunity.*

Source: Fortune *magazine (3 August, 1998) published for the first time 'The 50 best companies for Asians, blacks and Hispanics' under the banner 'Companies that actually do something about diversity'.*

The Cranfield diversity management performance project

Researchers at Cranfield School of Management asked the heads of diversity about the initiatives in their organisations. These were surprisingly varied, and emerged from their different business contexts. Their responses are captured below.

WORK/LIFE BALANCE

Work life balance and flexibility programmes were very frequently reported as diversity initiatives both in the public and private sectors. This was seen as the key way to attract and retain staff at all levels, both male and female. Flexible working was offered, and hourly paid contracts for those who could not commit to regular working hours on a part-time basis. Even managers were employed on this basis.

One company had moved to segmenting employees by their needs, rather than by sex, race and age. This worked well, and allowed different groups, such as those with caring responsibilities, to be catered for in imaginative ways. Where there were shortages of staff, employment was offered by the hour, day, week, month or longer. This allowed a new category of workers to be more involved in a relationship with the firm. These were the workers who did not want a career as such, and who preferred long periods away from the UK every year, for winter hotel breaks for instance in Spain or Florida. They did not necessarily need the money but liked to work part-time for social reasons. Another large group of employees were the women who only wanted to work during term-time, so that they could spend the school holidays with their children.

AGE

Some diversity managers talked about age initiatives. McDonalds had a large number of very young employees spread across the country and, for many of them, it was their first job. For them the induction process was not just into the company but also into work. Getting some of them to be reliable in terms of time-keeping proved a challenge. The company instigated a scholarship scheme to help some of the youth go back into education. They also had a campaign to attract workers over the age of 40, to provide more stability and leadership to the young crews. Old age pensioners were also employed. They often chose to work for the social interaction as much as for the pay, and many did not mind the early shifts that were so unpopular with the young employees. By being open to recruitment of all ages, the staffing problems at McDonalds were resolved, and there were beneficial social interaction effects as well.

RELIGION

One public sector organisation reported that they had been asked to provide prayer rooms, and although they were not able to give a dedicated meeting room, they did try to make local arrangements so that there was continuity of location as far as possible. Another company had a diversity calendar, which allowed them to develop location-specific actions to celebrate various religious festivals. For example, restaurants in towns with large Indian minority populations would have special plans for Divali celebrations, and managers in such locations would be forewarned of dates by the calendar. Generally, it seemed that there was goodwill to take seriously the needs of various religious groups as far as it was possible to incorporate them within the normal frameworks available.

DISABILITY ACT

Organisations interfacing directly with customers and clients in both the public and private sector had taken steps to ensure that disabled customers' needs were considered. They ensured access for mobility-impaired clients (and employees) by appropriate infrastructures. Other diversity initiatives included the provision of notepads in restaurants so that deaf people could communicate in writing, as well as Braille menus for the blind. Another company also provided notepads and induction loops for the deaf at supermarkets. In one area, they had a store near a deaf community. They recruited a deaf employee who was then trained to give deaf awareness and sign language training courses for hearing employees across several stores. They now have several deaf people working for them in the original supermarket, as well as a number of trained individuals who can help deaf customers in neighbouring stores. In addition, they recruit mentally handicapped staff, who also make a contribution as employees, with training. These small projects show that treating diversity with imagination can lead to good outcomes.

Perhaps the most startling aspect about disability for those without physical or mental impairments is that disability can strike anyone at anytime without warning. Able bodied men and women, even athletes, can suddenly, out of the blue lose their mobility or physical or mental capabilities through illness or accident. The apparent randomness with which it strikes ought to make everyone more alert to the needs and rights of the disabled. Yet it is only recently that public awareness has combined with a long overdue vindication of the rights of the disabled to ensure some measure of equality when it comes to employment opportunities and basic protection.

REALITY CHECK

CHRISTOPHER REEVE 'STILL ME'

Everything seemed to be rosier than ever before. One of the last movies I did before I was injured was called Above Suspicion, *in which I played a paraplegic. I went to rehab centre in Van Nuys, California, to do research on what it would be like to be a paraplegic. I learned how to transfer in and out of a car. I learned how to transfer in and out of bed and onto a rehab mat. And I spent time with a young woman who had been injured in the earthquake in California. A bookcase had fallen on her head, and she was in a halo. She was just learning how to walk. I remember I went about every other day for two weeks to do this research. Every time I would leave and get in my car and drive back to my comfortable hotel, I would thank God that that was not me. Eight months later I had the accident and joined the disability population.*

Source: Speech at the National Organisation on Disability Corporate Citizenship Award Luncheon, 8 October, 1997.

HUMAN RESOURCES MANAGEMENT – RECRUITMENT AND SUCCESSION PLANNING

In one company, recruitment of technical talent was a key issue, and women entrants were under-represented. This was tackled by linking employees to girls in schools and universities, encouraging shadowing, role model provision and presence at recruitment fairs. In another technology company, there were pre-recruitment initiatives to widen the talent pool by using placements, sponsoring young people, especially girls, in underprivileged areas to help them get access to university. Equal pay initiatives were reported by some of the private sector firms to ensure that there was not any indirect discrimination. In a banking firm, succession management was a key feature of diversity management. Several of the organisations mentioned career development initiatives such as leadership coaching and senior women's programmes.

CULTURAL CHANGE PROGRAMME OR TRAINING

Almost all of the companies had culture change programmes within which diversity management was dealt with. Public sector managers were guided by action plans from the Cabinet Office. The LEAP (local equality action planning) Programme had four key areas: leadership, working environment, staff awareness and planning, but was very much enacted as a local initiative, to ensure that the local community was best served in terms of diversity management. In the public sector, several departments had awareness workshops for senior managers, who would then take the initiative down to lower levels. One diversity manager said that it was important not just to have 'sheep-dipping' courses, but to build diversity competencies and capabilities into all training. Whilst some managers talked about the need for cascading down the changes, others felt that it was better to deal with the training of teams and groups of individuals so that the message was better integrated at grass roots level.

SUPPORT GROUPS

Many of the participating organisations had support groups for individuals with particular differences. These included networking groups for women at various levels, and even conferences and a global women's summit for senior women. There were support networks for ethnic minority individuals both as a group and as separate groups, and for disabled employees. In one organisation, a gay and lesbian group had been supported. In some cases, the groups were financially supported, whilst in others, there was advice but no funding. Surprisingly not every organisation had a women's network or support group. Some diversity managers said that there was no demand for ethnic minority groups, and in other cases, earlier support groups had simply disappeared. Most employers said they reacted supportively when asked for help, but they did not generally initiate such support.

Singh, Schiuma and Vinnicombe (2002) highlight that in order to progress, equal opportunities management has to be transformed into diversity management. From the organisational perspective, the authors emphasise the need for developing a diversity capability within the organisation that may be derived from a genuine desire for greater diversity management effectiveness or a need to avoid litigation or ensure for the basics of compliance. Irrespective of the start point, the steps Singh, Schiuma and Vinnicombe (2002) highlight are:

- cease ignoring differences,
- accept, recognise and respect differences,
- utilise such differences and
- make strategic use of diversity for the purposes of competitive advantage.

STUDY OUTCOMES – SUGGESTIONS FOR DIVERSITY MANAGEMENT

There were 15 suggestions from the diversity managers in the Cranfield study, which are helpful for those organisations that are starting initiatives on this issue. These are not prescriptive, as there was a strong view that each organisation would have to find what was best practice for its context.

- Embed diversity management into corporate strategy for best advantage.
- Locate diversity responsibility in the whole organisation (it should not just be a human resources issue).
- Give diversity an inclusive definition. What values does the definition highlight? Is this in alignment with corporate strategy?
- Create a high-level, visible 'diversity champion', and an organisation-wide 'diversity council'.
- Appoint a diversity director or manager and form a diversity task force to draw up an action plan.
- Allocate a central budget at least for preliminary initiatives. But remember that training costs should be the responsibility of the delegates' departments, as managers should be prepared to invest in this training. (If they pay for it, they may be more likely to make the resulting change happen in their departments.)
- Assess the current situation: the climate in the organisation, employee satisfaction surveys, focus groups and interviews. Look at the symbolic as well as the real – remember that perceptions are as important as reality in terms of influencing behaviours.
- Design relevant interventions, such as training to increase awareness and understanding about diversity. Be creative in designing support such as mentoring, coaching, executive education, as well as flexible ways of working. Monitor take-up and outcomes by different minority groups.
- Develop skills that employees can use to deal with diversity in the workplace as well as diverse customers. Diversity skills should address internal (employee to employee) and external (employee to customer) relationships.
- Create open channels of communication throughout the organisation using new technology.
- Have a local diversity co-ordinator to maintain contact with the central head of diversity so that there is sustainability.
- Hold managers accountable for diversity performance and build diversity management into the competency and capability frameworks.
- Monitor the diversity of the employee profile at group and organisational levels.
- Measure costs and effectiveness of each component of diversity initiatives (training, task-force, mentoring, employee networks, and so on) so that appropriate choices can be made for further action.
- Note that the impetus is easily lost. There may be a change of champion, loss of passion, other priorities and mergers (diversity management needs to be sustainable through such changes).

REALITY CHECK

JEAN-DOMINIQUE BAUBY: FROM EDITOR-IN-CHIEF OF *ELLE* TO A 'LOCKED-IN SYNDROME' VICTIM

Jean-Dominique Bauby was the witty, intelligent, at times abrasive editor-in-chief of *Elle*, the French high-fashion magazine. From his offices in Paris, he lived in the fast lane. He had left his wife and two pre-teenage children to live with a girlfriend. He was cool, his *savoir-vivre* became his hallmark personal trait.

Late one afternoon, a BMW salesman collected him at his office in the new car he was planning to buy. They drove to the outskirts of Paris to his former family home where he collected his 10 year old son, Theophile, to take him to the theatre that evening. As they set off to drive to the centre of Paris, with Bauby at the wheel of this new BMW, he had a massive stroke. He climbed into the back seat of the car and asked the salesman to drive to the house of his sister-in-law, who was a nurse. She ordered an ambulance to rush him to the hospital where he remained in a coma for 20 days.

Jean-Dominique Bauby emerged from the coma to discover that he had 'locked-in syndrome'. Although his brain was undamaged and in perfect working order, and his vision was unimpaired, he was totally paralysed. The only thing he could move was his left eye. With his eyelid blinking wildly he eventually attracted the attention of a nurse who devised a crude Scrabble-like system whereby Bauby could blink on to individual letters she pointed to on a board or recited, not in alphabetical order but in order of the most-used letters first. She turned the letters into words and then into sentences and he was able to communicate from within his human tomb. Bauby wanted to tell his loved ones, friends and associates that he was not a 'vegetable', that his brain was in fine shape and that he still retained his sense of humour. He wrote a letter and sent it to 60 of them. Editors at French publishers Robert Laffont, who had worked with Bauby before his stroke, were among the recipients of the letter. They suggested to him that he write a diary of his traumatic experience with the 'locked-in syndrome'. They assigned a young lady from their staff, Claude

Mendibil, to daily take down Bauby's dictation to her letter by letter.

He often composed the diary entries before dawn and then dictated entire sections of the book from memory, letter by letter. In this way he painstakingly produced a 139 page diary. It is a marvellous document of a human being's courage in the face of such a devastating disability. He would not be defeated by the 'locked-in syndrome', but rather used it to devise an amazing human account of struggling against despair, a testimony to his dignity and to an unconquerable human spirit. Three days after the diary was published under the apt title: *The diving bell and the butterfly* to marvellous reviews, he died on 9 March 1997, without recovering any further mobility. The previous year he had set up ALIS (*Association du Locked-in Syndrome*).

Bauby opens his diary with these words:

Through the frayed curtain at my window a warm glow announces the break of day. My heels hurt, my head weighs a ton, and something like a giant invisible diving-bell holds my whole body prisoner. My room emerges slowly from the gloom. I linger over every item: photos of loved ones, my children's drawings, posters, the little tin cyclist sent by a friend the day before the Paris-Roubaix bike race, and the IV pole overhanging the bed where I have been confined these past six months like a hermit crab dug into his rock.

He recalls the date of his stroke: Friday 8 December 1995:

Paralysed from head to toe, the patient, his mind intact is imprisoned inside his own body, but unable to speak or move. In my case, blinking my left eye is my only means of communication.

He relates how he escaped from his circumstances:

My cocoon becomes less oppressive, and my mind takes flight like a butterfly. There is so much to do. You can wander off in space or in time, set out for Tierra del Fuego or for King Midas's court.

You can visit the woman you love, slide down beside her and stroke her still-sleeping face. You can build castles in Spain, steal the Golden Fleece, discover Atlantis, realise your childhood dreams and adult ambitions.

He also described the task of writing the diary:

Enough rambling. My main task now is to compose the first of these bed-ridden travel notes so that I shall be ready when my publisher's emissary arrives to take my dictation, letter by letter. In my head I churn over every sentence ten times, delete a word, add an adjective, and learn my text by heart, paragraph by paragraph.

Source: Bauby, J.-D. (1998), *The diving-bell and the butterfly*, London: Fourth Estate Limited, pp 11–14.

Individual differences

Definitions of personality run into the hundreds. Perhaps one of the clearest definitions to emerge recently is given by the English psychologists Eysenck, Arnold and Meili in the *Encyclopaedia of Psychology*, Vol 2, 1972:

> *Personality is the relatively stable organisation of a person's motivational dispositions, arising from the interactions between biological drives and the social and physical environment. The term usually refers chiefly to the affective-cognitive traits, sentiments, attitudes, complexes and unconscious mechanisms, interests and ideals, which determine man's characteristic or distinctive behaviour and thought.*

This suggests that personality does not change very much (it is relatively stable), it is organised (there is an integration of components), it results from an interaction of internal drives and the external environment, and that each person is different (it is distinctive). So personality does not arise from purely inherited genes or environmental factors, but from a combination, an interaction, of the two, and all through our lives the two sets of factors interact with each other in complex ways, resulting in patterns of behaviour which are characteristic to us.

INDIVIDUAL CHARACTERISTICS

Type theorists hold that people have a particular type of personality (for example, extrovert or introvert), which they are either born with or develop at an early age. For instance, in the study of human stress, two different types of behaviour have been distinguished, type A and type B. Type A people put constant pressure on themselves to achieve results, always seeming to be hurrying towards their own ends. Type B are more laid back and relaxed about their goals. Type A and type B are seen as two quite distinct categories.

In contrast, trait theorists believe that people use different personal traits to different extents. They feel that certain behaviour shows, not the personality of the individual, but that the individual has used particular characteristics in the situation. It follows from this that people can learn to behave in certain ways. Later trait theorists developed a number of psychological (psychometric) tests that measure people's learned capacity to draw on particular traits. In these, extroversion and introversion, for example, are seen as two extremes of a behaviour pattern, and a person's score would fall somewhere between them.

In other words, a type theorist would proclaim somebody to be extrovert, while a trait theorist would describe the same person as more extrovert than introvert.

One particular measure that we find useful at Cranfield School of Management, based on the work of Carl Gustav Jung (originally a collaborator of Freud), is a particularly interesting example of type and trait theories combined. The American psychologists Katherine Briggs and Isabel Briggs Myers developed a personality test that reveals, how a person prefers to work (that is, work preferences). This test, termed the Myers-Briggs Type Indicator®, identifies two functions that in turn are influenced or modified by two attitudes showing how a person relates to the outside world. The model, outlined below, is easy to understand and is presented in a way that we consider attractive to practising managers.

The four dimensions of behaviour that Myers and Briggs studied are:

- relating to other people,
- finding out, generating and gathering information,
- making decisions
- deciding and setting priorities.

On each of these dimensions Myers and Briggs, a mother–daughter team of psychologists, defined a continuum of behaviour at each end of which there are two contrasting preferences. But what is meant by preferences? An individual's normal (preferred) way of doing something is discovered from experience and experimentation. Doing something in a certain way provides positive feedback, for example, a person may prefer to use a certain style when running or jogging because doing it that way produces reliable results. They would therefore continue to use that style more, to the exclusion of others, in order to become more accomplished at the sport. Suddenly to use a different style may result in poor performance. Not having fully developed in the new style, the person cannot produce the desired results. Similarly, when at work most of us like to work in familiar ways; it helps us get results, it makes us feel more confident, so we reinforce these styles to the exclusion of others.

FUNCTIONS

Two dimensions in the model highlight the preferred ways in which people tend to generate and gather information, and the ways in which they like to utilise that information to make decisions (see Figure 6.1).

People collect information either by relying on their senses, by using practical, measurable data (*sensing*), or by using their imagination, intuition and insight to recognise possibilities to pursue (*intuitive*). People make decisions based on logical, rational analysis of the situation (*thinking*), or rely on their own personal values, beliefs and experiences of people and hence respond more emotively (*feeling*).

While people can use either approach on either of these dimensions, they tend to have a preference for one more than the other on each dimension. There are therefore four basic conceptual types – intuitive thinking (NT), intuitive feeling (NF), sensing feeling (SF) and sensing thinking (ST).

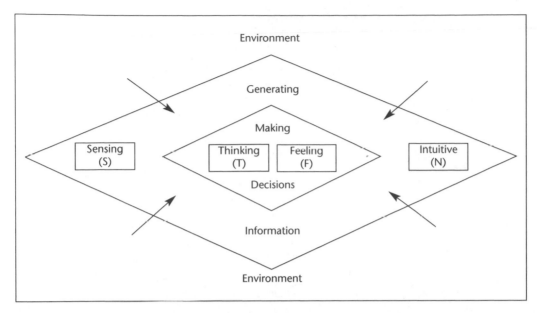

Figure 6.1 The two functions of the Myers-Briggs model (*Source*: *Working in Organisations*, First Edition, 1987)

MODIFYING FACTORS

Modifying factors concern the way in which people relate to others, and how they set priorities (see Figure 6.2).

In establishing and managing relationships with others, people will prefer to behave in either an *extroverted* or *introverted* manner. Extroverts need the company and stimulus of other people. Introverts are more content with their own company. When setting priorities, people will try to establish order and resolve issues by using their judgement (*judgemental*), or will seek more information and try to understand the situation (*perceptive*).

This theory has great relevance for managers in that it relates to activities which they have to pursue in their work life – they have to relate to other people, they have to decide on the priorities of their work, they have to collect information and they have to use it in making decisions.

The Center for Creative Leadership in North Carolina, USA, broke down the descriptions of these combinations into four managerial types: traditionalist, troubleshooter/ negotiator, catalyst and visionary.

- **Traditionalist** (ISTJ, ISFJ, ESTJ, ESFJ). Traditionalists (SJs) are factual, systems managers who are good decision-makers. Practical managers, who assess consequences and risks before acting, they place a high value on order and punctuality. They are dependable and tend to rely more on facts than on people. As a consequence, their managerial style is often formal and impersonal.

  They are loyal to the status quo, and may be slow to perceive the need for change and even be suspicious and afraid of change to existing systems. Very good at handling large quantities of data, they are excellent co-ordinators and integrators and manage time well.

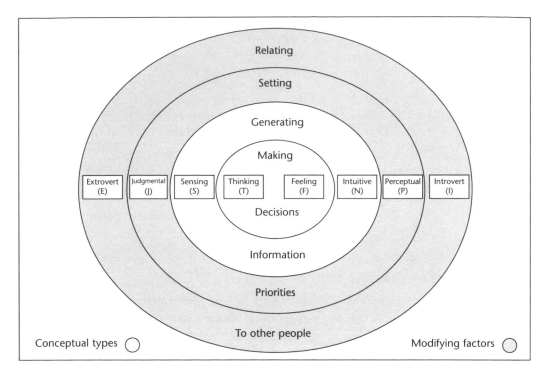

Figure 6.2 The eight Myers Briggs types of work preference (*Source*: *Working in Organisations*, First Edition, 1987)

- **Troubleshooter** (ISTP, ESTP); **Negotiator** (ISFP, ESFP). Troubleshooters and negotiators (SPs) are problem-solvers. Very flexible and aware of situations and their implications, they 'use' the system to effect change rather than trying to change the system. They live in the reality of current needs – they may shift positions to cope with these and thus sometimes appear unpredictable to their colleagues. They are stimulus-response managers and may appear disorganised and disorderly to traditionalists, but they are good at sniffing out and dealing with trouble before a large problem develops.
- **Catalyst** (INFJ, INFP, ENFP, ENFJ). Catalysts (NFs) are communicators, charismatic, committed managers who work well and intuitively with people. They care for people, and their decision-making may be influenced more by their own personal values and relationships than by the facts of the situation. If they are not nurtured, catalysts can become ineffective and discouraged. They are very useful in such areas as public relations, but prefer to work with few constraints, and may spend more time in interpersonal interactions than on task-related activities.
- **Visionary** (INTJ, INTP, ENTP, ENTJ). Visionaries (NTs) are the planners, the innovators, the creative force in organisations, the managers who are able to see the whole picture and relate it to the present situation. They look at possibilities and analyse them objectively. While they like to put new ideas into operation, they may quickly lose interest and search for new areas of challenge within their competence – and competence is one quality they expect in others. Because of this they may be insensitive to the problems of other people, and need to be reminded to expect less than perfection. They are good decision-makers, but because they expect everyone else to read situations as well as they

can, they often feel it unnecessary to explain their reasons. Visionaries are ideas-people who quickly conceptualise outcomes; it is therefore not surprising that they may equally quickly leave organisations where they feel their talents are not being used.

All these types are necessary in the running of any organisation: the traditionalist keeps the system running and provides stability; the troubleshooter or the negotiator senses developing problems and deals with them; the catalyst maintains communications and uses people to best effect; and the visionary looks to the future, senses needs for change, and stimulates its implementation.

Of a large sample of managers attending business school programmes from large organisations, 60 per cent fall into the traditionalist category, 20 per cent in the visionary category and 10 per cent each in the catalyst and troubleshooter/negotiator category. Interestingly across many samples of women managers this typical breakdown deviates. Essentially there is no clear dominant category for women managers, they vary across all four categories far more than their male counterparts. It is quite probable then, that many women managers and male troubleshooters, negotiators, visionaries and catalysts have to perform in organisational roles which are not to their preference. It is equally probable that organisations pay less attention to the talent spotting and training of those managers who do not fit the traditionalist role.

Perception

Perception is the process by which people select, organise and interpret external sensory stimuli and information into terms and categories that are consistent with their own frames of reference and personal views of the world. People use a selection mechanism when they are incessantly exposed to a multitude of sensory stimuli and have to filter out extraneous 'noise' to find and identify those that are relevant and important to them as individuals. Whilst listening to music on the radio, we know the baby is asleep upstairs. When she cries, we screen out the music and concentrate to hear whether the cry is a pain cry, a hunger cry or a temper cry, to help us decide what action to take. Selection enables us to avoid distracting or unimportant sensory stimuli.

This filtered information is then organised into clusters and categories that, through remembered experience, enable people to make interpretations in relation to their internal states and frames of reference. We may say someone who accepts all information as true, without checking, is trusting. Past experiences of ourselves and of others who were trusting may have shown that the information given was not accurate – even, in some cases, was deliberately inaccurate – and that acting on the assumption of accuracy has led to unexpected and negative outcomes.

UNDERSTANDING OTHER PEOPLE

Proper understanding of other people depends very much on interacting and communicating with them – 'getting to know' them. (See Chapter 8 for further discussion on managing communication.)

In Figure 6.3, A's and B's perceptions and impressions of C are different, even though the information passed from C to A and B is the same, because A and B have different values, beliefs, attitudes and experiences. When A and B communicate to each other their perceptions of C, and a process of disclosure and feedback occurs, A and B are more likely to understand each other's perception of C. Greater common understanding develops when A, B and C share and feed back perceptions of each other.

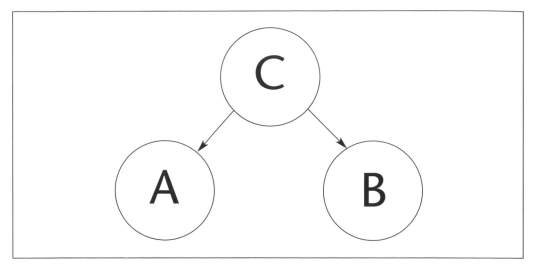

Figure 6.3 Unshared perception and understanding (*Source*: *Working in Organisations*, First Edition, 1987)

An even greater empathy and understanding occur when A, B and C share some common values, beliefs, attitudes and experiences.

Too often, however, in organisations, individuals have to make judgements of other people based on limited information. In these situations people face the conflict of needing to be as accurate as possible in their perceptions while needing also to make up their minds very quickly. Where time or information is short, individuals often tend to stereotype other people into categories which fit the aggregation of the limited information available, within the parameters of their past experiences. Prejudice occurs by simply categorising people on incomplete information, or by refusing to accept evidence about individuals which conflicts with previous experience.

However, people often have to rely on 'first impressions' in such situations as selection interviews. Three factors influence their judgement: the 'perceived' (the person they are meeting), the 'perceiver' (themselves), and the situation. We can all improve our ability to understand other people and their behaviour by being aware of these three factors throughout the relationship.

The perceived

People's perception and categorisation of, and their behaviour towards, other people, influence to a certain extent their apparent characteristics. Some factors that affect people's interactions are:

- *Physical appearance.* 'People with glasses are studious.' 'Red hair means a quick temper.' There are many old adages that link personality characteristics to physical appearance. Gestures, demeanours and facial expressions are also important influences on our perception. Two fingers raised in a victory sign by Winston Churchill in 1940 evoked admiration for his courage and defiance. Two fingers raised in benediction by the Pope, and two fingers (reversed) raised in vulgar contempt by a soccer hooligan, generate entirely different feelings in us when we have to form impressions based on public behaviour. Dress also affects our evaluation of other people – we dress smartly for an important interview in order to make a good impression, whilst perhaps feeling that people who wear individualistic clothing or hairstyles are not good team people.

- *Verbal and social cues*. One of the most influential factors in people's perception of other people is their verbal behaviour – how people speak, and what they say. We all have our own pictures of someone who speaks with a broad Yorkshire accent, or a Scouse accent, or a Scots, Cockney or German accent. Even UK and USA 'English' can lead to perceptual misunderstandings. In the UK, the cover on top of the engine is called the bonnet; in the USA, it is the hood. And in France, regional dialects (patois) give different meanings to common words, which the individual needs to understand in order to comprehend and be comprehended. Grammatical exactitude and the use of long words may also influence us to see people as intelligent, though this may not be the case. People's education and status are often categorised by their manner of speech. Those who attended and were pleased with public school could attribute positive characteristics to someone with a strong public school accent. People who speak loudly are often considered extrovert – or even vulgar – while people with soft voices are often thought to be shy and sensitive.
- *Motor behaviour*. 'People who won't look you in the eye are shifty and unreliable.' 'Strong handshake – strong character.' Certain personality traits are often inferred from people's motor behaviour.

These various cues – physical appearance, verbal, social and motor behaviour – help us to form impressions of other people in a first social interaction. Some may be valid, others not. There appears to be a low correlation between most of these factors and personality traits, and how, and which, cues are selected, organised and interpreted depends on the values, attitudes and beliefs of our particular culture and society, as well as on those of ourselves, the perceivers.

The perceiver

This is the factor over which we have most control. The more we understand and have confidence in ourselves, the more likely we are to understand others. Some of the factors specific to the perceiver that affect the perception of other people are:

- Individual values, beliefs, attitudes, prejudices and experiences.
- Level of awareness and knowledge of, and confidence in, self. People with accurate perceptions of themselves are likely to be more accurate in their perceptions of others. Positive attributes are also more likely to be given to people perceived to be like the perceiver, and vice versa.
- Current past experiences. People's perceptions, as well as their behaviour, are likely to be affected by their experiences. Dearborn and Simon (1985) conducted an experiment with a group of executives representing different functional areas of business. The executives were given a case study of a company experiencing business problems. The executives were asked to identify the principal problem. The majority of the executives identified the principal problem as one related to their own functional area.

- Expectations about other people. A person who is told someone is brilliant tends to see brilliance. People seem to see what they expect to see, and often the conflicting evidence needs to be overwhelming before it is accepted.

REALITY CHECK

EXPLAINING WHAT I SEE

The well known guru of international cultures, Gert Hofstede, captures his experience of teaching a session on perception using the classic picture of the young girl/old woman! (Boring, E.G. (1980), 'A new ambiguous figure', *American Journal of Psychology*, (July), p 444. Originally drawn by cartoonist W.E. Hill, published in *Puck*, 6 November 1915. As printed in *Games Trainers Play*, by J.W. Newstrom and E.E. Scanneil, McGraw-Hill, 1980.) Hofstede describes how he showed half of a class a slightly altered version of the picture, for only five seconds, in which only the young girl could be seen. He then showed the remaining members of the class another version of the picture, again for only five seconds, in which only the old women could be seen. After this preparation he showed the full ambiguous picture to everyone.

The results were, he says, amazing. Most of those 'conditioned' by seeing the young girl first saw only the young girl in the ambiguous picture, and those 'conditioned' by seeing the old woman saw only the old woman. He then asked each group to try to help the others to see what they saw until everyone saw both images.

Each group found great difficulty in getting its views across to the other, with considerable complaints about each other's 'stupidity'.

Source: Hofstede, G. (1980), 'Motivation, leadership and organisation. Do American theories apply abroad?' *Organisational Dynamics*, (Summer 1980).

The situation

Situational factors can be influential when forming first impressions of people. Since individuals have few behavioural cues to help them, the context (a board meeting), the environment (the executive suite at the top of the building) and the perceived value of the other person to themselves (the managing director) affects their perception.

ATTRIBUTES

As people interact more with others, they tend to infer from the behaviour of others certain characteristics about their motives, their feelings, their needs and their attitudes. Their observed behaviour is felt to be a more accurate external indication of the 'real person' than the earlier, non-behavioural cues on which first impressions were based. Attributes are inferences about people's internal states of mind and emotions based on their observed behaviour.

Reality is what we subjectively perceive to be real. Our own 'real world' – our frame of reference – shapes the way in which we behave in the external objective environment. It also tends to distort, sometimes consistently, sometimes erratically, the information that we receive from that environment, and the people who live in it. Some of the ways in which this distortion affects us are described below.

Stereotypes

Sometimes we have little information about a person apart from their demographic characteristics – their home, their education, their religion and nationality, and so on. From this very limited information a picture of the other person can be built and that person can be classified in categories based on our experiences or the frames of reference of others. With no further information, we tend to deal with such people as representatives of their category in our internal picture, and not as individuals. We expect certain types of behaviour from each category, and behave accordingly ourselves. This can help to reduce our own internal conflict and ambiguity as we reject dissonant cues, and if we can be accurate in our stereotyping it makes it easier to predict behaviour. It can, however, also lead to erroneous judgements about people.

Schein (1989) built on previous work into sex role stereotypes, which suggested that there were distinct characteristics, attitudes and temperaments that could be attributed to men and others that could be attributed to women. She argued that as management is a sex typed occupation due to the high ratio of men then it was likely that the managerial position would be seen to require personal attributes thought to be more characteristic of men than of women. She found across a number of male managerial samples a significant relationship between the ratings of men and managers and a near zero relationship between the ratings of women and managers. Her findings with women managerial samples showed a similar significant relationship between the ratings of men and managers and a less significantly relationship between the ratings of women and managers. The conclusion was that women, as a result of their sex, were perceived as less capable than their male counterparts.

REALITY CHECK

WHAT PREVENTS WOMEN FROM ADVANCING TO CORPORATE LEADERSHIP?

	Women directors	Male chief executive officers
1 Lack of significant general management/ line experience	47%	82%
2 Women not in pipeline long enough	29%	64%
3 Male stereotyping and preconceptions	52%	25%
4 Exclusion from informal networks	49%	15%
5 Inhospitable corporate culture	35%	18%

Source: Ragins, B.R., Townsend, B. and Matthis, M. (1998), 'Gender gap in the executive suite: CEOs and female executives report on breaking the glass ceiling', *Academy of Management Executive*, **12**(1), p 34.

As can be seen, the views of women directors and male chief executive officers vary considerably on the five key reasons for lack of career progress identified by Ragins et al. (1998).

Halo and horns effects

A manager may say: 'He's got all the technical know-how needed – he should be able to keep on top of the work and make a good supervisor.' An individual's perceptions of someone's behaviour in certain areas – whether favourable (the halo effect), or unfavourable (the horns effect) – can influence predictions about that person's behaviour in other areas. People who are like us, or come from similar backgrounds, or have had similar experiences, are likely to be credited with more positive attributes than people who are entirely unlike us, for example, what prevents women from advancing to corporate leadership?

Expectancy

Expectancy refers to the actual occurrence of something that is expected to happen. Perhaps we expect someone to be antagonistic towards us and so we display defensive behaviour, even being aggressive towards him or her (we are pre-emptively aggressive.) We reject any overtures of friendship as being inconsistent with our expectations. Eventually the person really does end up being antagonistic towards us. We then rationalise our behaviour by saying, 'See, I told you he or she was like that and that person lived up to expectations!'

Projection

Projection occurs when people attribute to other people their own feelings and perceptions. The 'them and us' attitudes between management and unions are an example of projection. Management may distrust a union and feel that under current circumstances the union also distrusts management. This, however, may not be the case. So instead of entering a negotiating situation with a win/win outcome in mind, management may ignore conflicting evidence of the union's attitudes and a win/lose situation develops.

Selective perception

We all tend to reject information that we perceive to be inconsistent with our own frame of reference and self-image. Selective perception means that we only listen to what we want to hear, see what we want to see. This is epitomised by the old adage, 'Love is blind!'

IMPROVING UNDERSTANDING AND INTERACTION

A framework called the Johari Window, developed by Joe Luft and Henry Ingham, two American psychologists, has been used in management training and counselling to help people understand the development of differences between their self-perception and others' perception of them. The Johari Window (named after a combination of their first names Joe and Harry) is useful in reducing perceptual biases such as stereotypes, halo and horns effects and selective perception (Figure 6.4).

In social interactions (see Figure 6.5) there are facets of ourselves, our attitudes, behaviour, and personality that are known to us and also apparent to others (the *open* area). At the same time, other people may observe aspects of ourselves of which we are unaware (the *blind* area). We also keep some of our attitudes and feelings private and do not disclose them to others (the *hidden* area). There are some aspects of ourselves of which we are unaware and which are also not apparent to others, but which do influence our behaviour; unless we make determined efforts to increase our self knowledge, we are unlikely to understand some of our actions and reactions (the *unknown* area).

	Known to self	Unknown to self
Known to others	Open	Blind
Unknown to others	Hidden	Unknown

Figure 6.4 The Johari Window (Adapted from Luft, J. and Ingham, H. (1955), 'The Johari Window; a graphic model of interpersonal awareness', *Proceedings of the Western Training Laboratory in Group Development* (Los Angeles: UCLA Extension Office)).

Open	Blind
Hidden	Unknown

Figure 6.5 First social interactions (Adapted from Luft, J. and Ingham, H. (1955), 'The Johari Window; a graphic model of interpersonal awareness', *Proceedings of the Western Training Laboratory in Group Development* (Los Angeles: UCLA Extension Office)).

In first social contact situations (Figure 6.5) we tend to reveal little about ourselves; others do not get to know much about us, and their view of us is based on non-behavioural cues. Our open area is small. As relationships grow we feel we can be more open with others, and the open area expands, while the hidden area reduces. This is achieved by *self-disclosure* (see Figure 6.6).

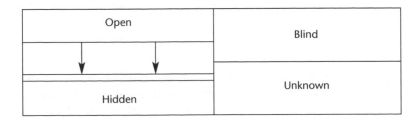

Figure 6.6 Self-disclosure effect (Adapted from Luft, J. and Ingham, H. (1955), 'The Johari Window; a graphic model of interpersonal awareness', *Proceedings of the Western Training Laboratory in Group Development* (Los Angeles: UCLA Extension Office)).

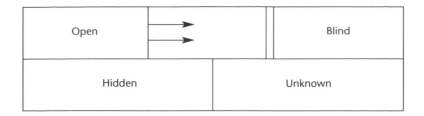

Figure 6.7 Feedback effect (Adapted from Luft, J. and Ingham, H. (1955), 'The Johari Window; a graphic model of interpersonal awareness', *Proceedings of the Western Training Laboratory in Group Development* (Los Angeles: UCLA Extension Office)).

Figure 6.8 Self-disclosure and feedback effects (Adapted from Luft, J. and Ingham, H. (1955), 'The Johari Window; a graphic model of interpersonal awareness', *Proceedings of the Western Training Laboratory in Group Development* (Los Angeles: UCLA Extension Office)).

The other mechanism by which the size of the open area can be increased is feedback from others (see Figure 6.7). This reduces the size of the blind area.

Where both self-disclosure and feedback occur, the size of the unknown area will also probably reduce, as our knowledge of self increases, and we can begin to understand the underlying motives for more of our behaviour.

Only by self-disclosure and feedback from others can the size of the open area be expanded and discrepancies between self-perception and perception of self by others be reduced (see Figure 6.8). To reduce perceptual biases and distortions we need to develop confidence in ourselves so that we can be open with others and willing to receive feedback. Feedback can sometimes damage our view of ourselves (that is, our self-concept); we can react defensively to feedback that (in our view) places us outside our comfort zone, our 'real world' – and, particularly in counselling situations, considerable skill is needed to maintain a positive, progressive climate.

Impression management

Impression management is the process whereby individuals seek to influence the perception of others about their own image. The prime reason for attempting to 'manage' the impression we create is that through the construction of 'desirable' social identities, our public selves come closer to our ideal selves. We seek to influence how we are perceived, and therefore the way in which others treat us. The effect of such behaviour may directly impact material outcomes. For example, giving the impression that one is competent and ambitious can lead to benefits such as improved performance ratings and career-enhancing opportunities. Impression management behaviours may be focused on one's self, one's managers and the job. Self-focused strategies include promoting one's successors and ambitions, whilst upward-focused impression management refers to building up a good relationship with one's boss and networking with senior management. Job-focused impression management refers to a high commitment to delivering an excellent performance. This usually involves working long hours.

Impression management is important because promotion decisions are very much influenced by the rating of potential or 'promotability' by bosses, which is a subjective assessment based on managerial perceptions and an estimate of the promotion decision's anticipated effectiveness.

Our research at Cranfield indicates the importance of informal influence processes in promotion systems, and the different inclinations that individuals have to use impression management strategies to play (or ignore) the unwritten rules of the game. For some, particularly men, the use of impression management seemed almost natural, whilst for others, at times there was an uncomfortable learning process. Some individuals, particularly women, did not wish to use impression management at all, despite recognising its potential.

Gowler and Legge (1989) comment that, 'the "successful" manager is the one who manages the good opinions of others'. (Gowler, D. and Legge, K (1989), 'Rhetoric in bureaucratic careers: managing the meaning of management success', in Authur, M.B., Hall, D.T. and Lawrence, B.S. (Eds), *Handbook of career theory*, Cambridge: Cambridge University Press, pp 437–453). Managers may have the right ideas and skills, but unless their reputation, or others' perceptions of their abilities, is valued, purchased and used by those in power, their management capital is worthless for their career advancement. We have identified that many women are aware of the potential of impression management but choose not to use it. If female managers are less inclined to use impression management, then their opportunities for upward career advancement become more limited.

Summary

DIVERSITY

Diversity means 'being diverse, unlikeness, different kind, variety'. It is 'otherness' or those human qualities present in other individuals and groups that are different from our own and outside the groups to which we belong.

Diversity describes the different kinds of employees in organisations. Individual differences will not be assimilated into organisations unless there is proper recognition and valuing of them. Diversity is inherently linked with social and group identity. It is critical that diversity is managed in the workplace. Instead of seeing diversity as a compliance issue, it should be positioned for competitive advantage. Compliance is motivated by an organisation's need to be seen to be a good corporate citizen, keeping the laws against discrimination, establishing equal opportunities and providing a level playing field for all out of social justice and ethical consideration.

In contrast, competitive advantage is at the heart of the business case for increasing employee diversity. Its driver is the belief that employee diversity is good for business and delivers on bottom line results. A diverse workforce is necessary today because of demographic factors (a falling population) in Western countries that compel organisations to cast their recruitment nets wider than ever before. Women and minority groups possess the skills and management abilities in scarce supply and without them companies will be disadvantaged. Yet unless these diverse people see that organisations have proven track records in managing diversity in a way that values their diverse contributions, they will not be attracted to them as 'employers of choice'.

Valuing diversity means recognising that recruitment and promotion must be based on talent and merit. The other benefits of a diverse workforce include: better decision-making and greater creativity springing from different perspectives; more cultural awareness in creating and marketing products to minority groups; more effective development of people resulting in their heightened loyalty and commitment to the organisation.

Diversity initiatives vary across organisations and include:

- diversity awareness programmes,
- achieving better work/life balance,
- respecting age differences,
- developing inclusiveness for all regardless of sex, religion, age, sexual orientation, race, ethnicity and disability,
- equal opportunities for promotion based only on merit,
- open recruitment and succession planning,
- developing cultural change programmes and
- establishing support groups.

Research shows that introducing diversity programmes and practices into organisations requires consideration of key factors ranging from the strategic importance attributed to the initiatives, who champions the programmes, how effectively the programmes meet employee needs, the focused communication and the maintenance of the programme.

INDIVIDUAL DIFFERENCES

Personality is the relatively stable organisation of a person's motivational dispositions, arising from the interactions between biological drivers and the social and physical environment. Theories of personality cover both type and trait. The Myers-Briggs Type Indicator® is an example of a psychometric instrument that combines type and trait characteristics. The test identifies two functions (generating information and making decisions), which in turn are influenced by two attitudes (managing relationships and setting priorities) showing how the person relates to the world outside them. The four dimensions measured in the Myers-Briggs Type Indicator® are:

- relating to other people,
- generating/gathering information,
- making decisions,
- allocating time priorities.

Combinations across these dimensions produce four managerial types: traditionalists, troubleshooters or negotiators, catalysts and visionaries. Sex differences in terms of type and trait characteristics are identified amongst managers.

PERCEPTION

Perception is the process by which people select, organise and interpret external stimuli into terms that are consistent with their own frames of reference. Increased understanding of other people comes through communication. Three factors affect how a person is judged: the perceived, the perceiver and the situation.

ATTRIBUTES

Attributes are inferences about people's internal states of mind and emotions based on their observed behaviour. Our own frames of reference shape the way we interpret information. Some of the ways in which distortion affects us are: stereotypes, halo and horns effects, the expectations we hold, projection and selective perception. Perception can be improved through self-disclosure and feedback.

IMPROVING UNDERSTANDING AND INTERACTION

Being more conscious of the nature of diversity in organisations and society, being sensitive to individual differences, recognising the variety of perceptions people hold and relating the attributes we feel people have to the behaviour they exhibit, help us understand the nature and 'psyche' of the individual. However, understanding is not sufficient, as making a positive impact on others is an important element of being a manager. Impression management is the process whereby individuals seek to influence the perception of others about their own image. The aim is to construct a desirable social identity.

7 *Leadership*

The chairman of a company is measured by success or failure in achieving financial and operating results acceptable to the shareholders. Divisional directors are measured by how well they have been able to integrate the work of their divisional managers to make a significant contribution to the company's profits. Sales managers are measured by their ability to organise and motivate their sales teams to meet or surpass their sales targets. Supervisors are measured by their effectiveness in allocating work and ensuring that it is completed.

Leadership occurs at all levels in an organisation, and the quality of a manager's performance is directly related to their management of their subordinates' performance.

The style adopted by a manager or leader is a critical dimension of their individual and organisational effectiveness. The quality of leadership is one characteristic that distinguishes the successful company from one that is performing poorly. Many business failures can be traced back to weak leadership. It is no surprise, then, that research into the nature of successful leadership has been pursued for decades, and only now are we beginning to put together a composite picture that makes sense.

Although studies of leadership and leaders have often generated conflicting data, progress has been made towards understanding them. Figure 7.1 gives a historical overview of leadership studies and research on the individual as leader.

The early assumption was that leadership qualities were innate: that leaders were born, not made. Later studies suggested that successful leadership derived from the leaders' personal values and beliefs, their attitudes, behaviours and styles of leadership. Today it is argued that successful leadership is a function of the leader's skill in diagnosing the people and tasks in a situation, and of the leader's ability to modify leadership style appropriately.

For managers to be good leaders, some may need to change their core values, but most are likely to need to change their style of interaction to fit the demands of the situation. The need to adapt style has produced many definitions of leadership, but all of them agree on these three features:

- Leadership is an influencing process.
- There are two or more people involved – a leader and one or more followers.
- Leadership occurs when people are trying to achieve given, implied or unconscious objectives.

The person with most formal authority is not necessarily the leader in any given situation. A potential leader is anyone who tries to influence someone else's behaviour, whether the other person is their subordinate, peer or boss. Thus a manager who aspires to be a good leader should choose the most appropriate style of influencing, managing or communicating to achieve the required goals with given persons. This implies two separate questions: how do effective leaders emerge? and what behaviour makes leaders effective?

Three further issues require examination: does the manager or leader operate within the current system or does he or she change things? Leading within the current system is called transactional leadership, whereas introducing dramatic and wholesale change is known as transformational leadership. Historically one branch of research has studied transactional leadership, while a different body of research has looked at how great men and women have instigated changes that have turned the world upside down. The third perspective recognises that a number of leaders exist in any one organisation and examines how these leaders, all of whom could hold transformational aspirations, integrate their efforts or clash with each other, thereby generating friction and disharmony in the organisation. This third school is termed the discretionary school of leadership, in effect, how transformationally inclined leaders make choices and act in the ways they do.

This chapter begins by focusing on the transactional view of leadership, goes on to examine the transformational aspects and then how a number of leaders utilise the discretion in their role.

Transactional leadership

Transactional leadership concerns the abilities and skills of a manager to lead for more successful performance of the team and the organisation through being better able to manage individuals and groups in the workplace. As Figure 7.1 shows, the exploration of leadership for managers has moved from early studies based on personality to the concept of situational leadership and finally to current models.

In one sense, little progress in transactional leadership thinking has been made since the 1970s; the emphasis is still on adapting style and behaviour to fit the circumstances. On the other hand, greater importance is now attributed to individual responsibility and what the person needs to do to make a difference. There has been an attitudinal change over the last 30 years from what is needed to work more effectively in situations, namely a concept of fit, to what the individual desires to do or not to do in any given situation, namely to make his or her contribution. The thinking on transactional leadership is now more concerned with each individual's maturity and sense of purpose.

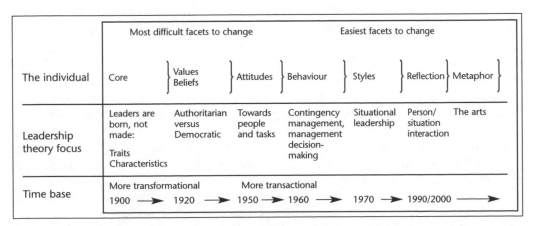

Figure 7.1 Historical overview: transactional leadership theory development (*Source*: *Working in Organisations*, First Edition, 1987)

Our own background, experiences, values and beliefs generate expectations as to how we should use a leadership position to involve ourselves and others for whom we are responsible in trying to achieve the desired results. Our natural learning and development affects our attitudes towards other people and the assumptions we hold about them. This, in turn, influences our leadership behaviour. Douglas McGregor (1960), with his theory X and theory Y, described two contrasting sets of assumptions. If a manager believes people are generally lazy, and will work only if coerced or tightly controlled and directed (theory X), he or she is likely to have a self-image as the boss, as their superior, and will spend time directing and monitoring what people are doing. If a manager believes people are inherently good and are willing to accept responsibility when given the opportunity for self-direction (theory Y), he or she is likely to stand back, let people get on with the task and act as a facilitator or co-ordinator, providing planning and services so that they can achieve the agreed targets. The manager's own expectations are vital factors in their behaviour. McGregor identified two contrasting sets of behaviour and leadership orientations. In fact, many more exist. We shall study transactional leadership from six viewpoints: (a) personality traits, (b) the varying behaviours, attitudes and styles that leaders adopt (behaviour approach), (c) why leadership style and decision-making behaviour needs to match (or be contingent with) the demands of the situation, (d) how managers go about making decisions, (e) how to analyse situations so as to know what style to adopt to what circumstances and (f) why transactional leadership is important when it may feel less glamorous than transformational leadership (hot managers).

TRAIT STUDIES

Studies of leadership assumed that there were certain qualities of personality which were common to good leaders. This research concentrated on personal factors such as intelligence, age and experience, or on personality traits (extroversion, dominance). Certain characteristics were considered inherent and God-given – if a person did not possess them, he or she was unlikely to be a good leader. It was easy to identify potential leaders. The main purpose of training therefore would be to develop the leadership characteristics in those who already possessed them. Training would be wasted on others. It was the leader's characteristics that were important, not the task in hand or the situation in which they operated.

The assumption that certain individuals are able to direct, control, guide and lead others because they possess certain qualities conflicts with democratic principles. The idea of a leadership elite perpetuated by heredity is little favoured by people today, who dislike the thought of being forever doomed to be followers. Although half a century of research has produced some evidence that leaders, particularly successful leaders, are more achievement-oriented, extrovert and intelligent than other people, it has not been possible to identify any significant traits or characteristics which are common to effective leaders. There is not even agreement on a list of leadership traits or qualities – one writer might include 'honesty' while another would insist that the leader can be duplicitous or even Machiavellian.

Was Alexander the Great a good leader in terms of leadership traits? After one successful battle he had 2000 people crucified to inspire fear. Joseph Stalin studied for the priesthood before becoming head of the Soviet Union and a mass murderer.

Continuing lack of success moved attention away from the trait approach. Certainly, personal characteristics and personality factors may feature among the determinants of great leadership, but if they are not the main factors, what are? Could it perhaps be the way in which leaders behave in the process of leadership, the way in which they tackle the demands of situations in which they have to display leadership that causes some to do better than others?

Researchers began to look more closely at leadership behaviour rather than what sort of people the leaders were. A leader is what a leader does. Studies were also made of the situations and environments in which certain different leadership behaviours appeared to succeed.

THE BEHAVIOURAL APPROACH

Leadership is a process whereby a person attempts to influence an individual or group towards the achievement of a given goal. Capable leaders therefore help people to work successfully on tasks; they are concerned with the task (production, goal achievement), and with the people doing it (relationships between the leader and his subordinates, or followers). The examination of leadership behaviour in managers and the styles they use to interact with their subordinates moved the focus of research from what leaders are to what leaders do. Leadership is viewed as an activity, not as a set of individual characteristics or qualities; leadership cannot be considered as dependent on the leader alone – it consists of interactions between the leader and their subordinates. Because leadership occurs between people, and is an influencing process, the behavioural approach assumes that subordinates will work better for managers who use certain styles of leadership than they will for others who employ different styles. Two schools of thought, the authoritarian and democratic, highlight the controls and facilitative approaches to leadership. Such contrasts are integrated through the managerial grid.

The authoritarian/disciplinarian school

Scientific management, as developed by Frederick Taylor in the early twentieth century, was concerned with increasing productivity by the use of improved techniques, work study and method study (see Chapter 2). Tasks and jobs should be broken down into clearly structured units, with specialisation of labour and well-defined and measurable performance targets. The emphasis was on direction and control by the manager, rather than on the needs of operatives. Leadership focused on satisfying organisational needs, not the needs of the individual. At this time, with poorly organised workers and weak trade unions, power lay in the hands of management; it had sole authority for decision-making and control of reward and punishment. Task achievement was the manager's prime concern. This style of management was called 'authoritarian'.

Unfeeling, inconsiderate and indiscriminate use of this style often leads to alienation and withdrawal on the part of subordinates, and also to feelings of powerlessness, which can manifest themselves in restrictions of output, absenteeism and the development of the kind of 'them and us' attitude that still exists today in many workplaces.

The human relations school

In the 1920s and 1930s Elton Mayo, one of the first of a series of behavioural scientists, suggested that in addition to using most appropriately designed methods to achieve productivity, management could perhaps reduce alienation and negative feelings towards the organisation by looking also at the human aspects of work. Interpersonal relations, particularly the feelings and attitudes within working groups, were important. He argued that people looked for satisfaction of their social needs at work. Moreover, the influence of groups on individual members was such that organisations should develop systems and styles to try to satisfy people's social needs in their workgroups. The leader using this human relations approach would act primarily as a facilitator, sharing power and authority with the group in moving towards goal achievement. Group harmony, satisfaction of individual needs and concern for people were consequently of prime importance. This style of leadership could be called 'democratic'.

It was felt that the styles usually adopted by leaders were based on the assumptions they make about people, determined by their own values, beliefs and attitudes, and their perception of their own bases of power (see Chapter 6 for analysis of attitudes and perceptions and Chapter 10 for an understanding of power bases).

The human relations school grew out of Mayo's philosophy. It maintained that a democratic style would be more likely to motivate people to work productively than an autocratic style. By being able to participate, being involved in decision-making, and exercising autonomy and responsibility, the individual would feel satisfied in terms of most of the Maslow hierarchy of needs (see Chapter 4) and thereby apply more energy and effort to getting the job done. There is evidence that democratic styles are linked to higher subordinate satisfaction, lower staff turnover and absenteeism and less intergroup conflict, and are often the styles subordinates preferred. Most research findings show a correlation between high group productivity and a democratic style of leadership. However, certain other studies also indicated that productivity is positively related to an authoritarian style – some people *do* prefer to be controlled and directed.

For some time these two styles, authoritarian and democratic, were thought to be opposite ends of one continuum of leadership style. Further observations of leader behaviour showed greater variations. Some leaders exhibited high task-directed behaviour and also a high concern for relationships with their subordinates. Some exhibited neither; some emphasised relationships but showed little concern for task achievement. Others focused on the task and spent little time on relationships. It became evident that managers used a mix of authoritarian and democratic styles. It also became clear that authoritarian and democratic styles are not two ends of the same continuum, but are in fact different dimensions of leadership behaviour.

The managerial grid

Robert Blake and Jane Mouton crystallised the earlier work of the famous Michigan and Ohio State research studies with their managerial grid (Figure 7.2) which described five managerial styles based on the concepts of task achievement (production) and concern for people (relationships) (Blake, R.R. and Mouton, J.S. (1964), *The New Managerial Grid III*, Houston: Gulf Publishing Company, p 12). They are:

- *Task management* (9, 1). The manager achieves high production by planning, organising and directing work in such a way that human variables are kept to a minimum.
- *Team management* (9, 9). The manager tries to gain commitment from his or her subordinates; high production will be achieved by balancing task achievement, organisational goals and the satisfaction of human needs.
- *Middle of the road management* (5, 5). Adequate performance is achieved by trading off production requirements against subordinate morale.

- *Country club management* (1, 9). Satisfying people's social and relationship needs leads to group harmony and a comfortable workplace.
- *Impoverished management* (1, 1). The manager exacts minimum effort to get the required work done and maintains warm relationships with his or her subordinates.

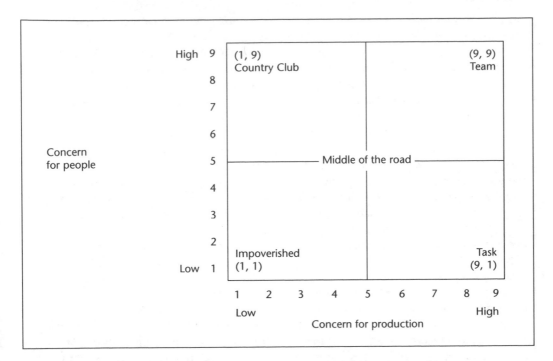

Figure 7.2 The managerial grid (*Source: Working in Organisations*, First Edition, 1987)

The popularity and simplicity of the managerial grid led many managers to infer that the best style of management was (9, 9) – team management – with high concern for production, high concern for people. Employing a style that emphasised concern for people, their development, their need for satisfaction, and also concern for task achievement, was felt by many to be the ideal leadership behaviour. Rensis Likert (1965) found that supervisors with the best records of performance concentrated on human aspects and tried to develop workgroups with high performance goals. His conclusion was that the most productive leadership behaviour was democratic, but his results also showed that favourable results were gained by leaders using tight control and supervision.

In the face of this conflicting evidence, can we say that there is any single ideal leadership or management style? It seems unlikely. The research findings suggest that managerial competence is not a function of task-oriented or people-oriented style alone. It includes a third factor – the situation.

CONTINGENCY STUDIES

The contingency model of leadership assumes that leaders are effective when their style matches the demands of the given situation, particularly the task or work group and the position of the leader with respect to the workgroup. Fred E. Fiedler (1967) defined

REALITY CHECK

MAYOR GIULIANI, THE DAY AFTER SEPTEMBER 11TH, LEADING THE RECOVERY

Only five survivors were pulled alive from the rubble of the World Trade Center after the attack left it a smouldering ruin. Only five. New Yorkers and people across the world had hoped for hundreds more. The great city was reeling from the attack and in need of leadership. As he had done so visibly on the day of the attack itself, Mayor Giuliani met this requirement masterfully. He went on the *Today* TV show to reassure everyone that New York was still standing and that its people would overcome the disaster. They would show the nation that they refused to be terrorised and, in doing so, become a role model for the country.

He then did what he always did. He led his daily morning meeting. He even started it on time at 8 am, using a police escort to negotiate the congested roads in Lower Manhattan. His staff, some of whom had no sleep the night before, were there for the meeting. The deputy mayors and commissioners began to report in detail on the challenges each of them faced in their respected agencies. The Governor of the State of New York, Governor Pataki and members of his staff also attended the meeting. Everyone listened to the reports and responded to them. Giuliani made some key decisions immediately. Other issues were debated or assigned task forces to deal with them. Some issues were postponed.

'We contacted the military and the Federal Emergency Management Agency to order 11 000 body bags and could pause for only a second to reflect on the horrific meaning of what we had just decided' Giuliani recalled.

The Mayor and his top team increased the size of the no-go area around the World Trade Center and decided to phone each of the business leaders who had lost many of the employees in the attack. Each member of staff contacted the leaders he or she knew best, leaving for Mayor Giuliani the firms whose work forces had been most affected.

'I called Howard Lutnick, chief executive officer of Cantor Fitzgerald, whose firm on the top floor of the north tower had lost over 700, including Howard's brother Gary. Howard was understandably upset during our call and I offered him whatever assistance he needed. I again spoke to Dick Grasso, Head of the New York Stock Exchange, concerned that the city might be in for additional attacks and that the Exchange was a possible target. I reached Phil Purcell, the chief executive officer of Morgan Stanley, at home.'

The company with the largest number of employees – 3700 – on site was benefiting from its own preparations. Morgan Stanley had planned for an attack following the bombing of the World Trade Center in 1993. Colonel Richard C. Rescoria, head of security at the bank, had in place a crisis management plan that he had drilled with Morgan Stanley employees.

The Mayor pointed out that Colonel Rescoria was an Englishman who had come to America to fight in the Vietnam War. In addition to the courage of the Fire Department of New York and the New York Police Department, according to the Mayor, it was 'because of the bravery and preparedness of Rick and his team, thousands of Morgan Stanley employees made it to safety on September 11. Tragically, six employees died, and Rick was one of them.'

Source: Giuliani, R.W. with Kurson, K. (2002), *Leadership*, London: Little, Brown, p 5.

situations in terms of their favourableness to the leader. The key component of favourableness is influence over the workgroup and he argued that the influence dimension is
composed of three main factors. They are:

- The leader-member relationship. A favourable relationship enables the leader to exercise
  greater influence over the workgroup.
- The degree of structure of the task. The more structured the task, the more favourable
  the situation for the leader.
- The leader's formal position of power. The greater the rewards or punishments the leader
  can award, the more influence he or she can exert.

The most favourable leadership situation is therefore one in which there are good
leader-member relationships, the task is well-defined and highly-structured and the leader
enjoys a high degree of formal authority. In favourable leadership situations, Fiedler concluded that an authoritarian style is likely to be more successful. In situations that are
neither favourable nor unfavourable, a relationship-oriented style (democratic) is preferable. In unfavourable situations, where the task is unstructured, the leader-member
relationships are poor and the leader has little formal authority, the leader is likely to
achieve best results by adopting a task-oriented style. Conversely, task-oriented leaders are
likely to achieve better results in group situations that are favourable or unfavourable to the
leader, while relationship-oriented leaders tend to achieve better results in situations that
are neither favourable nor unfavourable.

Despite Fiedler's emphasis on managerial style, he felt that it was more practical for
organisations to change a given situation than to hope that managers could adapt their style
to fit in. Task structure and formal authority were considered easier to change than a manager's natural and preferred style of leadership. Peter Drucker (1990) agreed that in a small
organisation, training and changing managerial styles would take one to two years, rising to
five years in a larger organisation. These changes need not necessarily be dramatic, for even
small changes can improve effectiveness. Fielder's conclusion also implied that leaders are
more often born than made and that leadership behaviour was one-dimensional along the
authoritarian-democratic continuum – whereas in reality most managers' styles are combinations of these two separate dimensions.

MANAGERIAL DECISION MAKING

In contrast to the 'born to be a leader' school of thought, Victor Vroom and Philip Yetton
(1973) began with the assumption that managers learn various styles and from that basis
they developed a series of rules whereby leaders should modify their preferred styles to meet
the requirements of given situations. They consider that there are situations where managers, in making decisions, should behave autocratically, or democratically, or should use a
combination of both these styles. They identified those situations where, for maximum
effectiveness, subordinates should participate, and the degree to which they should participate in managerial decision-making. They describe a model with three ranges of styles,
'autocratic', 'consultative', and 'group participation':

- *Autocratic*. The manager solves the problem or makes the decision himself or herself on the
  basis of the information available or supplied by subordinates at the time.

- *Consultative*. The manager shares the problem with subordinates, either individually, or as a group, then he or she makes the decision – which may or may not reflect the sub-ordinates' influence.
- *Participative*. The manager shares the problem with sub-ordinates as a group. Together they generate and evaluate solutions and attempt to reach agreement on a solution. The manager accepts and implements whatever solution has the support of the group.

Vroom and Yettin argued that the factors determining the best leadership style to adopt are:

- the quality of the decision to be made,
- the level of acceptability required by the subordinates to implement the decision and
- the time scale of the decision-making process.

When making decisions, managers should assess and weigh all these factors before deciding whether, or how much, to involve subordinates in the decision-making process. The technique used in this consideration is a decision tree, applying the seven questions shown in Table 7.1. Unlike the decision tree model that Vroom uses to illustrate an expectancy theory of motivation (see Chapter 4), this decision tree provides a model to help in the making of decisions.

Table 7.1 Vroom/Yetton decision tree questions (*Source: Working in Organisations*, First Edition, 1987)

A	B	C	D	E	F	G
Is there a quality requirement such that one solution is likely to be more rational than another?	Do I have enough information to make a quality decision?	Is the problem structured?	Is acceptance of the decision by subordinates important for effective implementation?	If I were to make the decision by myself, is it reasonably certain that it would be acceptable to my subordinates?	Do subordinates share the organizational goals to be attained in solving the problem?	Is conflict among subordinates likely in preferred solution?

Questions A, B and C relate to the quality and rationality of the decision required. Questions D and E refer to the acceptance of the decision by subordinates. Questions F and G concern the subordinates' attitude to the problem's context and the preferred solution.

Where the manager has or can obtain the information to make the decision, or no one decision is preferable, they can make the decision themselves. Where the manager does not have enough information, and acceptance is a problem, some degree of consultation and participation is needed.

The Vroom-Yetton model was a popular training tool throughout the 1970s and 1980s. What managers had to learn was how to integrate the logical process of decision making with the need to allow subordinates to contribute to the process in ways which can aid the manager in achieving their objectives.

Vroom and Yetton, through their appreciation that good managers have to adapt their styles to match the requirements of different situations, heralded the onset of a new approach to organisational leadership: situational leadership.

SITUATIONAL LEADERSHIP

Using these earlier studies, Paul Hersey and Ken Blanchard (1976) developed a model of situational leadership. They describe four leadership styles, based on the dimensions of task behaviour and relationship behaviour.

- *Task behaviour* is the extent to which leaders are likely to organise and define the roles of the group (followers); to explain what activities each is to undertake, and when, where and how tasks are to be accomplished. It is characterised by endeavouring to establish well-defined patterns of organisation, channels of communication and ways of getting jobs done.
- *Relationship behaviour* is the extent to which leaders are likely to maintain personal relationships between themselves and members of their group (followers) by opening up channels of communication, listening to them, providing emotional support and 'psychological strokes' and offering facilitating or supportive behaviours.

Task behaviour is characterised by the leader's use of one-way communication in direction and explanation, while relationship behaviour opens up two-way communication through encouragement, listening, friendliness and recognition.

Situational leadership theory suggests that there is no such thing as a common style of good leadership, no one best way to influence people. Leaders will be effective when they match their style to their own requirements, those of the subordinates and the task itself in the context of the situation. The individual manager needs to determine which approach to use and which combination of task and relationship behaviour is appropriate, depending on the circumstances.

Hersey and Blanchard argued that the main factor determining the best management style in any situation is the job-related development of subordinates, defined as the ability and willingness of people to take responsibility for directing their own behaviour, specifically in relation to the task to be performed. A subordinate or group working competently has the knowledge and skills to perform the task, is willing to take responsibility for the job and is highly committed to achievement of the task. A developed subordinate or group can be described as 'ready, willing and able'. The relative lack of these characteristics shows the degree of underdevelopment or immaturity.

This implies that individuals may be underdeveloped with regard to some tasks, yet developed with regard to others. Moreover, in a group of subordinates each member may be at a different level of development in respect of each task they have to perform. This means that leaders may have to use different styles towards individual members of their group when managing the same task, and also behave differently with the same member, who is carrying out different tasks. In Hersey and Blanchard's model (Figure 7.3), a curve suggests the appropriate style – the best combination of task behaviour and relationship behaviour – for the job-related development level (maturity) of the subordinates (followers).

When a group or individual appears to the leader to display, and be working at, a low level of development, the leader needs to provide a high degree of control, direction, role

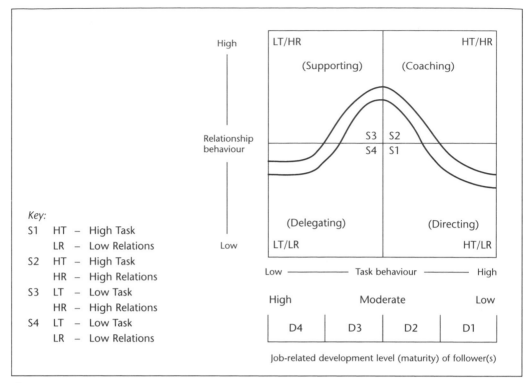

Figure 7.3 The situational leadership theory (*Source*: *Working in Organisations*, First Edition, 1987)

definition and structure with respect to the task, while positively reinforcing only that behaviour which shows increased motivation, job-related skills and increased responsibility. As the level of development increases, the leader should increase relationship behaviour while reducing the control and direction (task behaviour) given to the group or individual subordinate. As the level of task-related development approaches maturity, the leader can withdraw both task and relationship behaviour involvement and move to a delegating leadership role. However, when delegating he or she needs to have set up monitoring systems so that he or she is constantly aware that this style is appropriate. If the level of development is falling, if the group or individual is not achieving targets, then he or she should move their leadership behaviour back down the curve to a supporting, coaching or ultimately a directing approach. However, the individual must beware of moving directly from a delegating to a directing role. Sudden changes of behaviour are likely to make subordinates feel that the leader is inconsistent and may lead to resentment and resistance to change, which may be reflected in reduced productivity and performance.

The ideal manager is one who can modify behaviour across the four principal leadership styles to fit the job-related development of his or her subordinates. However, we all have a preferred style of managing and may find it difficult to behave in a role which is alien to our own values, beliefs and attitudes. A manager who feels that people cannot be trusted to perform adequately, and need constant control and direction, would be uncomfortable acting in a delegating role. A manager who is happiest when working as a member of a group would be uncomfortable as a delegator, or as a controller and director. If a manager is required by the nature of the situation to behave constantly in a role in which they feel uncomfortable, then they will eventually exhibit symptoms of frustration and stress. Likewise, if employees are over-managed they may experience frustration and stress.

The theory also implies that a manager needs to be able to diagnose the subordinates' levels of job-related development. The Hersey-Blanchard development scale helps managers to make this diagnosis.

REALITY CHECK

SIR CHRIS BONINGTON'S LEADERSHIP CONQUERS EVEREST

. . . the teamwork was good and there was a dynamism with the expedition that helped everyone feel we had a real chance of success. With such a strong team it was very important to work from a basis of consensus while avoiding running it by committee. I made my plans and then, where possible, called a meeting and asked for comments, only reserving the right of final decision to myself.

My effectiveness as leader was helped by the fact that I was climbing at around the same standard as my peers. It is hard for a leader to run an expedition from base camp (emphasis added) . . . I probably erred to the other extreme, finding excuses to get out in front making the route. But once there you tend to think emotionally and lose touch with what is happening to the rest of the expedition. The best position for the leader of a large expedition is at the camp immediately below that of the lead climbers. Here he can keep in touch with what is going on at the front and have a good feel for how the supplies are flowing up the mountain.

Source: Bonington, C. (1996), *Mountaineer: thirty years of climbing on the world's great peaks*, London: Baton Wicks, p 98–99.

HOT MANAGERS

Management consultant, Bruce Tulgan, in one of his recent flyers, has created the term 'Hot Leadership' to describe a particular style of leadership that has emerged. As he explains it HOT stands for 'hands-on' and 'transactional'.

These managers are in constant touch with the people they are managing. They work closely, helping them understand assignments, provide the resources required, anticipate problems and develop realistic schedules for results. They provide constructive feedback and coaching to keep their people focused.

These managers are also transactional as we have described in the leadership styles above – performance-orientated, always ready for personal negotiations to meet each employees particular needs in exchange for their meeting challenging goals within timeframes. By capturing the phrase 'HOT managers', Tulgan emphasises that transactional leadership is as vital a consideration as that of transformational. For today's managers, both are needed.

Transformational leadership

The quest to understand the complexities of leadership has been pursued for centuries. Military leaders such as Napoleon and Montgomery, great patriots such as George

Washington and Thomas Jefferson, who laid the foundation for a new nation, and leaders such as Martin Luther King and Nelson Mandela, who raised societies to a new level of social consciousness, have been endlessly analysed and discussed. The source of their greatness is still an open question, mainly because substantially different interpretations of leadership exist, namely:

- as a type of executive work that, depending on the circumstances, may or may not be required,
- as a motivator, which pushes the individual to act in extraordinary ways,
- as unnecessary, since success can as well be achieved through the sound application of management skills (that is, being more transactional),
- as one aspect of power, so that leaders are driven to mobilise resources to achieve their visions,
- as a form of knowledge, in that leaders use managerial disciplines like marketing, finance, operations management and human resource management,
- as possessing (or developing) superior conceptual skills, in that an analysis of potential opportunities helps to turn them into realities,
- as the verbal ability to articulate a vision in such a way that others share it,
- as aspects of character, such as ambition, conscience and concern for others. In balancing such contrasting emotions, a leader combines drive and desire with being held responsible for his or her actions, or
- as a journey through ambiguities, paradoxes and dilemmas, which require the leader to develop contrasting capabilities ranging from being innovative to being disciplined over detail, from having an unshakeable self-belief to practising humility in the service of others.

The perspective adopted often reflects the character of the writer or the leader who pronounces on the desired characteristics of leadership. In contrast to the command or control style of leadership discussed earlier as transactional, a transformational style involves encouraging participation, sharing power and information, enhancing the self-worth of others and stimulating enthusiasm about work.

Great leaders continuously attend to the handling of opposites. They are ethical and yet at times highly political. They are sensitive and yet disciplined, determined, even ruthless. They are aware of details and yet have a mind open to possibilities so that the slightest of chances can be exploited. Such apparent paradoxes distinguish those leaders who are transformational from those who are transactional.

Earlier in this chapter we explored the transactional elements of leadership, the managerial elements of the leader's role. Now we examine the varying interpretations of transformational leadership. It is argued that those who make a powerful impact on organisations and society are leaders who transform the status quo. To bring about this transformation leaders penetrate the very being and soul of others, fire their imagination and rejuvenate whole masses to strive for ever greater goals. In so doing, the leader often calls on personal charisma.

J. McGoldrick and J. Stewart (1996) single out leadership as the link between strategy, culture and employee commitment. Their view of leadership was built upon B. M. Bass's earlier work on transformational leadership that identified four components (Bass, 1985). They are:

- charisma,
- inspiration,
- individualised consideration and
- intellectual stimulation.

Transformational leadership was endorsed by the International Labour Organisation (ILO) which says leadership is a 'starting point for providing vision and sense of momentum and direction' (McGoldrick and Stewart, 1996).

First we shall explore transformational leadership in terms of charisma and its opposite, narcissism. In so doing, we shall not only explore transformational leaders, but also the needs of their followers.

CHARISMA

The term charisma (see also Chapter 10) is used to describe the inspiring, but nevertheless controlling and dominating relationship between leaders and their followers. Certain writers consider charisma an attribution, a quality that followers attribute to their 'adored' leaders. Others regard it as the manifestation of the innate characteristics of certain leaders. Why were so many attracted to J.F. Kennedy, or Charles de Gaulle? Was it the circumstances, or manipulation of the media – or was it those yet-to-be-defined forces that make for great men and women?

Charisma and the heroic leader

The military historian John Keegan describes how a central activity of primitive societies, hunting, brought out extraordinary qualities from the huntsmen. They were required to be heroes, facing wild animals with their primitive weapons; otherwise, the tribe would not eat. The idea that exceptional behaviour required extraordinary qualities was as widely recognised in primitive society as in today's complex world. Probably the battlefield, more than any other circumstance, promoted the view of the heroic leader, envied, feared, even mysterious, undoubtedly a role model for others.

The 2 Para Commanding Officer, Colonel H. Jones, was posthumously awarded the Victoria Cross at the 'Battle of Goose Green' in the Falklands war. Within military circles the debate continues whether he was a true hero or a rash leader following an outmoded style of leadership called 'Restrictive Control'. 'Restrictive control rests on the spurious premise that combat is a structured, mechanical affair which can be rendered orderly by detailed planning and strict adherence to orders. It results in superiors attempting to control the actions of their subordinates according to a predetermined plan often made in great detail in the wishful thinking that fate, the enemy, the weather, and other factors not subject to one's own command system can somehow be expected not to interfere with one's plans. On analysis it can be seen that the British command tradition has generally been of the restrictive control variety' (Fitz-Gibbon, S. (2001), *The history and mythology of the battle of goose green*, Cambridge: The Lutterworth Press, p xiv). One view is that Colonel H. Jones's belief in his plan cost him his life and endangered his own men.

The opposite of 'restrictive control' is 'directive command'. 'Directive command rests on an understanding that combat is inherently chaotic; that it cannot be tamed, but that the chaos can be exploited by the more flexible and quick-reacting command system. It implies a system in which orders are given in the form of 'directives'. A directive is an order which indicates an end-state to be achieved, but which leaves the method if its achievement to the imagination and on-the-spot judgement of the subordinate commander. This allows subordinates the freedom to act appropriately in response to unfolding events – whatever surprises may occur during the fighting – while still providing the guidance necessary to prevent diversification of effort. Empowering command values (in effect discretions see discretionary leadership section in this Chapter) can be identified, for example, in the writings of the ancient Chinese military philosopher Sun Tzu, and in the Prussian-German command philosophy since the eighteenth century. Such values have also been advocated from time to time in the British army, though empowering command has never been the predominant school of thought' (p xiv).

The nineteenth-century philosopher Frederick Nietzsche captured the great leader model through his concept of the 'Übermensch' (superman), emphasising the innate, extraordinary qualities of leadership. Nietzsche's analysis of a finite number of inborn leadership characteristics with which a few are blessed gained favour with two groups in the twentieth and twenty-first centuries, namely search consultants and biographers. The mission for search consultants is to find the 'fit', the right top person for the right job! In fact, the very concept of fit adds to the mystique of searching for this extraordinary human being. For biographers, the Übermensch concept has helped sell books, justifying their glorification of the great leader. Biographers, historians and even headhunters have had a profound impact on promoting charisma, the image of the great leader as a product or brand.

Charisma and attribution

The German philosopher and sociologist, Max Weber (1968) adopted a different approach from Nietzsche. Weber's view is that charisma arises according to the level of attribution bestowed on the leader by his or her followers. Those individuals that stand apart and are considered to display superhuman qualities do so only because they are 'allowed to' by those who follow them. In the more primitive societies of the past, such deference was accorded to the great and powerful warrior who distinguished himself in battle by his size, strength, cunning and skill. As society became more civilised, other qualities came into high regard, such as intellect, analysis and the skills of communication. Hence, charisma continues to be bestowed on religious leaders, like prophets and popes, politicians, business leaders, scientists and writers. The strength of charisma depends on the degree of recognition of the leader, and dependency on the leader by those who subordinate themselves to him or her. Weber did, however, acknowledge the fact that certain individuals are exceptional, in that they stand out and their impact on society will outline them, irrespective of the opinion of others. These exceptional people, however, may not be attributed with charisma by their peers, as the position they adopt may be considered unwelcome. In their earlier careers, they may be seen as villains or revolutionaries, although history may ultimately honour them as heroes, as in the case of Ghandi and Nelson Mandela.

Weber identified an additional element of charisma: the 'routinisation of attribution'. Hereditary wealth, and titles, are examples of such routinisation of charisma. Certain individuals are considered the natural heirs to a position of power or the family's wealth. In politics, certain constituencies were passed down from father to child, simply on the basis that the family were viewed as 'having the right' to be that community's representatives. This analysis can be applied to whole societies, such as India, with its caste system. Charisma is an attribution awarded not to an individual but to a position, or even a ruling elite. A classic example of hereditary charisma is the house of Nehru, whereby political leadership passed from Nehru senior to daughter Indira Ghandi, to son Rajiv Ghandi and, on his assassination, was offered to Rajiv's wife Sonia. She at first refused high office. However, Sonia, Italian by birth, from a poor background, was re-invited to become Prime Minister of India because she was next in line of the house of Nehru; her hereditary charisma placed her in an exalted position.

Charisma is concerned with attraction, enticement and being able to persuade others to do one's bidding. The charismatic leader influences the ideas, values and beliefs of others through the way their own beliefs and values are lived. Self-confident charismatic leaders believe what they preach.

Similarly, the self-developed leader exhibits the same powerful image, but in addition he or she displays a sensitivity to context, sensing people's pain and needs and reflecting empathy in their words and actions.

The self-developed leader also listens to others. The most famous of Kennedy's speeches, 'Ich bin ein Berliner . . .', captured the plight of the isolated West Berliners in the Cold War period. The words themselves hold no meaning. Kennedy was neither born nor resident in Berlin, but to conjure up words that identified him with the plight of a worried community made him a hero. The impact on the listening crowds of his words was so great that the authorities were afraid they would attack the hated symbol of the Berlin wall. Later TV reports of the powerful speech edited out some of Kennedy's more explosive sentences.

The American researcher Bob House (1997) examined the psychological characteristics of great political leaders by inviting panels of historians to judge the power and charismatic qualities of their speeches and writings. House distinguished the outstanding US presidents from the less effective by analysing four traits of charismatic leadership:

1   the capability to promulgate a vision (goals, agendas, an expectation around which others can converge),
2   communication skills (verbal, non-verbal and symbolic),
3   the capability to build trust or, as some would put it, dependency-creating skills, by being consistent, reliable and dogged and
4   the strength to promote respect and self-esteem in others by nurturing their strengths and talents.

The values and sentiments of the charismatic leader are captured in phrases such as Martin Luther King's 'I have a dream . . .', reflecting the repression and trauma of a troubled people, or John F. Kennedy's, 'Ask not what your country can do for you; ask what you can do for your country', inviting the American people to become more involved in the public life of their nation and in the service of American idealism abroad.

From the perspective of followers, the image of the powerful leader feeds the need of others to sacrifice their personal interests for the sake of some collective goal, a goal that they, as followers, feel unable to set themselves or know how to achieve. It was such thinking that over 60 years ago led the social researcher Wilfred Bion to explore how groups behave when they do not wish to, or even know how to, protect themselves from unpalatable experiences. Bion suggests groups fall into patterns of dependency or pairing or display fight or flight behaviours.

In dependency, the group needs a powerful leader to resolve their present problems and relieve their trauma. The leader is idealised. The more the leader is venerated, the more the group members accept their own shortcomings and see themselves as inadequate. A strong leader gives the group hope and with hope emerges emotional comfort. Leaders have greatest influence in times of crisis, as the inadequacies of the followers are then at their most extreme.

Should the leader fail or fall short of expectations, the group is likely to react initially by denial or betrayal, then by anger, and eventually by a 'character assassination' of the leader, followed by his or her removal and a search for a substitute.

Bion's pairing reflects a strong sense of expecting a saviour or a 'Messiah' to appear, who will lead the group out of its present difficulties. As with dependency, the group is too paralysed to attend to its own problems. The difference is that the followers fail to act because they are waiting for the leader-to-be. For this reason pairing is a more pathological state than dependency.

The third of Bion's responses is 'fight or flight', the projection of the group's fears onto an enemy, such as a competitor, a hostile nation or even a particular person. When the leader does not know what else to do, the temptation is to find a third party onto whom all the group's frustrations can be projected. The fight or flight dynamic glorifies the group's leader, focuses energy and resources, motivates the followers but also distorts the group's ability to assess their circumstances as the frenzy of fighting the enemy clouds people's judgement.

Margaret Thatcher, for example, was accused of using the Falklands war to divert attention from her unpopular restructuring of the British economy. The war made Thatcher a heroine but allowed her to continue transforming Britain into a market-based economy through deregulation and privatisation.

Tony Blair has been both praised and criticised for his charisma. In continental Europe there is criticism of his close alliance with America, particularly over Afghanistan and Iraq, while in the USA he is seen as the most charismatic supporter of that country's anti-terrorist campaign, and his support for the war in Iraq has won him praise.

Charismatic leaders who introduce fundamental change are vulnerable, as witnessed by the rate of executive succession in Anglo-American organisations over the last decade. For example, research in the USA shows that the average reformist police chief lasts about two years before the internal network gathers momentum and secures their removal, often unduly influencing their replacement.

REALITY CHECK

SHACKLETON WAY

While the rest slept, Shackleton kept quiet watch. Ever since the Endurance *had gotten stuck in January 1915, he had taken bottom-line responsibility for the life, health and safety of every one of his men. Back in August, on the ship, Orde-Lees wrote, 'I know for a fact that he did not once lie down for three days and I don't think he has undressed for ten days. Even when he did condescend to rest a little, it was only for about three hours at a*

time . . . He seems always on the alert, especially at night, having certainly been up every night for the last three weeks.'

Sleep was to become an increasingly rare luxury for the boss. His ceaseless vigilance would save a life that night of 9 April 1916, which happened to be his twelfth wedding anniversary. The boss had been in his sleeping bag only about an hour when he got up to survey the floe. As he approached the seamen's tent in the dark, an unexpectedly large swell tossed the floe and it split under the men's tent. Someone yelled, 'Crack!' and one man hit the water, letting out a yelp. Shackleton quickly threw himself onto the edge of the ice, and as the others watched, he heaved the man and his sleeping bag back onto the floe. The seaman, Holness, seemed more annoyed than grateful. When asked if he was all right, he replied, 'Yes, but I lost a

****** tin of baccy,' Wild later wrote, omitting the expletive. When someone suggested he should be thankful the boss had saved him, Holness snapped: 'So I am, but that doesn't bring the tobacco back.'

Source: Morrell M. and Capparell S. (2002), *Shackleton's way*, Harmondsworth: Penguin Books, p 163.

NARCISSISM

Saddam Hussein's exploitation of Iraq for three decades provides a case study in narcissism. Statues, paintings and mosaics of the dictator were ubiquitous. Every school book began with a photograph of Saddam Hussein. The self-promulgation of Saddam as a heroic figure took place at the expense of his own people as he led Iraq in three failed wars and squandered oil revenues for personal gain and self-glorification. Once free to express themselves, the people of Iraq pulled down the statues and pictures of their flawed leader and applied the soles of their shoes to his image – the ultimate insult.

A number of Freudian psychologists hold that emotionally healthy individuals have little need for adulation, recognition or self-projection. Manfred Kets de Vries (1989) of Insead argues that those who are poorly developed emotionally need extraordinary recognition and acclaim. This raises the interesting question of the difference between self-confidence and self-love. From the point of view of transformational leadership, knowing what to do and knowing when to stop, even if the image of the leader is tarnished in so doing, exhibits self-confidence. Narcissism, or self-love, is exhibited by someone who continuously needs attention and does not know when to terminate their action because of their insatiable need for acclaim. In using need for acclaim as the measure, Kets de Vries distinguishes three types of narcissism:

- reactive, or pathological, narcissism,
- self-deceptive narcissism and
- constructive, or more healthy, narcissism.

Reactive narcissism

A pathological, or reactive, narcissist is someone with little confidence who needs reassurance. Narcissistic desires are driven by the unrealistic expectations of early parental figures. However, instead of experiencing an emotional collapse, the instinct for self-preservation is so great that what emerges is a powerful, 'greater-than-life' personality. Independent, aggressive, action-oriented, such a leader exudes self-confidence and loves no one but themselves. However, when their inner drive becomes so pathological, the leader becomes unable to distinguish desire from reality. Reactive narcissists distort external events in their favour, partly, according to Freud, to prevent loss and disappointment, and partly to attract even more attention. In the crisis-ridden spots of the world, reactive narcissists emerge. Often they start by pursuing a good cause but in time their psychopathic desire to dominate, allowing no rival near them (often executing any contender for power) promotes the darker side of their transformational desires. Their tendency to be ruthless, grandiose and exhibitionist, often to the obvious detriment of their people, knows no bounds. Robert Mugabe of Zimbabwe is one example. During 2002 and 2003, the spectacular economic deterioration of his country in no way deterred his striving to remain in power and to eliminate those who stood in his way. Yet Mugabe was once viewed as a bright economist capable of leading his new nation into a new era of social justice for all.

Self-deceptive narcissism

Self-deceptive narcissists combine a need to be liked with certain tendencies of the reactive narcissist. The desire to dominate, the striving for recognition and the intention to bully one's way forward are mediated by the need to be seen in a positive light. As with the reactive narcissist, their deficiencies in bonding relationships with early parental figures, arising from the unrealistic ideals given to them and the need to please their parents, emerge in the adult as guilt and questioning. Did I do the right thing? Did I over-react? If I do not attend to all the details, can I cope with being seen to fail? Unlike others who experience self-questioning, the self-deceptive narcissist lives in a continuous state of 'controlled anxiety'. Others who self-question do so because of the circumstances and problems they face. In contrast, the self-deceptive narcissist self-questions perpetually and has to 'learn' to accommodate guilt.

People who experience self-deceptive narcissistic tendencies are likely to explain their lives as balancing positive and negative emotions, or an inner struggle between good and bad. As a leader, the self-deceptive narcissist would tend to be less exploitative, more approachable and more tolerant of dissenting opinion. The reluctance to upset relationships induces them to adopt a transactional approach to leadership, attentive to details, making small advances, justified in terms of taking a balanced approach, but also unduly concerned with other people's relationships. Their fear of being unpopular, or making a mistake, inhibits their pursuit of transformational change. Some would interpret the attention to detail and to other people's relationship as sensitive concern. Others see it as prying. However, the underlying motivation is fear of not knowing what is going on.

Where the need is to build up the organisation's infrastructure, or to provide sound management, the self-deceptive narcissist can make a substantial contribution. However, when circumstances change and the desire for tactical success is no longer paramount, a radically different philosophy of leadership is required.

Constructive narcissists

Driven to succeed, but with a quieter nature, the constructive narcissist falls into the category of the balanced transformational leader, taking responsibility for his or her own actions, and open to comment and criticism. Many famous leaders in business and politics, whose resolve to address known concerns is high and yet who seem to take a balanced view on issues, are constructive narcissists. The Jack Welch image of an intelligent, driven man from a humble background who, on reaching senior office, is well able to steer the organisation through difficult times, acting in the interests of the enterprise and not of his own self-promotion, provides a good example. Another is Alexei Mordashov, a former general manager of a steel works in Russia and now billionaire chief executive of the Severstal

Group, whose interests range from steel and oil to transportation, motor vehicle manufacture, to name but a few. Apart from running the lives of over 200 000 people, Mordashov supports the city of Cherepovets as well as untold charities. He is only 38 years old. Interestingly, although Alexei Mordashov and Jack Welch are successful, driven and intelligent, both are also regarded as team players. The original group that started around Alexei Mordashov remain with him today. Jack Welch nurtured his own successor at General Electric, an epitome of the teamwork culture he inspired.

An example of teamwork at General Electric was given by a senior manager who was recently 'headhunted' for a top job in another company. He described how, on joining any of the companies in the General Electric group, a newly appointed executive spends a day with their new team and is then sent home for the following two days. During that time the team discuss their new manager and identify questions and issues they wish to raise with him or her. Then the newly appointed top manager again meets the team on day four, listens to their feedback and concerns, and responds to the issues they raised. Such openness establishes the basis for a robust team. 'The first time it is a daunting experience,' said the manager. 'After a while, you get to like it. The experience is invaluable!'

Radiating self-confidence and purposefulness, being flexible and focused, promotes a willingness to take responsibility for one's own actions and to help others when events do not proceed as planned. These considerable strengths are counter-balanced by the weak point of constructive narcissists, their tendency to react badly to personal criticism on the basis that they can see little wrong with themselves.

Sex and leadership style

Judith Rosener (1990) pointed out that women managers are more comfortable with transformational leadership rather than the somewhat masculine models derived from research on male leaders managing male subordinates.

However, in male-dominated industries women managers lead in ways that are more similar than different to the men in those industries. This is consistent with Rosabeth Moss Kanter's work on tokenism (1997), which found that where women are in the minority they alter their management style to reduce their visibility or to lessen perceived differences and stereotyping by men.

The Centre for Developing Women Business Leaders at Cranfield has produced many research studies that illustrate the differences between men and women in terms of executive performance, highlighting the benefits of femininity in terms of cooperation and teamwork. These studies also describe the disadvantages women face in mastering the aggressive politics often encountered in organisations. They conclude that 'impression management' for women is a challenging but necessary skill to develop whereby they promote their own talents and achievements.

Earlier surveys undertaken at Cranfield positioned masculinity/femininity as one of many demographic factors, and concluded that no significant executive performance differences exist between men and women. Men and women can be equally effective and ineffective as leaders. The main determinants of effectiveness are the contextual challenges facing the leader and the individual's capacity to adjust, not sex.

Two different points of view encapsulate the sex debate. One is that the nature of masculinity and femininity produces performance differences. The contrasting viewpoint is that sex is simply one of many demographic factors, all of which have to be taken into account to appreciate the leadership challenges that need to be tackled, which vary according to circumstance.

However, whether or not women are more inclined to cooperation and men are more aggressive and competitive, does little to enhance understanding of the discrimination women face in the workplace. Considerable research demonstrates that discrimination does exist and acts as an impediment to the movement of talented women into executive positions. In fact, a whole terminology has emerged highlighting such barriers, with phrases such as 'an uneven playing field', 'glass walls' and 'glass ceiling' entering common usage. The poor utilisation of women's capabilities, particularly in senior management roles, has now reached the national political stage.

The British government has a hundred or more female members of parliament frequently in the headlines. Female MPs and Ministers have thrown their support behind the campaign to get more women on the board of FTSE 100 companies. Thus, the distinction to make, which has not emerged sufficiently clearly in the literature, is between 'getting there', that is, career progress and the barriers women face, and 'having got there', which refers to the capabilities required for effective performance once in a senior position.

Discretionary leadership

Discretionary leadership explores the choice-making behaviour of leaders. Certain roles in the organisation are structured to be more leadership than management oriented, thus requiring leaders to exercise much greater choice over a broad range of resources in order to pursue and realise their sense of vision and mission. Thus, the discretionary school of leadership distinguishes leaders from managers on the basis of role and not personal characteristics.

Over 50 years ago, in his analysis of the Glacier Metal Company, Elliott Jaques (1951) drew a distinction between roles that are prescribed and those that are discretionary. A prescriptive role is one that leaves little room for the manager's judgement. The parameters of the role, the activities that need to be carried out and the objectives that are required to be met, are fixed. More than half of the role is pre-determined. The role occupant must do what is required. In contrast, a discretionary role is not clearly structured, in that half or more of the activities are left for the role incumbent to decide how to do them. The degree of discretion varies according to the goals the individual is required to achieve, their ability to influence others, the demands of the role incumbent's boss and the particular circumstances of the day. A discretionary role requires an individual to be a leader and provide direction, whereas a prescribed role is more akin to a middle manager's job, demanding the application of certain skills. The distinction between prescribed and discretionary activities is echoed in the 'management versus leadership' argument, as well as in the more recent debate about transactional and transformational leadership.

Discretionary role analysis highlights the number of leader roles in the organisation, many of which are likely to be at the top of the organisation, but some of which could be positioned lower down because of the peculiarities of the role and organisation. Further, discretionary role analysis also surfaces the range of views held by these leaders.

The leaders of an organisation may well hold contrasting views concerning its future direction. Complex corporate structures, overlaid by partnerships and alliances and a series of outsourcing relationships, may engender over fifty key discretionary leader roles of varying status, such as president, chief executive officer, vice presidents, directors and general managers. The managers occupy either corporate or functional roles, regional responsibilities and line of business responsibilities. The manner in which discretion is exercised will vary according to the individual's ambitions and aspirations, their professional judgement, the demands of the market place or stakeholders and the imperatives laid down by the centre.

Certain relationships are formally predetermined. The managing director or president of a subsidiary will be held to account for the performance of his or her organisation by the chief executive officer or president of the corporate entity, located at the centre. A corporate director, for example, with a regional responsibility in Europe/Africa is likely to hold directors, who have country responsibilities in the subsidiaries, to account for the performance of their country. On this basis, a country director could have two or more reporting relationships: to the managing director or president of the subsidiary and to the corporate director in charge of a particular region. Likewise, a specialist functional director at the centre, for example, human resources or information technology directors, hold their functional counterparts in the subsidiaries or regions to account, while at the same time being responsible to the line managers of that subsidiary, country or region to provide the necessary level of service. Every leader will form their own view as to what are the most productive synergies to pursue. The role incumbents' vision for the future of their organisation is a key determinant of how accountabilities will be exercised.

Analysing the different actions and reactions adopted by individuals occupying discretionary roles can identify the potential conflicts that may arise at senior management levels. The inability to work together as a team could severely damage the organisation. Senior managers may pursue different courses of action based on differences of vision, or in attempting to satisfy varying stakeholder demands. Senior management may not be able to draw upon the required qualities of leadership to confront known challenges. Conflict at senior levels in an organisation can be widespread.

The Cranfield School of Management surveys of many thousands of organisations, spanning fifteen countries, indicate that more than 33 per cent of top teams are seriously divided in terms of pursuing a clear vision and 66 per cent of teams are unable to generate a sufficiently robust dialogue for them, as a team, to confront the challenges their companies face. The lack of openness of discussion is usually attributed to 'sensitivities' of relationships between the senior team members. Only 33 per cent of top teams have managed to develop a cohesion and openness of discussion that enables them to focus the whole organisation on achieving its goals. Ironically, research shows that continuous exposure to pressures and challenges leaves management fully aware of what needs to be done. Knowing what needs to be done is not the issue; it is how the team pull together that counts!

Thus, from the perspective of the individual, what one writer may see as inborn qualities, another may view as the result of experience. Manfred Kets de Vries makes an interesting interpretation of the entrepreneur Richard Branson, highlighting those of his qualities and attributes visible since childhood. Other commentators on Branson put more emphasis on the 'on-the-job' learning that entrepreneurship brings. 'Richard Branson's gift was his genial enthusiasm which disarmed those whom he approached for help,' wrote Tom Bower of the 17 year old Branson whose self-confidence produced a magazine *Student* in a first edition of 50 000 copies. He soon assembled corporate ads for the magazine and volunteers whom he paid £12 per week to sell it (Bower, T. (2000), *Branson*, London: Fourth Estate, p 15). A similar mixture of views emerges when examining leadership tasks such as goal setting or communicating particularly when applied to senior teams. Do these leadership behaviours arise from inborn traits or are they learned by leaders as they develop? Discretionary leadership emphasises the need to be mindful of diversity and the importance of being aware of changing circumstances.

Summary

In this chapter we looked at three different approaches to examining leadership – transactional, transformational and discretionary leadership.

TRANSACTIONAL LEADERSHIP

Transactional leadership concerns the abilities and skills of a manager to lead his team in the workplace to achieve better performance. It involves management activities such as setting targets, appraising performance, giving constructive feedback and coaching team members.

Trait approach

Early studies of leadership concentrated on traits or qualities of the leader. If these could be identified, the search for good leadership in organisations could be simplified. However, very few common leadership traits have been identified and agreed on after over a half century of research. If a list of traits could be found that were inborn, one could argue that leaders are indeed born and not made.

Behaviour approach

Leader behaviour indicated that jobs should be broken down into clearly structured tasks to introduce specialisation of labour and well-defined performance targets.

Later it was recognised that attention needed to be paid to interpersonal relationships at work as well as output and productivity. It was learned that people expect their social needs to be satisfied at work. The human relations school considered the leader to provide a facilitative function, sharing power and authority with the group towards goal achievement.

Further, observations of management and leadership behaviour suggested that managers adopted different degrees of task-orientated and people-oriented behaviour. This concept, spawned from the original Ohio studies, revealed the relationship between a leader's concern for production and concern for people. A similar vein of thinking led to the concept of the managerial grid. The styles identified are task management (emphasis on productivity), team management (achievement through negotiating commitment from others), middle of the road management (trade off between production requirements and market morale), country club management (satisfaction of social needs) and impoverished management (minimum effort to tasks and relationships).

Contingency studies

Under the contingency model, successful leadership is attained when the leader's style matches the demands of a given situation. The closeness of the match is determined by the degree of favourableness to the leader. Three elements are considered; (1) the leadership-member relationship, (2) the degree structure of the task and (3) the leader's formal power. Assessing the situation according to the combination of these three should show the appropriate leadership style to adopt.

Managerial decision-making

In order to assist managers in making decisions, Vroom and Yetton developed a series of questions, which could help leaders modify their styles to suit the circumstances of different situations. Three alternative styles were identified, autocratic, consultative and participative. Which style to use depends on the answers to seven key questions.

Situational leadership

The situational leadership model was based on the idea that good managers need to adapt their styles to meet the needs and characteristics of individual situations. It describes four leadership styles based on the two dimensions of task behaviour and relationship behaviour. Although a manager may prefer a particular combination of styles, the best manager is the one deemed capable of adjusting their style to the demands of the situation. The 'situational requirements' relate to the needs of subordinates or followers measured in terms of their developmental level. A follower with a lower development level requires a more directive leadership style, while a follower with a high level of development for a particular task is ready for delegation from the leader.

Hot managers

The term 'hot managers' has arisen in order to emphasise the importance of transactional leadership in the running of today's organisations. Paying attention to detail on tasks and being both firm and flexible with people highlights the nature of managerial performance in today's organisations.

TRANSFORMATIONAL LEADERSHIP

Transformational leadership, with the emphasis on change, is not a requirement of all organisations to succeed. Some can rely on the application of sound management principles alone.

Charisma

So often transformational leaders are acclaimed as charismatic. The concept of charisma includes inspiration, adornment and an unequal relationship between the leader and followers.

Some writers see charisma as attribution, namely the qualities given to a leader by the followers (sometimes because of their own inadequacies). Others consider charisma as emanating from the individual, innate qualities that people find attractive.

Narcissism

Narcissism was viewed as the opposite to charisma. It is the tendency of some successful leaders to indulge in vanity and selfishness. There are three forms of narcissism; (1) reactive, (2) self-deceptive and (3) constructive. Reactive narcissists are so self-obsessed that they find it difficult to distinguish sense from reality. Self-deceptive narcissists are people who need to be liked but have a better hold on reality than the reactive narcissist. Constructive narcissists are more in the mould of a balanced leader with transformational aspirations.

DISCRETIONARY LEADERSHIP

Discretionary role analysis focuses on the leadership demands of particular roles. Not every role has a leadership component. As the label implies, there is a lot of scope for individual choice in discretionary leadership.

As Elliott Jaques identified in his research, certain managers hold prescribed roles whilst others occupy discretionary roles. A prescriptive role leaves little room for individual judgement. In contrast, a discretionary role offers scope for initiative, judgement, imagination and individual decision-making. The critical questions discretionary role analysis addresses are: how many leaders exist in any one organisation?, how do these leaders interact and interrelate? and how can these leaders enhance their relationships so that they can more cohesively pursue the vision and strategy of the organisation?

2 *Working the Organisation*

8 *Communication and Conflict*

In problem-solving groups, when managers use brainstorming to identify their work problems, someone always shouts out 'communication' as a major problem. Others in the group nod their heads in agreement that communication is a critical problem in the work group or the entire company. They usually mean that organisational communications are poor, inadequate or insufficient, too casual, ill timed or too infrequent, or misleading or false. But communication is much more of a broad theme to be dealt with rather than a problem to be solved. It is a vital element in developing organisational effectiveness.

In this chapter we look first at the nature of communication and then at the two basic types: interpersonal and organisational. Interpersonal communication includes verbal and non-verbal forms. We examine first the dynamics of listening and then 'active listening' as a critical part of understanding what is being communicated.

Powerful communication on the part of chief executives can be used to share visions and missions. We review extracts from speeches by three American presidents. We then focus attention on conducting communication systematically through the organisation. Here we explore one popular type of organisational communication, team briefings, as an effective way of cascading messages through the entire workforce. We find examples of the wide variety of other forms of organisational communications. In-house bulletins, magazines, in-company TV stations, videos, e-mails and websites all form part of an organisation's modern communications machinery. One airline, for example, relays the latest company news to its highly mobile employees through audiocassettes containing weekly messages from the managing director.

We look at how people negotiate and sort out their differences. We examine 'principled bargaining', a new approach to negotiations developed at the Harvard Law School.

The topic of communication leads on to an exploration of conflict at work. People are right to claim that poor communication often leads to conflict. The opposite can also be true. Clear communication sometimes leads directly to conflict because your message is apparent and understood by the recipient, but not seen to be in their interest. Conflict is seen not as an aberration, but as a natural process arising from the divergence of interests of the stakeholders who make up any enterprise. We view conflict resolution through the approach adopted by two American psychologists, Thomas and Kilmann (1974). We end the chapter with some ideas on creative conflict as opposed to dysfunctional conflict and describe how management teams can have a good fight and yet remain effective.

The nature of communication

Communication involves the sending of messages by a person or a group and the receiving and understanding of those messages by another person or group. For true communication to take place the meaning of the message has to be clearly stated and received or understood. Hence, Marcouse et al. (1999) defines communication as 'the process by which information is exchanged between one group or person and another'.

Communication involves both the transference and the understanding of shared meaning. It is a managerial competency and a skill. As a competency it is 'the ability to understand the choices involved in communication and the ability to choose the appropriate action to influence outcomes and to achieve one's objectives'. As a skill, good communication is 'the ability to execute the communication in the chosen way' (Black, O. (1996), *People management*, (25 July), p 44).

Interpersonal communication

Many people who fail to achieve at work do so because they lack the skill of interpersonal communication. So central is interpersonal communication at work that it is difficult to think of a job that is not enhanced by the holder's ability to communicate well. At whatever level managers find themselves in an organisation, they need to communicate with their colleagues, subordinates and superiors verbally, in writing and with their body language. Good clear, interpersonal communication is vital to get the job done, to facilitate teamworking and to meet customer requirements in face-to-face situations. People need to project care and concern about the products and services they deliver to both the internal customer (anyone who receives their work outputs) and the external customer (the consumer).

Personal presentation involving body language, appropriate dress and common courtesy form part of interpersonal communication. 'What you *are* speaks so loudly, I can't hear a word you're saying,' could be a statement printed on a poster and hung in many offices and shop floors. The message refers to the sincerity and integrity we expect from the person speaking with us. Insincere apologies for poor work or shoddy customer service mean nothing at all. Careless or unclear work instructions can be downright dangerous. Interpersonal communication has two purposes: information passing and relationship building.

INFORMATION PASSING

The effectiveness of information passing can be measured in terms of the quality of the information received. Both the source and the manner in which it has been acquired have to be scrutinised in order to assess its quality. How useful or how adequate is the information? These two questions have to be answered in the context in which the receivers find themselves – the challenges and problems they face; the supports and constraints that surround them; their aims and objectives; their expectations and assumptions.

Information, once received and digested by the recipients, in turn, affects their perception of their roles and accountabilities, the quality of their decisions and ultimately their job performance. If the information they receive is considered to be satisfactory and helpful and supportive, they are likely to respond to it by working harder, taking more calculated risks and being more open and honest about their job performance. The reverse will occur if the information received is considered unsatisfactory. So the quality of the information itself can either be a positive, motivating and empowering experience or a negative and demotivating one.

RELATIONSHIP BUILDING

The effectiveness of communication to achieve the aim of relationship building can be measured in terms of employees' ability to relate to one another, psychological closeness, supportiveness and approachability. Understandably the quality of relationships people develop at work affects the way they identify with the organisation, their degree of commitment to the goals of the organisation and finally their overall motivation and satisfaction.

Individuals need to think about the impact they make on others; is it positive or negative? Some may not care what others think of them at work. Such people risk being seen by others as obstructive, uncooperative, the source of tension or conflict – in short, as undesirable work colleagues. Positive communication with our work colleagues is a prime source of job satisfaction and enjoyment. Many people come to work for the social interaction it offers. Diminish that interaction and you diminish their job satisfaction. In fact, on a philosophical level, we are creative of ourselves and others in our interpersonal communications. The French existentialist Gabriel Marcel has coined the phrase 'personal communion' to describe how we are creative of one another. 'When someone's presence does really make itself felt, it can refresh my inner being; it reveals me to myself, it makes me feel more fully myself than I should be if I were not exposed to its impact,' Marcel wrote (Marcel, G. (1960), *The mystery of being*, Chicago: Regnery).

LISTENING AND ACTIVE LISTENING

Over half of communication, personal or organisational, should be listening. It is not a skill many people possess. 'Conversation in the United States is a competitive exercise in which the first person to draw a breath is declared the listener,' joked the humorous Nathan Miller.

In English, the average person speaks about 125 words per minute. Yet the mind is capable of processing 400–500 words per minute. Hence people have spare capacity to process incoming information and if they are not careful, their eyes can glaze over as their minds wander on to other things, while they pretend to listen. (It happens often in conversations when a friend or colleague goes on and on in great detail about a summer holiday.) One of the ways of dealing with this tendency to think of more than one thing at one time and failing to listen is to engage the spare capacity of the mind and to use the technique of 'active listening'.

To stay alert the listener reflects back what the speaker has just said, mirroring his or her words or ideas. Or the listener asks questions to clarify what has just been said or to expand it. The listener may also summarise what is being said to assure the speaker of the listener's attention.

Active listening is a skill that, with practice, can be used very effectively in counselling others and helping them to solve their problems. Reflective listening, sometimes known as active listening, is a way of helping people focus and explore key issues, so that they are better informed on how to proceed. Carl Rogers (1961) considers active listening a key part of the client-centred approach to counselling. In this approach to counselling, people are encouraged to explore their assumptions about the world, both rational and irrational. The irrational feelings are the ones people find most difficult to explore and change.

In the work context, this technique can obviously be of great benefit. Instead of looking for solutions all the time and giving people advice based on their own experience, managers can listen to employees and help them develop their own solutions to their problems.

Listening is not a passive process, it is an active, time-consuming one. Active listening involves paying attention to the other person on three separate levels: mind, emotion and body (Figure 8.1). The mind deals with words leading to understanding. The emotions deal with feelings leading to contact with the emotions of others, whilst the body refers to position or stance, showing interest simply by the way the individual stands or sits.

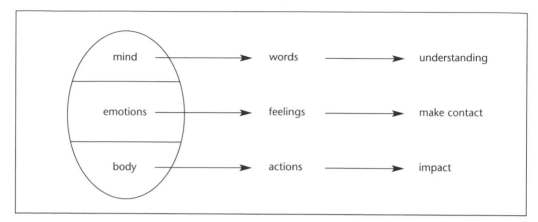

Figure 8.1 The three levels of active listening (*Source*: *Working in Organisations*, First Edition, 1987)

Listening actively to the words of a message can be achieved by asking appropriate questions and by giving encouragement. Open questions are best – those that do not invite a 'yes' or a 'no' reply, but that encourage the other person to share thoughts, opinions, facts, observations, experiences, worries and so on, to explain the nature of the problem. Probing questions can be used to acquire additional information. Interjections such as: 'Yes', '. . . Mmm . . .', 'Uhuh . . .', will encourage the person to talk. They may seem inconsequential, but they work in practice to show that one is listening.

READING BODY LANGUAGE

The body signals that people transmit through their posture, gestures, facial expression and voice characteristics are important because they express actions that reveal their inner feelings. For example, a man with his shoulders hunched forward, his face creased and his voice breaking on the edge of tears is obviously deeply troubled. It would be quite wrong for his supervisor not to notice this and to pass him in the hallway with a hearty: 'Everything alright, Bart?' (see Figure 8.1).

As Julius Fast put it: 'We all, in one way or another, send our little messages out to the world . . . And rarely do we send our messages consciously. We act out our state of being with non-verbal body language. We lift one eyebrow for disbelief. We rub our noses for puzzlement. We clasp our arms to isolate ourselves or to protect ourselves. We shrug our shoulders for indifference, wink one eye for intimacy, tap our fingers for impatience, slap our foreheads for forgetfulness. The gestures are numerous, and while some are deliberate . . . there are some, such as rubbing our nose for puzzlement or clasping our arms to protect ourselves, that are mostly unconscious.' (Fast, J. (1971), *Body language*, New York: Pocket Books, pp 7–8). Someone can decide to stop talking, yet cannot not communicate, because we send messages through our behaviour all the time. Our stance, posture, facial expressions, gestures, movements – in fact all of our observable actions – communicate what we are feeling and experiencing deep down.

The ability to read body language, then, is part of the skills of active listening. The observation of body language is important to the listener since it conveys those things that are vital to the person speaking. This is especially the case when the speaker is hesitant about showing their true feelings or putting them into words. Usually, even when the speaker is trying to hide their true feelings in the matter, they momentarily leak out or manifest themselves in body language clues we call 'non-verbals'. Tell someone, who has been at a company for 23 years, that their now head the list for redundancies due to a downsizing and, however a brave face is put on their acceptance of the dismissal, that person's body language will probably betray their true feelings of disillusionment and deep disappointment.

Organisational communication

Leaders of organisations use communication to share their visions of the future. The objective of such visionary speeches is to get their followers to become caught up in the vision and thereby share the sublime mission. Experienced leaders know how to blend idealism with achievable, if challenging goals. They capture our collective imagination, harness our energies and fill us with resolution to dream the impossible dream with them.

REALITY CHECK

THREE AMERICAN PRESIDENTS SHARE THEIR VISIONS

Excerpts from three speeches by three American presidents demonstrate effective communication of the visions these men shared with their fellow citizens. The first is the Gettysburg Address by Abraham Lincoln; the second is the 'Man on the Moon' speech from John F. Kennedy; the third is from Ronald Reagan's words on the loss of the Challenger astronauts.

1. Lincoln's vision of America after the Civil War: the Gettysburg Address

In a three minute speech at the dedication of Gettysburg Cemetery in Pennsylvania, Lincoln gave an account of the country's recent bloody past and his own vision of its future. His speech does not mention the victorious North or the defeated South or even the issue that tore the nation apart – slavery – or the Union. But what he said radically changed all of them. His words spoken in November 1893 became one of the most influential speeches in modern history.

The world will little note, nor long remember, what we say here, but it can never forget what they did here. It is for the living, rather, to be dedicated here to the unfinished work which they who fought here have thus far so nobly advanced. It is rather for us to be here dedicated to the great task remaining before us – that from these honoured dead we take increased devotion to that cause for which they gave the last full measure of devotion – that we here highly resolve that these dead shall not have died in vain – that this nation, under God, shall have a new birth of freedom – and that government of the people, by the people, for the people, shall not perish from the earth.

2. John F. Kennedy's 'Man on the Moon' speech

In a short speech on 25 May 1961, John F. Kennedy proposed the aim of placing a man on the moon before the end of the decade. It was a strategic, mission-defining speech that captured the imagination of the nation. The mission was achieved when Neil Armstrong and Buzz Aldrin landed on the surface of the moon on 20 July 1969, and returned safely to earth.

Now it is the time to take longer strides; time for a great new American enterprise; time for this nation to take a leading role in space achievements which, in many ways, may hold the key to our future on earth.

I believe we possess the resources and talents necessary, but the facts of the matter are that we have never made the national decisions or marshalled the national resources required for such leadership. We have never specified long-range goals on an urgent time schedule or managed our resources and time so as to ensure their fulfilment.

I believe that this nation should commit itself to achieving the goal, before this decade is out, of landing a man on the moon and returning him safely to the earth. No single space project in this period will be more impressive to mankind or more important for the long-range exploration of space, and none will be so difficult and expensive to accomplish.

But in a very real sense, it will not be one man going to the moon. If we make this judgement affirmatively: it will be an entire nation! I believe we should go to the moon.

3. Ronald Reagan: tribute to the crew of the space shuttle Challenger

On 31 January 1986 President Reagan faced the grim task of articulating his country's feelings at the failure of America's space shuttle Challenger. He focused first on the nation's grief and then on the heroism involved in continuing the exploration of space:

We shall never forget them nor the last time we saw them this morning as they prepared for their journey and waved goodbye and slipped the surly bonds of earth to touch the face of God.

The future is not free: the story of all human progress is one of a struggle against all odds. We learned again that this America, which Abraham Lincoln called the last, best hope of man on Earth, was built on heroism and noble sacrifice. It was built by men and women like our seven star voyagers, who answered a call beyond duty, who gave more than was expected or required and who gave it little thought of worldly reward.

However, as highlighted in Chapter 7, a number of leaders may exist in any one organisation. On this basis, organisational communication is viewed on a broader basis. Most chief executive officers, boards and senior management teams spend much time defining their organisation's missions. They use as many media channels as possible to communicate their vision to their employees, their customers and suppliers, shareholders and other stakeholders, and the public at large. At times an organisation's vision may include merger strategies. In recent years, for example, there have been many mergers of pharmaceutical companies, oil companies and automobile companies. The communication process involved in constructing these deals provides a fascinating study.

With the deal constructed and the parameters for the merger or strategic change programme agreed, the key messages can be efficiently spread through the organisation using team briefings.

REALITY CHECK

A 17 MINUTE PRESENTATION THAT MERGED MERCEDES AND CHRYSLER

Jurgen Schrempp, the chairman of the board of management of Daimler-Benz, flew in a private jet from his headquarters in Stuttgart in Germany to Wayne County airport in Detroit, Michigan to make a presentation to the board of Chrysler at their offices in Auburn Hills, a smart suburb of Detroit. His briefcase contained the paperwork that supported a radical idea – a merger between Daimler-Benz and Chrysler. The deal he put to Chrysler had no precedent in the 115 year old history of the automotive industry. It would completely change the way the major players operated. The executive was lost in thought as his chauffeur drove him and his assistant in a black Mercedes-Benz S-Class car through the outskirts of Motown, USA.

Journalist David Waller takes up the story:

Arriving at Chrysler's imposing corporate headquarters 40 minutes later, he is shown to the chairman's office on the fifteenth floor. He follows his instinct and the meeting with Bob

Eaton is over almost before it has begun. Schrempp leaves behind the contents of his briefcase . . .

It was a short visit to the Chrysler headquarters, lasting no more than 17 minutes, but the consequences were profound. It set in motion a sequence of events which would culminate ten months later in the merger of Daimler-Benz AG with Chrysler Corporation to create DaimlerChrysler AG.

The day before the DaimlerChrysler merger took place, a well-informed article about the pending merger appeared exclusively in the Wall Street Journal *– one of the business news scoops of the decade. No one was admitting to a leak, but after all journalists are there to be used by organisations, who treat the press as just another channel of information to advance their corporate objectives.*

Source: Waller, D. (2001), *Wheels on fire: the amazing story of the DaimlerChrysler merger*, London: Hodder & Stoughton, pp xiii–xiv.

Team briefing

Verbal communication in organisations can take many forms. A vital, popular method of communication is called 'team briefing'. The name has a military ring to it. Pilots are briefed before a mission and debriefed afterwards. But there is nothing particularly military about this important way of communicating with the workforce. It is used in many different kinds of organisation throughout the world to achieve efficiency and competitive edge.

One of Britain's great industrial leaders, Sir John Harvey-Jones, made communication a central element of his leadership style. His central theme is communication down the organisation and up the organisation. Why both top down and bottom up? So that the necessary commitment from those within the enterprise can be fully gained.

Employees cannot be involved and cannot cooperate fully with corporate goals unless they know about them firsthand and understand what is required of them. Their response is most often in a team effort. Hence team briefing is a very natural way of building people into effective groups with synergistic performance. In this process, managers formally raise their profiles. The team briefing procedure actually strengthens the manager's position as visible leader of the work team.

Team briefing is a system of communication operated by line management. Its objective is to make sure that all employees know and understand what they and others in the organisation are doing and why. It is a management information system. It is based on leaders and their teams getting together in groups for half an hour on a regular basis to talk about issues relevant to their work.

Briefing the team is part of the manager's job; a team briefing system merely formalises something that good managers and supervisors do anyway. It is only one way of communicating, but an effective one. There is a 'cascade' element in team briefing. There are things that the chairman or the chief executive officer or the senior management team wants communicated. This information is called the 'core brief'. The system is so structured that this information from the top of the organisation – the core brief – is added to the local team's brief and so cascades through the entire workforce. But the focus is always on the local brief first because it is most relevant and useful to the work team. The core brief should form no more than 30 per cent of the entire brief; the remaining 70 per cent should be work team information. It is best if the manager writes the local brief before incorporating the core brief. The question the manager needs to have in mind while preparing and delivering the team briefing is: 'What information should my team have to help them do their jobs better?'

The benefits of team briefing are:

- It reinforces management as team leaders.
- It increases commitment.
- It helps prevent misunderstandings.
- It helps people accept change.
- It provides a control for the 'grapevine', or the natural gossip in the organisation.
- It improves upward communication.

A popular poster displayed in offices and on shop floors in a humorous way expressed the need for clear communication. It read:

I know you believe you understood what you think I said, but I am not sure you realise that what you heard is not what I meant.

REALITY CHECK

ACTIVE COMMUNICATION VALUES AT BRITISH AEROSPACE

By communication I mean something more than the common expression of thoughts and impressions in language. In a culture change programme, the only communication that counts is communication that connects with people at all levels of the organisation. It must have the simplicity of a good advert, but also other dimensions. Parables, stories, examples and legends do the heavy lifting here . . . The primary communicators have to be the chief executive and his top team . . . Real communication depends on managers who have internalised the values and communicate them in everything they do – in tone of voice and style of interaction. Leadership and communication are inseparable.

> *Communication will not be effective unless it is heartfelt; and this applies from the chairman to the foreman on the shop floor.*
>
> *Source:* Evans, R. and Price, C. (1999), *Vertical take-off: the inside story of British Aerospace's comeback from crisis to world class*, London: Nicholas Brealey Publishing, pp 94–95.

Emergence of e-mail

In many companies e-mail has become the swiftest and most popular way of communicating. It is instantaneous and can be super efficient. Drafts of strategic plans fly across the Atlantic with the speed of light and are instantly discussed and responded to by e-mails. Entire marketing plans are shared electronically with employees across the planet. Architectural drawings zoom to clients for their instant feedback by e-mail. Estate agents can offer potential buyers virtual tours of properties thousands of miles away over the Net and accept bids by e-mail.

Not only distances but time zones are diminished by e-mail. The office for managers with a laptop has never been more portable. The main issue for most managers is overload. This is particularly associated with e-mail, because it feels more immediate and urgent to the recipient. The balance has shifted between paper and electronic forms of communication. Although volumes of e-mail are greater than before and increasing exponentially, there should be a corresponding drop in the amount of paper people receive, but there is little sign of that occurring. In addition there is the all-pervasive problems of 'spam' and the use of e-mail for personal communications.

Since e-mail is now one of the main ways for managers communicating both within organisations and with external partners, it is reasonable for senders to expect that e-mails are read at least once a day and acted on. Another expectation is that there will be arrangements in place for e-mails to be dealt with in the recipient's absence. However, the problems of overload, partly due to people being 'copied in' on other people's correspondence, and with comparable volumes of paper being utilised, have made the need for introducing codes of practice for e-mail evident.

CODE OF PRACTICE FOR E-MAILING

The Department for Education and Employment (DfEE) felt the need to develop helpful e-mail standards (full details are published on the IT Guidance website on Prism via Pathfinder (ntweb1/itguidance/desktop/frontends/A-Z.htm)).

Under the title 'Helping other people', the DfEE listed its *rules for senders*:
Do:
* make sure the title of your message tells people what it's about.
* use markers to show importance (high, normal, low).
* use indicators and dates in the subject line, for example, 'for information', 'for action'.

Supporting standards and good practice:
Do:
* make clear what action is required of both 'TO' recipients and 'CC' recipients.

- avoid jargon and explain abbreviations where necessary.
- show consideration for others' working patterns.
- keep attachments to a minimum – list and describe them in the body of the document.
- sign off with contact details, particularly to external correspondents.

Don't:
- use e-mail if phone or paper might be better.
- automatically reply to all recipients – limit copy lists to those who really need to know.
- send an e-mail late at night, expecting a reply first thing in the morning.
- use colour or font combinations which are difficult for people with visual disabilities to read.

Principled bargaining

Negotiation is one of the most frequent forms of communication. We negotiate all the time about everything. It is the most basic means of getting what we want from other people. It is a back-and-forth communication that is used to come to an agreement with a partner who shares some interests with you but also has interests that conflict with yours. Most decisions are arrived at through negotiation. The process is used widely in our personal lives and in our political activities. It looms large in business activities.

The problem with the communication process in traditional negotiations (positional bargaining) is that it produces an outcome that is often not sensible, one that wastes time and leaves the participants at odds with one another. The very different approach to negotiations called 'principled bargaining' aims at producing wise agreements that are efficiently arrived at and that leave the participants at the same level of friendship as when they started the negotiations, if not a higher level.

Principled bargaining was developed by the Harvard Research Project, which rather surprisingly arose not at the Harvard Business School, famous for its innovative research, publications, new management techniques and scholarship, but at the Harvard Law School.

The Harvard Project (Fisher and Ury, 1991) collected data about negotiations for over a decade to develop the new principled approach. They found that although negotiations occur frequently they are often poorly done. Normal styles of negotiation leave the parties dissatisfied, exhausted or alienated – or all three.

People usually adopt a hard negotiating strategy in which they turn the process into a contest of will where the one with the most extreme position, who can hold out the longest, wins. The win is often a costly one as it comes at the expense of the other party, thereby damaging the relationship and encouraging the 'loser' to seek to 'get even' in the future. (Historians agree that the seeds of the Second World War were sown during the punitive and one-sided negotiations at the end of the First World War that left Germany humiliated, impoverished and feeling victimised.) The alternative to the hard approach to negotiating is soft negotiations, where the party who wants to avoid personal conflict, and to reach agreement at any costs, makes the necessary concessions, but feels bitter and exploited by the experience.

Principled bargaining charts a new course in negotiations where issues are decided on their merits and the negotiating partners become problem-solvers exploring solutions based on common interests. Fairness for both is the goal.

The five principles that underpin this method of negotiation are:

- *Focus on interests, not positions*. Don't bargain over positions. This starting point is the most difficult. Taking positions in negotiations is a reflex; these are false positions from which we strategically retreat over time, making concessions to reach a compromise. It often does not lead to agreements that are wise. 'A wise agreement can be defined as one which meets the legitimate interests of each side to the extent possible, resolves conflicting interests fairly, is durable, and takes community interests into account.' It should be noted that positional bargaining also often fails on the other criterion of producing an agreement efficiently and amicably. Instead of taking a position, the Harvard method advocates focusing on common interests, mutually satisfying options and fair standards.
- *Separate the people from the problem*. The core idea here is to recognise that people have different perceptions of the issues under negotiation. It is important to separate relationships from the substantive problem, and to avoid defensive behaviours. Parties must think of themselves as partners in a difficult search for a fair agreement that brings them both advantages. They need to deal with each other as human beings and with the problem on its merits.
- *Invent options for mutual gain*. Invent first, decide later, is the watchword. Participants are encouraged to approach the issues as joint problem-solvers, generating as many creative solutions as possible. They are advised to use brainstorming techniques to open as many windows on the problem as they can and to produce a range of potential agreements satisfactory to both sides before selecting the preferred option.
- *Insist on using objective criteria*. Facts, not opinions, are needed at some stage in the negotiations. Usually there is more than one objective criterion to support one's case. For example, in establishing the value of a house for sale there are data from estate agents indicating the sale price of comparable houses in the area. The valuation a mortgage company or bank might put on the property could be used. The worth an insurance company might place on the property or what it might rent for could also be a basis. An appeal to objective criteria helps establish a sense of fairness among the negotiating partners. In using objective criteria in the negotiating process, it is important to frame each issue as a joint search for objective data and to reason together as to which standards are most appropriate and how they should be applied.
- *Before the negotiations, develop for oneself the 'best alternative to a negotiated agreement' (BATNA)*. Doing so will protect the negotiators from entering into an agreement they should reject. It will also help the negotiators make the most of the assets that they do have. The stronger one's BATNA, the less need they have to enter into an agreement that does not serve their interests. Remember that the agreement should be wise and efficiently arrived at and it should not harm the relationship, but if possible enhance it.

Dealing with conflict

Conflict is a natural phenomenon in modern enterprises. It is systemic and to be expected. It is a product of pluralism. In a pluralistic society, there are many stakeholders in any enterprise. There are the employees and the owners, the shareholders, the managers, the financial institutions, the government at all levels, the trade unions, the suppliers and consumers at either end of the supply chain, the regulators, consumer-protection groups, environmental-protection organisations and other pressure groups. Each of these stakehold-ers has its own interests and agendas that at times are incompatible with those of the other stakeholders. Sometimes, where one might expect a unity of interests, as between those of the employees and their trade unions, it does not exist. Employees might be interested in fighting the scope of a downsizing whereas their trade union is more focused on its own sur-vival through a merger with another stronger union.

Given the range of issues confronting most organisations today, the level of dysfunc-tional conflict between its stakeholders is surprisingly low. Enterprises, after all, are not analogous to sports teams or happy families where there is unanimity of interests and clear leadership. But neither should they be dichotomous, a battleground for two opposed war-ring camps, whatever labels we choose to give them. (Them and us, capital and labour, capitalists and proletariat are the most common labels.)

Given that conflict, then, is natural and not the work of poorly developed or unthink-ing people, it is the management of conflict and the minimisation of dysfunctional conflict that is the focus of our attention. How does a manager deal with conflict?

The Thomas-Kilmann conflict mode instrument (see Figure 8.2) helps people identify their preferred style for dealing with conflict. The individual is presented with conflict situ-ations – ones in which the concerns of two people appear to be incompatible – and asked to choose a course of action. In such situations a person's behaviour can be measured along two basic dimensions: 1) assertiveness, the extent to which the individual attempts to sat-isfy his or her own concerns; and 2) cooperativeness, the extent to which the individual attempts to satisfy the other person's concerns. These two dimensions of behaviour can be used to define five specific methods of dealing with conflict.

The five conflict-handling modes are:

- competing/collaborating,
- compromising,
- avoiding/accommodating,
- uncooperative/cooperative and
- cooperativeness.

Through recognition of one's styles of handling conflict, the manager can re-appraise his approach and adopt styles that he considers more appropriate for the situation.

Creative conflict: how management teams can have a good fight

The best organisations encourage creative conflict. Why not? It is a healthy sign when sen-ior managers disagree about issues and have understandable differences when making difficult decisions. These managers challenge one another and that keeps them on their toes. They develop a wide range of possibilities and explore many options. Without creative conflict, an organisation could lapse into apathy.

People should be allowed to argue their points of view without destroying their ability to work together. Three academics, Kathleen M. Eisenhardt, Jean L. Kahwajy and L.J. Bourgeois III (1997), set out to demonstrate the benefits of creative conflict. They studied a

Competing	**Collaborating**
• No change to my position • Clearly communicate my position • Most rational view is mine • Best way is mine • Threats • 'I know best' • Order	• Work together • Mutuality • Identify areas of disagreement • Find common grounds • Jointly explore • Declare each other's positions • Jointly problem solve
Compromising	**Avoiding**
• Quick solution • Give and take • Find acceptable some way point • At what point will you be satisfied? • At least both of us gets something	• No wish for responsibility • Leave it till later • Not my problem • Cannot discuss this • Will not discuss this • Do not want to see your point

Accommodating

- Give way
- Concede
- Agree with the others
- Accept what you say
- Non-threatening
- Charming
- From me to you
- Work on your preferred outcomes

Figure 8.2 Conflict-handling skills: five modes (*Source*: Adapted from Thomas, K.W. and Kilmann, R.H. (1974), Based on the Thomas-Kilmann Conflict Mode Instrument, CPP Inc., 3803 E. Bagshore Road, Palo Alto, California, CA 94303)

dozen top teams in technology-based companies over a ten year period. The companies were similar; global, highly competitive, selling into rapidly changing markets. 'The study's design,' they wrote, 'gave us a window on conflict as top-management teams actually experienced it and highlights the role of emotion in business decision making' (Eisenhardt, K.M., Kahwajy, J.L. and Bourgeois III, L.J. (1997), 'How management teams can have a good fight', *Harvard Business Review*, (July-August), pp 77–85).

The research team found that the very best companies in their sample actually encouraged conflict in their top teams and actively managed it. They developed a model for arguing while still getting along and performing to a high standard.

Their model was derived from their direct observations of the more successful top teams. It echoes some of the ideas of principled bargaining, particularly in its emphasis on creating multiple alternatives based on facts, separating the issues from the personalities involved and insisting on fairness. The research suggests that autocratic leaders who manage through centralised power bases generate dysfunctional friction and conflict. The same is true of leaders who are weak. A more democratic process, which steers a middle course and better balances power, generates greater participation in strategic decisions and a sense of fairness, with respect to the team's decision-making process.

Kathleen Eisenhardt and her colleagues recommend:

- focus on factual information,
- focus on issues,
- accommodate multiple alternatives,
- decisions should be framed on a collaborative basis,
- get the best possible solution for all,
- introduce humour in the discussions,
- do not push for consensus and
- aim for fairness and equity for all.

In linking their findings to those of others, the researchers said: 'A considerable body of academic research has demonstrated that conflict over issues is not only likely within top management teams but also valuable. Such conflict provides executives with a more inclusive range of information, a deeper understanding of the issues and a richer set of possible solutions. The evidence also overwhelmingly indicates that where there is little conflict over issues, there is also likely to be poor decision-making. 'Group think' has been a primary cause of major corporate and public policy debacles [see Chapter 5]. We found that the teams that engage in healthy conflict over issues not only made better decisions but moved more quickly as well.

'Without conflict, groups lose their effectiveness. Managers often become withdrawn and only superficially harmonious. Indeed, we found that the alternative to conflict is usually not agreement but apathy and disengagement. Teams unable to foster substantive conflict ultimately achieve, on average, lower performance' (pp 84–5).

On the practice of creating constructive disagreement within a team, the researchers offered advice in the form of five tips:

- Build a heterogeneous team. It should be made up of people of different ages, sexes, functional backgrounds and industrial experience.
- Meet as a team on a regular basis and frequently. Getting to know the team members well builds mutual confidence and allows people to express dissent without fear.
- Encourage team members to take on new roles. Let them branch out from their normal functional duties, territorial boundaries or product responsibilities to play devil's advocate roles or 'blue sky' roles.
- Apply multiple mindsets to issues. Use role-playing techniques, 'what if?' scenarios, put yourselves in your competitor's shoes and so on, to generate fresh perspectives.
- Manage conflict actively. Do not allow issues to be settled too soon or too easily. Apparent consensus can be apathy in disguise.

Summary

Communication involves the sending of messages by a person or a group and the receiving and understanding of those messages by another person or a group. Communication is about both a transference and or understanding of shared meaning. It is also a competency and a skill that can be developed with practice.

INTERPERSONAL COMMUNICATION

This is important to do one's job, to facilitate teamworking and to meet internal and external customer requirements. It has two purposes: (1) information passing and (2) relationship building. When information received from us is deemed adequate, helpful and supportive, it becomes a motivation at work. If, however, communication is judged to be unsatisfactory, the effect is demotivating in terms of relationship building. Communication can draw people closer together in the work groups or drive them apart. Positive communication with work colleagues is a prime source of satisfaction and enjoyment.

ACTIVE LISTENING

Over half of communication is listening. Listening is often undertaken reluctantly. There are techniques to engage one's mind fully whilst listening to another. These techniques are called 'active listening'. They include mirroring back the speaker's words or ideas, summarising what is being said, using questions to clarify what is being said and to demonstrate to the speaker that one is truly listening to them. Active listening is part of the process of non-directive counselling in which the problem-holder is introduced to options but encouraged to find their own solution.

Active listening pays attention to the other person on three separate levels: mind, emotion and body.

ORGANISATIONAL COMMUNICATION

Sharing the vision or mission of the organisation is one of the most frequent uses of communication by an organisation to its employees, customers and suppliers, shareholders and the public. However, to communicate critical themes or messages effectively through the organisation, team briefings are extensively utilised.

Team briefing is a formal process for communicating information operated by line management to make sure that all employees know and understand what they and others in the organisation are doing and why. As a management information system, team briefings require leaders and their teams to assemble in groups for about half an hour on a regular basis to talk about issues relevant to work. About 70 per cent of the team brief should contain local news, with about 30 per cent allowed for the 'core brief' – information from the top of the organisation about organisation wide issues that affect everyone.

Additionally, e-mail has become a popular mechanism of communication. Due to the overload of e-mails people receive, certain organisations have introduced codes of practise, highlighting the 'dos' and 'don'ts' of e-mailing.

PRINCIPLED BARGAINING

Principled bargaining was developed at the Harvard Law School by Roger Fisher and William Ury. It is a new way of bargaining where the parties avoid taking positions, but instead become problem-solvers exploring solutions based on fairness and common interests.

DEALING WITH CONFLICT

Conflict is a natural phenomenon, something that is systemic in any enterprise. It arises from a conflict of interest among the stakeholders of an enterprise. The Thomas-Kilmann conflict mode Instrument helps a manager identify their normal way of dealing with conflict – competing, collaborating, compromising, avoiding or accommodating.

CREATIVE CONFLICT

The very best organisations actually encourage creative conflict. They view disagreement as a healthy sign. Creative conflict provides executives with better information, a deeper understanding of issues and a richer range of possible solutions. Ways for building teams to creatively address constructive disagreement are identified.

9 *Politics in Organisations*

Political skills are just as important as business and professional skills, chairmanship skills, counselling skills and motivational skills. Knowing how to restructure and integrate the various parts of the organisation often depends on a manager's political insight. To deal with complex issues the manager needs to apply a variety of functional skills, but also has to be able to influence the views and opinions of others, particularly if conflicts of interest or a rivalry for scarce resources or a clash of values exists.

In this chapter the desire for personal influence is equated with politics. Organisational politics is examined because conflict and contradiction are normal, everyday occurrences that require political strategies if a manager is to handle them properly. Since the organisation is a community of people, it is natural for political activity to thrive within its boundaries.

We look first at the nature of politics in organisations. In particular, we explore the ways in which differences and problems arise between people. We discuss the concepts of shared and unshared meaning as the basis of political behaviour and describe seven political strategies for managers. Throughout, we stress that politics in organisations is a natural process that should be managed rather than viewed as something to be avoided.

Nature of politics in organisations

At an informal meeting at Cranfield School of Management, Professor Lyman Porter reported a study he had conducted of successful and unsuccessful promotion bids by management executives. He discovered that:

- Those successfully promoted attributed their success to their various personal skills and abilities.
- Those whose promotion bids failed attributed their lack of success to politics; they thought either that they were 'out of favour' or that someone else was more acceptable than themselves.

The unsuccessful candidate saw politics as an unpleasant, negative yet powerful experience. Porter concluded that politics is a critically important influence on a manager's development.

Most people in organisations recognise that simply doing a good job is not sufficient. For people who are more ambitious, attaining professional competence is only the first step to success. To achieve high office quickly requires skills in negotiation, in planning, in managing projects and in getting on with people. Being different from others in terms of excelling, yet at the same time being able to fit in with superiors, colleagues and subordinates, is important. Others who are ahead in the promotion race may spend their time at work vying for limited resources simply to get a good job done, competing for limited status positions or just attracting the attention of a senior executive. It is easy to see how politics comes to be perceived as negative for those who are not gifted with political skills or who find themselves outmanoeuvred.

Consider the situation at the group level. Certain groups or group leaders in organisations may wish to preserve an identity based on a professional ethos, geographic location or previous traditions and thereby put themselves in opposition to the wishes of corporate management. Other groups may likewise attempt to preserve their values and identity but avoid open confrontation with their superiors. These employees may seem to accept new systems of working but covertly tamper with the systems to meet their needs. Both groups are engaging in political behaviour.

If the actions and intentions of others can be easily misinterpreted; if groups and individuals confront and oppose each other; if the skills of negotiation and manoeuvre are as important as task skills for promotion to senior management; why then is politics in organisations not given greater attention in the training of managers? After all, politics seems to pervade our lives. There are two reasons:

- Writers, researchers and managers are not able to agree on the true meaning of the term politics. Despite this, it is clear that politics involves factors such as interpersonal influence, the skills of negotiation and devising means to an end. Politics is action based. It is individually determined and the actions can be practised in any organisational setting, limited only by the norms, values and foresight of each individual. However, certain actions, such as influencing others principally for self-gain or deliberately withholding information, are likely to be considered unethical. Therefore, an inability to agree on basic principles, coupled with the taboo nature of the subject, has made politics an under-examined area of study and one that is difficult to teach.
- Writers, researchers and managers have not quite come to terms with the fact that organisational life has as much to do with differences as with similarities between people. Theorists and practitioners alike have preferred to believe that similarities bond people together, for example, believing that everyone in the corporation is working together; that managers should be sources of energy and inspiration (that is, motivators). For them the most appropriate way to live in organisations is to accept the principle of *downward influence*. Yet all too often the strife and conflict show that downward influence is more supposition than fact.

Politics is an integral part of life in organisations. Differences, as much as similarities, between people form the reality of life. As a prelude to understanding politics in organisations, it is necessary to establish what sorts of differences exist in organisations.

Differences in organisations

How do differences arise? In all organisations, individuals and groups compete for resources, for attention, for influence; there are differences of opinion concerning priorities and objectives; clashes of values and beliefs occur frequently. All these factors lead to the formation of pressure groups, vested interests, cabals, personal rivalries, personality clashes, hidden deals and bonds of alliance. Managers spend much of their time managing conflict, competition and the formation of alliances. The first step to dealing successfully with differences is to understand how they come about.

There are five main sources of conflict in an organisation, represented by the possible tensions between:

- a global perspective and local issues,
- bosses and subordinates,
- people with professional backgrounds (doctors, scientists and the like) and the line managers,
- the centre (headquarters) and the divisions or subdivisions, and
- colleagues.

GLOBAL VERSUS LOCAL

Table 9.1 Global versus local (*Source*: compiled by Andrew Kakabadse)

Global	Local
Corporate reputation	Local concerns
Responsibility to corporation	Responsibility to county or region
Governance	Meet targets
Tax reduction	Local or national obligations

The number of organisations that operate globally is increasing. Whereas global ambitions are attractive to some, for others the term global arouses deep resentment (see Chapter 1). The demonstrations in Seattle, London, Washington, Melbourne and Stockholm in the period 1999–2001 indicate the degree of disquiet that exists over the global integration policies of large multi-nationals. The demonstrations were not against the concept of global trade. What is being demanded is corporate responses to social concerns, such as attention to the environment, labour rights and greater support for progressive social policies. The resentment towards globalisation is not without justification. According to a recent report:

- the 225 richest people in the world have a wealth comparable to the combined income of the poorest three billion people,
- of the world's 100 richest economies, just over 50 per cent are not countries but multinational corporations, with no constitutional obligation to the welfare of the countries in which they trade or reside and
- 30 million people in Africa suffer from AIDS. Pressure is being brought to bear on major multinational drug companies to lower the cost of medicine to treat these AIDS victims (Kakabadse, A. and Kakabadse, N. (2001), *The geopolitics of governance: the impact of contrasting philosophies*, Basingstoke: Palgrave).

The potential tensions and contrasting sense of obligation between those at the centre (that is, the headquarters) and those in localities and regions is considerable (Table 9.1). For the corporate directors of large multinationals, reputation is critical. A successful organisation can be damaged if its reputation is tarnished, and that odium is reflected in its share price. The pressure to exercise social responsibility in the country or region in which the corporation operates is considerable. However, from the organisation's point of view, corporate reputation can equally be tarnished, particularly with shareholders, if costs rise. Global outsourcing is the result of a search for economies of scale, which conflicts with meeting social obligations. Whether the centre pursues economy of scale or social obligation strategies – or both – local managers are required to implement those strategies. Most country managers, as well as being located in a region are often citizens of that country. (Expatriation is expensive. From a cost and motivation point of view, it makes sense for local management be given the responsibility for their territory.) However, local management needs to be sensitive to and responsive to local concerns. Local managers are likely to feel responsible for the social issues facing their countries or regions. Hence differences can arise between the territory managers and the centre. For example, the centre may seek to reduce tax by creating tax havens to avoid payment, in part or wholly, of local taxes, leaving local managers vulnerable to the accusation of being members of an exploitative multinational organisation. Whatever local management may feel about the demands made by the centre, their exposure to public criticism through the media means that they are the first to be blamed for policies over which they have no control. In the eyes of local management, top management is protected, doing what they want and also accumulating greater wealth. Local management, with salaries and bonuses befitting their context, regard themselves as under attack while earning substantially less. Unless the global–local dynamic is well managed, resentment can run deep.

BOSS VERSUS SUBORDINATE

The boss–subordinate relationship has attracted substantial attention in the study of organisations. As early as 1911, Frederick Taylor considered this relationship crucial to developing a successful organisation. His writings concentrated on establishing the key factors in the roles people held that would lead to an efficient and workable relationship.

Other researchers and writers have examined the superior–subordinate relationship from the point of view of the manager learning to collaborate with colleagues, superiors and subordinates, and from the point of view of appraising individuals in their current job in order to identify those suitable for further training and promotion.

The underlying characteristic of most of the studies has been the search for ways of improving the relationship. Rightly so, for the boss–subordinate relationship frequently leads to serious differences between people in organisations (Table 9.2). The reasons for such differences lie with roles, personal reasons and expectations:

- **Role reasons**: the manager may not have been given sufficient authority to carry out the duties required of him or her.
- **Personal reasons**: the manager may not be sufficiently skilled to establish a positive, comfortable working relationship with his or her subordinates. The subordinate, for example, may be obstructive towards the boss because of the boss's lack of social, technical, planning or administrative skills. It becomes difficult to achieve a productive working relationship when, from the subordinate's point of view, someone of lesser ability but earning more money has the right to direct other people as he or she desires.

Table 9.2 Boss versus subordinate (*Source*: compiled by Andrew Kakabadse)

Boss	Subordinate
Authority	May or may not respect authority
Accountability concerns	Responsibility challenges
Required to direct or coordinate	May or may not relate well to individual boss
Salary; status; bonus	Status or salary difference
Motivated to meet targets	Motivated to work; driven by projects
Achievement-oriented	Loyalty concerns

People may eventually oppose and undermine the individual manager and reduce their commitment to the organisation.

*   *Expectation reasons*: a successful manager is likely to be motivated by targets and obsessed with taking costs out of the business and manipulating people and resources ruthlessly to achieve those targets. The manager expects a career and a future in the organisation. However, the subordinate may hold different ideals. In the era of self-reliant employees, loyalty to the organisation is reduced as they more easily move into and out of organisations. Hence, although the subordinates may be motivated to work and be driven by projects, their expectation of a longer-term future in the organisation could be slight. (See Chapter 4 on the new psychological contract.) Where employment markets are fluid, where people are seen as resources and where loyalties can change by the day or by the project, how long can any boss rely on any subordinate?

Although managers may be charged with bringing people together and developing high-quality teamwork, the boss–subordinate relationship can incorporate more differences than similarities.

REALITY CHECK

POLITICS AT SHELL

From the top of the Shell Group down there is no traditional mechanism to resolve conflict. The group has no chief executive officer. The chairman of the managing directors is only primus inter pares, first among peers. One way or another, the members of the committee of managing directors and the two boards of directors have to agree among themselves on solutions that are acceptable to all. In practice, there will not always be real unanimity, but there is no good way to force through a decision to which one or more of the members is actively opposed. The minimum required is a 'quasi-unanimity'; otherwise the decision has to be referred back to the next lower level. Quasi-unanimity does not mean that everybody agrees with the proposal. It means that no one is so violently opposed that he or she will show a veto card. The chairman has no other power than his persuasion; he has no casting vote or final decision.

> It is not easy in Shell to exclude people from a decision if they are to be involved in implementation.
>
> *Source:* de Geus, A. (1999), *The living company: growth, learning and longevity in business,* London: Nicholas Brealey, pp 225–226.

PROFESSIONAL VERSUS MANAGER

What do research scientists feel about their management when asked to be more attentive to costs in research and development programmes? How do consultants react if their organisation requires them to spend more time on internal bureaucracy, rather than fee-earning work with clients?

People identify with their profession. Consider the factors that determine professional action and identity (Table 9.3).

Table 9.3 Professional versus manager (*Source*: compiled by Andrew Kakabadse)

Professional	Manager
Professional ethos	Organisationally focused
Loyalty to profession	Loyalty to self/organisation
Work to standards of profession	Work to targets
Team identity	Hierarchical identity
Like or dislike for management	Irritation with professionals

Professional executives or consultants or top specialists will place great emphasis on the quality of work they produce. They may see each new task as a challenge to their professional expertise. The task may have to be tackled slightly differently from all previous tasks. Consequently, the professional, whether engineer, doctor, lawyer, teacher or social worker, would probably attempt to undertake each job as he or she sees fit in professional terms and not refer to the organisation for guidance.

In contrast, managers are less ready to hold dual allegiances. Their work performance and career aspirations would be directed by the demands of the organisation. The classic – if not entirely accurate – image of the manager is of someone who identifies with his employing organisation: do no more or less than what is required of you; preserve the hierarchy; actions should be determined by your role requirements.

Not conforming to organisational norms can lead to a lack of trust between the line manager and the specialist, especially in each other's ability to manage work-related problems. With the growth of specialisation, line managers should be able to delegate certain tasks to specialists. For delegation to take place, line management must have sufficient confidence in the ability of the specialists and *vice versa*. Such trust, however, may be difficult to generate. Where the professional has little influence over his employing organisation, he is at a distinct disadvantage for he is just one more resource to be developed or discarded according to the organisation's current objectives. Certainly, professionals in research and development units, human resources and training have traditionally been vulnerable. During times of stringency, training and research and development are among the first to have their budgets reduced, irrespective of how well or badly they have performed in the past. Such conditions do little to endear the professionals to the organisation.

Some organisations have made a determined effort to improve the relationship between their managers and their professionals. Certain hospitals in the USA, run as separate profit centres, have evolved an integrated working relationship with their medical faculty. Such positive relationships arise as the result of individual initiative and leadership, driven by one or more well-respected managers or professionals. Until organisations attempt to improve the relationship between the professional cadre and the management, tension between professionals and management is likely to persist.

CENTRE VERSUS SUBSIDIARY

As is highlighted in Chapter 11, the centre–subsidiary relationship is one of continuous tension. The role of the centre is to attend to the interests of the organisation and not to any one subsidiary, division or strategic business unit. From the point of view of the organisation, changing the portfolio of interests of the group may or may not match with the needs of any one subsidiary (Table 9.4). Moreover, the centre will be focused on maintaining and enhancing share price and, in so doing, look for opportunities to introduce economies of scale. Corporate centre directors may decide on policy changes or new areas of investment; they may see a need to move plants and offices. Equally, a newly appointed senior executive may feel it necessary to stamp their authority on the organisation by introducing changes which represent their unique contribution.

Table 9.4 Centre versus subsidiary (*Source*: compiled by Andrew Kakabadse)

Centre	Subsidiary
Share price	Customer satisfaction
Corporate portfolio	Product or service portfolio
Economies of scale	Support services available
Value adding to group	Cost of centre
Top team focus	Conflict of loyalties
Audit	Resistance

From the subsidiaries' perspective, attending to the product or service portfolio and organising the corresponding support services are the main concern. Revenue and cost targets need to be achieved. Customers will only return if they are fully satisfied. Working hard to enhance market share and be competitive is likely to be applauded by the centre but equally may be the reason the centre needs to sell some of its operations. Hence, being operationally successful does not guarantee a long-term future in the corporation. With the centre's emphasis on improving share price, it can be sensible to sell any of the divisions, whether they are less profitable or more profitable. Thus whatever strategies the centre considers to add value can also be seen as undesired by the subsidiaries. The subsidiaries will support the cost of the centre but may feel they enjoy little value in return. The heads of the subsidiary (managing director, chief executive officer or director) may consequently find themselves in a conflict of loyalties. The need to introduce greater economies of scale across the group could undermine the quality of service support, for example in information technology, that the subsidiary may require. Moreover, the sale of a subsidiary to improve the company's share price could result in redundancies among the very people who have substantially contributed to the success of the subsidiary.

Where does the head of the subsidiary place his or her loyalties? For some, it is the centre as the subsidiary directors sees themselves as part of the central top team. For others, it is the subsidiary, with the director representing the views of the division or strategic business unit at the central executive committee meeting. One of the prime tools of the centre must be to audit the value of the total interests of the corporation. Yet certain executives located in the subsidiary consider that it is their duty to resist the centre by fighting a rearguard action against change.

COLLEAGUE VERSUS COLLEAGUE

Whatever other tensions and differences exist in an organisation, some are just the result of the interaction between particular people. For certain people, the hostility between them is a matter of conflicting style and personalities (Table 9.5).

Table 9.5 Colleague versus colleague (*Source*: compiled by Andrew Kakabadse)

Colleague	Colleague
Likes or dislikes	Likes or dislikes
Multiple team membership	Single team membership
Maturity/immaturity	Maturity/immaturity
Competitive	Competitive
Short term oriented	People values

The likes and dislikes of people for one another can affect how others behave towards them, whatever the reason(s) for the tension. Individuals talk to their own friends and colleagues and in so doing may discredit the person they dislike. When personal rancour becomes public and influences the way people work, interact and even think about each other, the maturity of the individuals involved has to be questioned. A more experienced person, witnessing potentially destructive behaviour, would intervene and probably tell all those concerned to act more sensibly.

However, certain tensions arise that have nothing to do with personality. Dislike, which can appear personal, may come about because of membership of particular groups or teams. The legacy of rivalry between two or more teams can continue long after the original reasons have disappeared. New members to the team are influenced to continue the rivalry but do not know why. Individuals with greater maturity would stop, think and question. Those whose reflective capacity is more limited, unthinkingly go out of their way to embarrass members of the other team.

Individuals who have been employed by a number of organisations, or who worked in a number of different departments and teams in the same organisation, are likely to adopt a more mature view than those who have worked in the same unit for a considerable time. Those with a broader perspective are more likely to question the decisions and behaviours of the long-standing members of the group. Genuine attempts to introduce improvement in relationships between two or more teams and units could be misinterpreted as someone making no attempt to 'fit in', or even as being disruptive. Suspicion of the more mature person's motives starts to grow in the minds of others. The more mature and sensitive newcomer is likely to become aware of the negativity of emotions that they are attracting and will adjust their approach, or leave. Those less sensitive, or less compromising, would persist with the questions and comments, thus making themselves more isolated.

As differences of attitude and orientation can lead to tensions between individuals, so can similarities. Two highly competitive individuals, pursuing the same job or attempting to become the favoured candidates for promotion, can cause 'sparks to fly'. Further, two dominant characters, even though they may not be competing for the same role, can generate tense and difficult interactions. In other circumstances, the two warring individuals might be friends. Even a single competitive, focused individual can generate tension. Their orientation towards short-term results can frighten others whose prime concern is to co-operate with colleagues and build satisfactory working relationships. What makes things worse is that all parties involved have a legitimate point of view. One wishes to achieve particular objectives. Others desire to preserve the current pattern of relationships. With little understanding of each other's perspective, the tension continues.

SHARED AND UNSHARED MEANING

With such differences between people who need to work together simply to achieve outputs, is there a permanent state of crisis? Is it quixotic to believe that people can live, work and share problems and personal experiences with each other?

Differences do exist; and people think, feel and see the same situation differently. However, that does not have to be a serious constraint to harmonious working. The problem is that managers have been misled. Consider certain basic values which many managers hold:

- Managers are paid to manage.
- It is a manager's job to motivate his or her people.
- It is a manager's responsibility to get others to work to common objectives.
- Good managers are the backbone of any company.

The common theme underlying the above values is 'shared meaning'; people sharing similar norms, attitudes, values, views of the world, feelings about situations, common experiences and viewpoints. Unfortunately, people do not behave in such a predetermined manner; individuals do not pursue the same objectives; stability and equilibrium are not necessarily the norm. In fact, there is as much unshared meaning as shared meaning in organisations. There are as many differences between middle and senior management as between management and operatives.

A senior manager may be irritated with his superior and consider that managers in his or her organisation cannot manage. In complete contrast, a shop floor operative may prefer managers to manage, as their own concern is to maintain a steady and secure income. A middle manager may think managers have the right to manage, but consider his or her own boss incapable. They may try to undermine and usurp the particular boss's position and yet still believe in the structure of the hierarchy.

People in employment are led to believe in shared meaning, and nowhere more than in management training. Managers who attend management-training programmes find themselves under strong pressure to get involved, take part, make a contribution, work with their study team. The underlying dynamic is to achieve 'best fit', that is, to come to terms with the environment and the people around you.

Notions of shared meaning are valuable. The 'pulling together' philosophy, especially when a group or organisation faces difficulties, is vital. But too often shared meaning becomes compulsive and enforced. The idiosyncratic and creative person can be excluded. Creativity often stems from the unusual person, the mutant gene, the persistent lone voice.

Living and interacting with other people has as much to do with unshared meaning as it has to do with shared meaning. Understanding politics in organisations involves analysing how people manage both shared and unshared meaning.

POLITICS IN PRACTICE

Politics in organisations means bridging the gaps between the individual and their motivation (the needs of the person), the group they deals with and their norms and behaviour (the shared attitudes of people), the general situations in which individuals find themselves and the acceptable and unacceptable ways people interact with each other.

One way of bridging the gap is to understand politics as the process of influencing individuals and groups of people to one's own point of view. The individual may wish others to accept their ideas, do what they want them to or simply get them to re-examine what they are doing so that they can improve their performance. Holding a position of formal authority is not sufficient. All too often an unacceptable boss finds that they are blocked, outmanoeuvred or even out-talked by smarter subordinates. What is required is to influence others sufficiently for them to accept one's own ideas and efforts.

Here are seven approaches to interpersonal influence:

- identify the stakeholders,
- work within comfort zones,
- fit the image,
- use networks,
- make deals,
- be 'economical with the truth' and
- confront or withdraw.

Identify the stakeholders

The stakeholders are the people with a commitment to act in particular ways in a situation. They have invested time, effort and resources to ensure that their objectives are adopted by the other people involved. The stakeholders are likely to influence what should be done and how it should be done. They are the key to the pressures and strains in a situation. How influential they can be depends on their own skills of interpersonal influence and their determination to pursue certain issues. It is not important that the stakeholders hold formal role authority, for pursuing particular objectives is a matter of influence and not command. Further, it may be difficult to recognise the stakeholders. They may take refuge behind others, especially those who hold formal role authority. People who wish to have their view adopted do not always have to make themselves visible to show their hand.

REALITY CHECK

IDENTIFYING THE STAKEHOLDER

Library suit backfires on Bottomley

Virginia Bottomley, former Conservative Heritage Secretary, faced the embarrassing prospect of seeing her attempts to find someone to blame for the delays and mistakes in the building of the British Library come to nothing.

Bottomley is thought to have overruled her advisers to make a £10m claim against Steensen Varming Mulchany, a private firm that designed and supervised the laying of 3000 km of cabling under the library floors.

The cabling, laid by Balfour Beatty, part of the BICC Group, was later found to be defective. In some cases it had been ripped down to its copper core in places where it had become snagged.

So what was the result?

- A hand inspection of 3000 kilometres of cabling.
- Court action to recover costs to the tune of £4m for repairing cabling and £5m for project delay.
- A view by industry experts that it would be difficult for SVM to be held liable for the damage.

If the claim against SVM is upheld it could mean financial ruin for its partners, who have worked on a number of other big projects, including the Sydney Opera House.

It should also be noted that a National Audit Office report published recently indicated that '. . . a total of 230 000 mistakes had occurred.'

The complex was officially opened by the Queen last month, 10 years overdue and at an eventual cost of £511m, against an original budget of £116m. It took 36 years of planning – almost as long as she has been sitting on the throne.

Even the Queen could not resist a reference to time when she spoke to the assembled architects and engineers at the opening ceremony. She said 'This labour of love must have seemed at times to be endless.' There were few who disagreed.

Source: Waples, J. (26 July 1998), 'Library suit backfires on Bottomley', *The Sunday Times.*

Work within comfort zones

Helping someone to feel comfortable involves concentrating on those behaviours, values, attitudes, drives and ideas that they can accept, tolerate and manage – that is, keeping within their comfort zones. The reason the 'comfort zones' are emphasised is that every person has developed a range of values and behaviour that they find acceptable and wish to put into practice. The range of values and behaviours is part of one's identity.

People will pay attention to the concerns of others as long as their own are not thereby threatened. Once an interaction with another concentrates on the issues important to only one party, and is threatening to the other party, that interaction is likely to be terminated. People interact sensibly only when they have sufficient interest in a situation.

In any situation people have two interests:

- the final objective, that is, what is the benefit to them and
- the manner in which the final objective is achieved, that is, the process.

By handling the interactions so that the receiving party feels comfortable, outcomes can be managed so as to satisfy both parties.

Working on the 'comfort zones' is synonymous with stimulating people positively and gaining their confidence. Different people require a different approach. Each person should develop some idea as to what other individuals can and cannot accept, otherwise a sincere attempt to help may be interpreted as manipulation.

There is always the danger that in meeting the needs of others one will relegate one's own needs to second place. It is all too easy to lose ownership of one's ideas and to have to deal with one's frustrations if one's efforts are not acknowledged. There is a fine dividing line between working on other people's comfort zones and ensuring that they recognise and reward one's own contribution.

Fit the image

By working on their comfort zones one can influence the stakeholders to one's own way of thinking. However, to gain the recognition and acceptance of superiors or individuals considered powerful and influential, it is necessary to work continuously on their comfort zones. As a result, one becomes aligned to the powerful other; one fits their image.

Maintaining that image is no simple task. Rather than becoming a fallen star, it is important to consider what one wants from the powerful other, how long it would take to obtain it, and whether one needs to realign with another powerful individual. Working on the comfort zones and fitting the image of an influential person is only likely to be effective in the short to medium term. Adjustments are required when the relationship ceases to be fruitful.

Use networks

Most people in organisations hold a number of identities. First, all employees have a role or job. All jobholders are held accountable for certain tasks and authority responsibilities inherent in their role. In addition, most individuals belong to certain interest groups that are formed for non-organisational reasons and may attract members from a number of separate organisations. These interest groups are called networks.

The network acquires its identity from the values and objectives of its members. Essentially, a sufficient number of like-minded people gather to debate, exchange information and achieve consensus about the issues that concern them. Depending on the prevailing issues and the dominant personalities, a network can be a more powerful determinant of the objectives to be pursued and how they are to be acted upon than the formal organisation.

Consequently, attempting to influence people who belong to networks is as necessary as attempting to influence particular individuals in an organisation. The principle of working on the comfort zones has to be extended to influencing individuals and groups. The key to networking is to determine the dominant core values of the network, identify the individuals who are generally seen as upholding the values of the network and influence them by working on their comfort zones.

Getting oneself known and becoming recognised as someone with a worthwhile contribution to make is achieved by entering one or more networks. To enter a network and be seen to make a contribution quickly involves the following processes:

- *Identify the gatekeepers*. The gatekeepers are individuals who are influential in the network and trusted by the network members, but spend as much time outside the network as within. Naturally, they meet with others who may wish to join the network or have a contribution to make to the network. The gatekeepers will assess whether the individual is worthy of introduction to the network. To have a gatekeeper as your sponsor will save you much time and effort, for you will then become quickly acquainted with the senior network members.
- *Adhere to network norms*. Once inside the network, it is important to recognise that it has certain values and norms of behaviour that should not be challenged. Whether one intends to advance one's own career through the network, or to promote or even prevent changes in a particular profession or the community at large, one should not introduce too many issues too quickly. Each network has its own way of doing things. To raise too many issues in too short a time could upset the other members. It is as important to fit into the network as it is to do anything new.

Management training programmes, workshops, dinner with top managers and even lunchtime or evening seminars all provide excellent opportunities to meet and exchange views and ideas about work, relationships, and how to resolve differences and improve co-operation in order to win and resource cross-function or inter-unit contracts. Such experiences facilitate the building of relationships in order to continue the education process once the workshop or management programme has finished. These processes, which are essentially the formation of networks, help managers to resolve managerial problems as more open, informal patterns of relationships are developed. In such circumstances people feel comfortable enough to discuss sensitive issues!

Make deals

Making a deal with other individuals or groups is a widespread practice in most large organisations. Whether resources are limited or not, different individuals or groups may agree to support each other to achieve a common purpose as long as they all benefit. It is realistic to expect individuals and groups in the organisation to wish to promote their own goals, which may be at the expense of others. Consequently, coming to some sort of agreement about common policies, reciprocity or at least not disturbing each other's aims, may be necessary.

The way deals are made is as important as the actual deal itself. For some a deal is seen as an honourable agreement which has to be kept. For others, it is a different matter: agreements may not be adhered to. Either party may break the agreements if they see this to be to their advantage. More probably, however, circumstances change, so people's needs alter and new agreements need to be negotiated. If both parties are aware of the new develop-ments, then change can be negotiated openly. If, however, one of the parties is unaware of new developments, or finds that changed circumstances are not in their favour, they may then attempt to hold the other party to the agreed arrangement. Even if the other party is willing to stand by the agreement, it is unlikely they will do so for long. The second party will simply cease to adhere to the agreement without informing the first party.

Whenever deals are struck between two or more parties, it is worth considering the true intentions of the other party and for how long one could realistically expect the arrange-ment to stand.

Be 'economical with the truth'

The notorious '*Spycatcher*' trial in Australia in 1986 produced a telling phrase, 'being eco-nomical with the truth'. A senior British civil servant, arguing that the book 'Spycatcher' should not be published, let slip how 'being economical with the truth' is an option in mat-ters of government policy. The phrase became a headline in Australia, highlighting, as much as anything, British duplicity. In fact, it originated with Edmund Burke, the eighteenth cen-tury statesman and constitutional theorist. In his analysis of political practice, 'an economy of truth' is permissible. It emphasises the need to consider how a case is presented, bearing in mind the impact of statements made, irrespective of their accuracy, on their audience. In effect, the idea of 'being economical with the truth' underlines the challenge any manager or public servant faces – that unguarded, inappropriate, or even appropriate comment can lead to damaging and undesirable reactions.

Although the phrase was first coined in a political context, it applies to any sensitive sit-uation. Judging audience reaction is critical. To be frank and open in sensitive circumstances, no matter how accurate the statements made, could mean being seen as inappropriate or even insensitive. However, if a manager makes more appropriate com-ments, so that others at least listen, and if they influence people who then use these revelations and it is discovered later that the manager has not been entirely forthcoming, they may be accused of misleading others. Should one be candid? That could make others feel alienated! Should one attempt to win people over by disclosing information gradually and selectively? The prevailing wisdom favours being selective even at the risk of a subse-quent accusation.

People in the organisation still need to be brought together and helped to tackle diffi-cult issues. The truth is that in complex enterprises, particularly in the international organisations of today, no simple solution exists to many of the challenges facing any man-ager. 'Being economical with the truth', as well as being robust in countering criticism, are both legitimate options.

REALITY CHECK

US BANKS' DAY OF RECKONING AFTER 'BETRAYAL' OF INVESTORS

'Ten of Wall Street's biggest investment banks signed a landmark settlement with US securities regulators yesterday, hoping to draw a line under the worst financial scandal in a generation.

'The final deal included findings of fraud against three banks – Citigroup's Salomon Smith Barney unit, Credit Suisse First Boston and Merrill Lynch. The regulators also released new evidence showing alleged conflicts of interest at other leading banks including Goldman Sachs and Morgan Stanley.'

William Donaldson, Chairman of the US Securities and Exchange Commission, stated, 'I am profoundly saddened – and angry – about the conduct that's alleged in our complaints. There is absolutely no place for it in our markets and it cannot be tolerated.'

Central was the 'promise' of attractive stock research as exchange for work in the area of investment banking.

'Under the settlement the banks will pay US$1.4bn (£880m) in restitution and to supply independent research to investors. It also requires the banks to introduce structural reforms to insulate research analysts from the influence of investment bankers.'

However, this initiative is likely to end the multimillion dollar pay packets some analysts enjoyed in the bull market. Moreover, pundits expect banks to pay out multimillions of dollars resulting from investors legally pursing their own grievances.

'Citigroup's Salomon division came in for the harshest punishment. Its US$400m payment includes a US$150m fine, the biggest civil penalty ever assessed by securities regulators. Along with Credit Suisse First Boston, Salomon was found to have issued "fraudulent research reports" to investors and to have awarded stock in hot initial public offerings to executives in a position to steer their companies' banking business back to them – a practice known as "spinning".'

Furthermore, Bear Stearns, Credit Suisse First Boston, Goldman Sachs, Lehman Brothers, Merrill, Piper Jaffray, Salomon and UBS issued research reports that were 'not based on principles of fair dealing', regulators said.

Source: Chaffin, J. in Washington (2003), 'US banks day of reckoning after 'betrayal' of investors', *Financial Times*, (April 29), p 1.

Confront or withdraw

It is impossible to satisfy everyone's needs in an organisation. One way of ensuring that certain groups do not over-react to issues that they see as important is to withhold information, which is one step beyond 'being economical with the truth'. By preventing certain information from becoming common knowledge, the manager can achieve his or her objectives without facing opposition that could thwart his or her plan. In such circumstances, the manager should be fairly convinced that the plan is valuable but that others have not recognised, or will not recognise, its worth. To withhold information constantly is not recommended, for such behaviour is symptomatic of a manager who cannot confront certain problems. Continuously withholding information protects the manager and not the policy and could lead to mistrust.

Withdrawing from a situation may also be necessary at times. Sometimes the presence of a manager in a dispute or negotiations is of no help. It is quite usual to withdraw and allow the different factions to negotiate their own terms, or for management to withdraw an unpopular policy for the time being. The larger and more diverse an organisation becomes, the more important is the timing of actions, the introduction or withdrawing of plans and information.

When all else fails

Of course, adopting strategies to increase one's personal influence does not guarantee success. Things go wrong and situations can get out of hand. What to do then, when all else fails?

The options are limited. The most obvious is to leave the job, situation or organisation. However, suitable alternative employment may not be easy to find. Job searches take time. What is more, a reference from the previous boss would be needed for any potential new employer. If the relations between boss and individual have been strained, then procuring a worthwhile reference may not be possible. In fact, it may be more difficult to leave than to stay.

The second alternative is to stay on. Working in an unpleasant environment is, however, not easy. It is both distasteful and demoralising to continue collaborating with people who do not appreciate one's contribution and who may wish to prevent one's growth and development. The only real advantage in staying is the chance to reassess one's own values, beliefs and action strategies. Was one trying to do too much too quickly? Were the underlying issues so important? Certain uncomfortable experiences simply have to be accommodated. It is possible to use the time to re-examine one's own purpose and objectives, if for no other reason than to prevent similar experiences from occurring in the future.

The third option, if adopted, is a risky one. It involves getting rid of the stakeholders. A superior putting pressure on one person in the hope that he or she leaves makes others uncomfortable. They wonder when their own turn will come. Trust, respect and performance are all likely to suffer severely.

For a subordinate to try to get rid of the boss is equally dangerous. The only realistic way is to conspire with the boss's boss to remove the troublesome superior. However, the boss's boss may feel uncomfortable about dealing with a subordinate outside their own role boundary.

Even if the individual succeeds in getting rid of their boss, there remains the danger that they may be the next to go!

Summary

Politics in organisations have been examined from four angles.

THE NATURE OF POLITICS IN ORGANISATIONS

Politics is equated with the way life in organisations is managed: in effect the way matters are discussed and affairs conducted. To analyse how managers in organisations behave, it is assumed that they are influenced by both similarities and differences between themselves and others.

DIFFERENCES IN ORGANISATIONS

Five types of differences were explored:

- *Global versus local*, that is, the differences between a global perspective – and even sense of responsibility towards the corporation – and a concern for the locality or country in which part of the corporation.

- *Boss versus subordinate*, that is, the differences that can emerge when one individual holds authority over another. This relationship is prone to tension, mistrust and sometimes an inability to confront such problems.
- *Professional versus manager*, that is, the differences between those who identify with a strong professional or expert ethos and those who preserve and defend the systems and morals of the organisation.
- *Centre versus subsidiary*, that is, the differences of outlook concerning the overall organisation's investment strategy and achievement of shareholder value as opposed to meeting local market demands and equally contributing to the costs of the centre when the value of the centre may be regarded as small.
- *Colleague versus colleague*, that is, the tensions that may arise between people of the same status and level in the organisation due to differences in expectation, ambition, maturity, outlook and personality.

SHARED AND UNSHARED MEANING

Shared meaning involves people identifying with similar norms, attitudes, values, views of the world, feelings and sentiments. Unshared meaning denotes an inability or unwillingness to hold similar views, values and sentiments or pursue comparable objectives or work towards stability and equilibrium by generating shared meaning.

There is as much unshared as shared meaning in organisations. Both differences and similarities are natural, inescapable experiences.

POLITICS IN PRACTICE

How can people influence each other? Politics is a process, a way to influence other individuals or groups towards one's own views. Hence, politics involves using negotiation skills to increase one's own interpersonal influence. Seven approaches to increased interpersonal influence were described:

- identify the stakeholders,
- work within the comfort zones,
- fit the image,
- use networks,
- make deals,
- be 'economical with the truth' and
- confront or withdraw.

10 *Power*

Eighty per cent of non-executive directors get their jobs by personal invitation of the chairman. The selection process is all to do with power.

Power definition

Writers and theorists in the behavioural sciences agree that the topic of power is vital to the understanding of organisation behaviour. David Lawless (1979) describes three prerequisites for the use of power:

* *Resources*. Wielding power nearly always involves the use of resources. The resources can be individually or organisationally based. A role which allows an individual to recommend someone for promotion or demotion qualifies as an organisational resource. Attractive appearance, private fortune, personal experience or high energy are examples of individually based resources.
* *Dependency is linked to resources*. The value of a resource is not determined solely by its possession. Its value is influenced by the degree of dependency of one person on the other. For example, a person is more powerful if they are not only in a position to determine the promotion of others, but if others actually depend on them to do so. If the person enjoys the sponsorship of a much more senior executive, their dependency on the lesser manager is diminished. In certain universities all of the full tenured professors in a department have to agree unanimously on the promotion of any faculty member from that department. Hence junior faculty depend on them to be promoted. Contradicting one's professor or offending all of the professors in one's department can be an exercise in career limitation for a junior faculty member. Such a dependency on the part of junior faculty stifles academic freedom and hampers robust debate. But it is part of the political reality of those universities.
* *Availability of alternatives* can also influence the power positions of people. If an individual is able to call on alternative resources, it is possible for them to reduce their dependency on others. A skilled, experienced person whose skills are in demand can take a job with a competitor if they find promotion blocked by a manager.

Seven power levers

From the authors' experience and from their research, an individual can employ seven power levers or strategies. They are: reward, role, personal, knowledge, network, information and corporate memory power.

REWARD POWER

Reward power is used by people in a position to influence the rewards given to others. Naturally for reward power to be used successfully, the individual must be able to control resources desired by others.

The resources include material (that is, money) or non-material resources (that is, status). Money can be viewed as a motivator or as a basic life commodity. Either way, a manager, who can utilise money as a reward, holds substantial power to influence the performance of his employees. This power increases if they also have the power to hire and fire. However, in many continental European organisations, which operate fixed pay scales and established conditions of employment, including procedures and agreements on hiring and firing, the power of the manager to reward or punish is drastically reduced. Under such conditions they have little discretion. Hence the parameters of the manager's resource power over employees can be closely defined.

Non-material based power such as status and privilege can also be a powerful lever. Access to exclusive clubs or restaurants, the key to the executive washroom and the opportunity to use the company's credit card are examples of non-material resource that increase a manager's status.

The success of reward power depends on people desiring the rewards on offer. What one person considers 'exclusive' may well be commonplace to another. Even rewards that are desired may be given in a way that is displeasing.

Reward power needs to be handled extremely carefully. No one enjoys having their manager behaving as a high profile, powerful determinant of their future.

Employees in paternalistic organisations may despise their managers if people believe high rewards are offered only to those who are subservient. Senior management in such organisations may find it difficult to understand why substantial rewards are, at times, only grudgingly accepted. If they are treated like children, employees may bite the paternalistic hand that feeds them.

The converse to reward is coercion, where punishment-centred methods are used to enforce compliance.

Coercive power depends on others realising that the manager will punish them. There is a significant difference between threatening to use coercion and actually using it. If bosses threaten retribution for not meeting deadlines and it is known that in the majority of cases they do not, then their capacity to apply coercive power in this instance is substantially diminished.

ROLE POWER

Sometimes referred to as 'legitimate power', role power stems from the formal organisational position held by one person. Role power comes from the authority, accountabilities and controls inherent in each role in the hierarchical structure of the organisation.

Occupying a certain role entitles the incumbent to all the benefits of the role. Equally, of course, the entitlement ceases once a person leaves a particular role. In a managerial role a person is usually allowed to redistribute work, re-set priorities and transfer personnel to various teams as needs arise. A manager is entitled to conduct checks on standards of work of operatives and supervisors to ensure quality products and services.

Analysing a person's job or role is useful to define the boundaries of activity and influence for the role holder and to know what can and cannot be done. Understanding which factors support managers and which constrain them is an important consideration. Supportive of role power are:

- **Positive attitude of the boss**. A manager who is willing to back his or her subordinates, particularly in making difficult decisions, provides legitimacy for the use of role power.
- **Transparency of information**. 'Information is power' is a well-known slogan. Legitimate use of role power requires having relevant information that enables sound decision-making. A manager needs to know the big picture and to be able to communicate relevant information to his or her team to empower them.
- **Accessibility**. Access to various networks in the organisation further supports the exercise of power. The manager's role permits access to personal, professional or informal networks.
- **Setting Priorities**. Setting priorities for subordinates' work is part of a manager's job.

The main constraints of the use of role power are:

- **Negative attitude of the boss**. If the legitimacy of role power is to be protected, what backing does the occupant of the role need? Who is the guarantor? The manager needs backing from other authority figures, otherwise the legitimacy of the power base is seriously undermined.
- **Withholding resources**. If the resources required for a manager to proficiently deploy rewards and coercion are withdrawn, the role holder is unable to influence.

PERSONAL POWER

Personal power depends on certain characteristics, loosely termed personality, and physical characteristics, which make an individual attractive to others. Managers with personal power are said to be charismatic, popular, possessing panache or flair. Rather than use role, rewards, coercion or knowledge, the manager influences others through pure personal power. The manager's ability to make contact with others, to connect with them emotionally, is at the core of personal power. The manager makes such an impact that others want to be in his or her presence, gain favour or simply be liked by the charismatic person. They will give him or her what he or she wants just to be allowed 'near them'.

Successful application of personal power depends on two factors:

- Others are attracted to the individual and
- Personal contact.

It is a mistake to assume that everyone will be attracted to the same person. Some senior executives have personal styles that work well with one group of people, but not with another. Charisma depends on personal physical contact. Charisma is best experienced on meeting the person.

KNOWLEDGE POWER

Someone with specialist knowledge in a particular field is considered an expert. The use of expert or knowledge power is especially pertinent to solving complex problems. An expert is called in to examine the problem, if necessary, to find appropriate solutions and to help

REALITY CHECK

PERSONAL POWER – CHARISMATIC BILL CLINTON

. . . the handshake is the threshold act, the beginning of politics. I've seen him do it two million times now, but I couldn't tell you how he does it, the right-handed part of it – the strength, quality, duration of it, the rudiments of pressing the flesh. I can, however, tell you a whole lot about what he does with his other hand. He is a genius with it. He might put it on your elbow, or up by your biceps: these are basic reflexive moves. He is interested in you. He is honoured to meet you. If he gets any higher up your shoulder – if he, say, drapes his left arm over your back, it is somehow less intimate, more casual. He'll share a laugh or a secret then – a light secret, not a real one – flattering you with the illusion of conspiracy. If he doesn't know you all that well and you've just told him something 'important', something earnest or emotional, he will lock in and honour you with a two-hander, his left-hand overwhelming your wrist and forearm. He'll flash that famous misty look of his. And he will mean it.

Anyway, as I recall it, he gave me a left-hand-just-above-the-elbow plus a vaguely curious 'ah, so you're the guy I've been hearing about' look, and a follow me nod. I didn't have time, or presence of mind, to send any message back at him. Slow emotional reflexes,

I guess. His were lightning. He was six meaningful handshakes down the row before I caught up. And then I fell in, a step or two behind, classic staff position as if I had been doing it all my life. (I had, but not for anyone so good.)

We were sweeping up into the library, the librarian in tow, and now he had his big ears on. She was explaining her programme and he was into heavy listening mode, the most aggressive listening the world has ever known: aerobic listening. It is an intense, disconcerting phenomenon – as if he were hearing quicker than you can get the words out, as if he were sucking the information out of you. When he gives full ear – a rare enough event; he's usually ingesting from two or three sources – his listening becomes the central fact of the conversation.

Source: *Primary colors: a novel of politics,* written anonymously by a political journalist. It tells the story of a campaign-staff member who is recruited by the governor of a small state who has set his sights on the presidency. The candidate is a very thinly disguised Bill Clinton (New York: Random House, 1996, p 3–4).

implement them. The application of knowledge power is not normally resented, as the majority of people involved will recognise the expert's knowledge and experience.

Managers use the application of knowledge power frequently to achieve their aims. But they need to exercise great care. In the fast moving field of information technology, individuals with specialist knowledge are often commercially involved in promoting their company's hardware or software and in so doing are biased. Knowing whom to turn to for the best offer is confusing for those managers without information technology expertise. Where there are conflicting opinions and a knowledge base that is quickly out of date it is understandable that people cling to the suppliers they know and trust. Hence, one aspect of information power is that the individual with an acknowledged expertise needs to be recognised as such for some considerable time.

NETWORK POWER

A manager enjoys network power when he or she has both personal and professional access to a larger number of people and groups within and outside the organisation. The essential feature of network power is making large numbers of contacts who could be valuable. Making friends at conferences, getting to know people at meetings and exhibitions, and joining professional and trade organisations are ways of making contacts. (See Chapter 9 on how to influence through networking.)

The traditional vertically integrated organisation has been almost superseded by an array of horizontal links, extending internally and externally across a number of organisations. Networking is now more than ever an integral part of organisational life. Thus, the manager needs to develop the skills of networking, which include contact-making skill and an appetite for further interaction with the contacts.

INFORMATION POWER

Information can provide an important power base. Raw data in itself means little. But data processed and interpreted becomes information that can support a point of view or disprove people's arguments, and therefore represents a useful basis for action. The skill is in knowing what information to acquire. There are three separate categories of information.

Concrete information is information already compiled and stored, such as facts, figures, trends, projections, financial statements, reports examining the effectiveness of the enterprise or its parts or even personnel reports on particular individuals.

Most organisations generate and tabulate substantial amounts of concrete information. Such information is an important aspect. Access to it is largely a function of role and position in the organisation. Confidential reports concerning the profitability of the enterprise are likely to be available only to the chief executive and a selected few. The financial and marketing data upon which the report is based may be available to many. Clerks, secretaries and team leaders may record the performance of particular product lines or teams for which they are responsible. However, as they do not have access to further information concerning the performance of the organisation, and are not in a position to discuss long-term trends, they may be unable to understand the full implications of the data they hold.

Process information concentrates on the processes by which people relate to and interact with each other. Unlike concrete information, which comprises tabulated facts, figures and trends, process information is non-tabulated data about people's feelings towards each other and the organisation. Hence it involves having access to particular people or groups in the organisation, so as to influence their thoughts and actions. The secretary or personal assistant to a chief executive has potential access to process information, partly because they have close personal contact with the chief executive and partly because they have access to most confidential concrete information.

Self-disclosure information is information of a personal and private nature that is freely offered by one individual to another on a basis of trust. One person trusts another sufficiently to discuss some personal matter that could be embarrassing if it became public knowledge. It is important for the person making the disclosure to feel that the other will listen and help if they can, but most of all maintain confidentiality.

Access

A vital consideration in information power is access. Access is a function of role and position in the organisation for factual and process information. Potential for access not only allows the individual to be privy to factual or process information, but also gives him or her the chance to influence the quantity or quality of that information. In contrast, self-disclosure information depends far more on the relationship between two people.

CORPORATE MEMORY POWER

Innovations in information technology, the greater influence of shareholders on corporate strategy, increasing demands for the organisation to perform and the possibility of take-over, mean that change is now a central feature of commercial and even public service organisations. Such volatility encourages greater turnover of staff and management. People seek opportunities for themselves elsewhere. The organisation requires new or additional skills and terminates the contracts of employees whose skills and experience are considered no longer necessary.

One casualty of continual change is 'corporate memory'. What is meant by 'corporate memory'? Experienced employees, who are 'long stayers', are intimately acquainted with the organisation. They know whom to ask for particular advice or skills. They can describe the history of the organisation, its development, its strengths and weaknesses. Within the organisation, they are considered to be the 'sages' or wise ones. Because of their understanding of others they can indicate whom to call on when an individual or group in the enterprise face a particular challenge or crisis. Their intimacy with the organisation could be viewed as a 'wisdom' that has taken years to build. The sum total of this collective experience, held in a memory bank, is what is meant by 'corporate memory'.

There are three reasons for preserving corporate memory:

- *Access*. Those with intimate knowledge and access to the various parts of the organisation save time in finding the right people to contact. They also save money, since there is no need to evoke external assistance, as the necessary skills are already available. Someone with corporate memory knows where to locate them.
- *Stability*. People who are intimately acquainted with the organisation provide a link between the past, present and future. Challenges and problems that occur today can be better managed if someone can recall how similar difficulties were dealt with in the past. Those with access to corporate memory power can exercise a calming influence: 'We've seen it before. Don't worry, this is the way it was handled before and this is what we should do now.' Thus access to corporate memory power promotes stability.
- *Respect*. Effectively applied corporate memory power induces a respect from others. Those who contribute to corporate memory become a focal point where people go for advice on how to tackle problems and challenges with which they are unfamiliar, but which someone has previously faced in similar circumstances. From the point of view of a customer or supplier, going to someone with insight into how the organisation works and who knows the appropriate people to contact, saves time and provides a valuable service.

Of course, excessive attention to corporate memory power may be regarded as being 'stuck in the past'. The skill is to recall those elements of the past that truly help in solving today's problems without being seen as 'a relic of yesteryear'.

Power levers in context

Organisational cultures differ as much as national cultures. When a manager moves from one organisation to another, becoming acquainted with the technical aspects of the new position is not sufficient. To be considered successful means making a determined effort to understand new colleagues, superiors and subordinates and their attitudes towards work, supervision and the organisation itself. In their previous position the managers may have been hardworking, conscientious and recognised by their colleagues as making a positive contribution. In the new job, to work too hard may be undesirable and to interact too closely with colleagues and superiors may be considered 'social climbing'. After a time, these managers come to realise that there are certain people one can afford to displease, and others one should keep on good terms with.

Their likes and dislikes reveal the attitudes that determine the behaviour of people in organisations. After a time, these attitudes and behaviours can become characteristics of a particular organisation. Various organisational characteristics such as leadership, management styles, organisational design and flow of communications interact to produce the culture or identity of an organisation.

Organisation culture is difficult to define. It is best described as feelings and values that a number of people share consistently about situations in the organisation. If a sufficient number of people perceive a situation in a similar light, does it then become reality? The answer is probably yes, and if such thinking is applied to organisations, then a culture or a number of cultures may form among the various groups operating within the organisation. Charles Handy goes further by suggesting that cultures are deeper phenomena than just commonly agreed ways of perceiving a situation. He states:

> *In organisations, there are deep-set beliefs about the way work should be organised, the way authority should be exercised, people rewarded, people controlled. What are the degrees of formalisation required? How much planning and how far ahead? What combination of obedience and initiative is looked for in subordinates? Do work hours matter, or dress, or personal eccentricities? . . . Do committees control an individual? Are there rules and procedures or only results? These are all parts of the culture of an organisation.*

Handy, C. (1976), *Understanding organisations*,
London: Penguin Educational Series, p 177.

Culture can take on many meanings ranging from the types of buildings, offices or branches housing the organisation's employees, to the kind of people it employs, their career aspirations, their perceived status in society, their degree of mobility, level of education and so on. Hence, culture refers to the way people in different (or sometimes similar) organisations view the world, their life and the way they go about their work. Even within one organisation, different cultures will co-exist; the views prevailing, for example, among those working in research, line management, policy determination, marketing and branding will all be different.

Keith Ward and Cliff Bowman together with Andrew Kakabadse, of Cranfield School of Management, describe different organisational identities principally derived from the process of organisational ageing. They identify four different organisational contexts in which the seven power levers are applied differently. These are: creative context, leverage context, scope context and cost discipline context.

CREATIVE CONTEXT

Driven by a sense of uniqueness through working from a distinctive knowledge base, the quality of relationships, robustness of debate and openness of relationships are typical of an organisation that has adopted a creative identity. In such a context, the seven levers of power take on particular meanings (Table 10.1). Reward power involves reward alone, not reward and coercion. Inappropriately or inequitably applied, coercion results in the best people leaving.

The most powerful reward is recognition. Developing the knowledge base of the organisation, enhancing the unique identity of the organisation through discoveries and research and development, are the basis for reward. Although promotion and financial reward are welcomed, the greatest reward is acknowledgement by one's own peers that one's contribution is truly of value.

Recognition, as a form of reward, emphasises the informal nature of an organisation with a creative context. Informality and respect, two important considerations in using personal power, highlight that those who effectively utilise personal power are already highly regarded. People who display a capability for advancing knowledge may also be considered charismatic. In other contexts, charisma is likely to mean something quite different. As

Table 10.1 Power levers in context: creative (Compiled by Andrew Kakabadse)

Reward	Role	Personal	Knowledge	Network	Information	Corporate memory
Knowledge oriented; if coercive, best people leave; enhance unique base of knowledge; promote further research and development; recognition is reward itself.	Authority counts for little; respect from task skills; use of authority or formality frightens; use of formality can undermine credibility of power user; informality; decentralised	Be highly regarded; respect each other; works well when works – emotional and damaging if not; charisma and knowledge linked.	Fundamental to creativity identity; professional expertise; the more unique the knowledge, the greater the power; research and development driven knowledge has greatest credibility.	Viewed as more important than organisation; source of inspiration or debate; source of status; acceptance in network is critical; 'tall poppies' valued; meeting point of similar niched knowledge workers.	Knowledge power is valued; financial performance data constraining; organisation or process information seen as bureaucratic; informal; trust is valued.	Short; team memory important; network memory important; loyalty to team or network; corporate memory seen as constraining; valuing corporate memory is being stuck in the past.

respect, rather than charm and influence, is the basis for personal power, it is ironic that those with poorly developed people skills may be judged to use personal power effectively, which may surprise those new to the organisation. When personal power, on the basis of respect, works well, it really does work well! When personal power is used inappropriately, particularly if respect is not forthcoming, it can be counter productive. Others can react negatively, especially if the individual wielding personal power is regarded as charming but untrustworthy.

As informality is characteristic of creative organisations, the weakest of the 'levers' is role power. In a truly creative enterprise, authority counts for little. In fact, using authority and formality could arouse fear. Certainly, excessive formality is likely to undermine the credibility of the role power user.

Gary Withers, chief executive officer of Imagination regards himself as an enabler of the talents of others. His multi-disciplinary design company, based in central London, operates design projects in over 35 countries. Withers can be seen moving from one team of creative designers to another with an encouraging word, a helpful gesture of support in Imagination's headquarters – two converted Victorian schools knocked together, on Store Street, off Tottenham Road. He is also the recruiter of talent, sifting through hundreds of unsolicited letters and curricula vitae to identify the few new employees who would make a contribution to his high-powered, creative workforce.

If role power is the least likely effective lever to use in creative organisations, the most effective is knowledge power. Knowledge, professional expertise and research and development based contributions are the heart of the creative organisation. As new knowledge is fundamental, equating knowledge with power would be regarded as unhelpful. In fact, using power would be seen as a negative and an unwelcome way of working.

Linking knowledge with informality illustrates how networking, both within and outside of the organisation, operates. The network is a crucial mechanism of communication between similarly minded knowledge workers. As an informal chain of colleagues sharing ideas, the network is likely to be regarded as more important than the individual's employing organisation. It is the source of and, for many, the inspiration for new ideas that may result in new products or services. And in academic circles it may determine the tone of academic publications. Networks often cluster around particular academic or scientific journals, so that the people who meet at the annual conferences of professionals, are the writers, reviewers and purchasers of the relevant journals. Academics, physicians, research scientists working in the nuclear industry or those in pharmaceutical companies feel a need to gather together to debate how to proceed, particularly with research and development programmes. Thus the network becomes a focal point. Being offered honorary positions in certain networks could be the ultimate accolade. Conversely, in certain professions, not to be part of the network would be tantamount to leaving the profession. Assuming acceptance in the network, then 'tall poppies' are valued. Tall poppies are people who stand apart and aside from others due to their achievements. They can be resented for their success and for standing out. The more unusual the individuals, the more noteworthy their accomplishments, the more acceptable they are to the network.

Information that is most valued is knowledge based. Procedural, organisationally driven information is likely to be labelled as bureaucratic and constraining. In some organisations, financial performance data may be viewed as historical, constraining and for the accountants to grapple with, or alternatively as an important lever to adopt in order to make progress. At General Electric, Jack Welch's approach was to create a dynamic climate in their markets. Unlike many niche-oriented enterprises with a creative context, General Electric is large, but with its chief executive officer promoting a culture of dynamism, the knowledge that was most valued was financial and the manner in which it was used was informal.

Corporate memory is short for two reasons, either people leave or they pay little attention to the workings of their own organisation, resigning its management to those who have accepted managerial responsibility.

LEVERAGE CONTEXT

In contrast to the individualistic and team-oriented nature of the creativity context, organisations that are driven by a leverage identity aim for consistency (Table 10.2). The consistent spread of knowledge and skills across the organisation (or the group, if it is not a single corporate entity) is pursued in order to gain and maintain competitive advantage. Spreading the expertise in the organisation across the enterprise to achieve sustained growth is the objective of the management. The more organisation-oriented power levers will accordingly have greater impact than informal tacit ways of working. Reward and coercion are likely to be used in equal measure. The focus is on the performance of the individual, assessed through formal appraisal. High performers are rewarded through promotion or financial enhancement. Poor performers are at first shown how and where they should improve. If they fail, they are dismissed.

Influencing through role power is likely to be extensive. Clarity as to the accountabilities and responsibilities of the role will be matched by equal clarity concerning relationships. Who reports to whom and who has a dotted line relationship with others, are likely to be clearly spelt out. Knowing one's role and working to clearly specified objectives, as much as possible through formal channels, are fundamental to an organisation with a leverage identity. Being centralised and working towards set objectives, is the mode of operation. Personal influence could be considered undesirable. People who exude charisma and inclination towards entrepreneurship could even be seen as dangerous. Personal influence is likely to be of advantage only when new developments emerge in the market place requiring an acquisition or the introduction of a new skill base. New developments are likely to mean re-aligning corporate goals. Managers are likely to be given the discretion to make changes. Thus, charismatic personalities with entrepreneurial flair are accepted at senior levels as long as they are seen to 'fit' the organisation.

Knowledge that is valued is directly linked to the promotion and enhancement of corporate identity. The promotion of the corporate brand and how staff and management should support the brand is made known throughout the organisation. If the unique knowledge base of the organisation lies in branding, the way to deploy these skills across different products or sectors is shared through the enterprise. The purpose of knowledge power is not to display a superior level of expertise but to make that knowledge available to all. Even with a new acquisition, the aim would be to integrate the new entrant into the organisation and ensure that its expertise becomes understood and known throughout the organisation.

As the emphasis is on enhancing the corporation's image there is little need for external network power. Loyalty is to the corporation. Any knowledge and insights gained from external networks is shared across the organisation. The only value of external networks is that they provide a platform for benchmarking. For example, an outsourcing provider or

Table 10.2 Power levers in context: leverage (Compiled by Andrew Kakabadse)

Reward	Role	Personal	Knowledge	Network	Information	Corporate memory
Reward and coercion used in similar measure; performance based, formal appraisal; rapid promotion or financial gain.	Formal; clarity of accountabilities and responsibilities; clarity of role relationships; know your role; work to clear objectives; centralised.	Work within system; charisma or entrepreneurship could be viewed as dangerous; work towards corporate goals.	Brand promotion; corporate identity promotion; purchase unique knowledge; sharing of knowledge.	Needs to be supportive of mission and goals: used for benchmarking; little loyalty to external networks; 'tall poppies' tolerated.	Numbers or target driven; explicit although tacit tolerated; structured; process driven.	Important; need to maintain so as to turn tacit into explicit knowledge; focus on best practice; historical unimportant; source of best practice critical.

consultant organisation may well send its specialists and managers to various academic and professional conferences and meetings to keep itself up to date with the latest thinking, research and best practice. Such information is brought into the organisation and shared amongst all other relevant staff and managers. The prime purpose of network power, internally or externally, is to provide insights on how to support the mission and goals of the organisation. Individuals with new ideas and practices are welcomed. 'Tall poppies' are tolerated and admired. What is not tolerated is someone using the network for personal advantage. Corporate loyalty is alive and well.

Information that is respected is explicit. Information power is based on numbers. Have the managers reached their targets? Have the profitability and cost ratios been achieved? Those who use numbers to drive through change are viewed as powerful. Tacit, informal, 'understood between us' information is tolerated, particularly if new ways of tackling interesting challenges are being explored. However, the aim is to turn tacit information into explicit, structured information. In this way, information that needs to be shared is distributed across the organisation in a disciplined manner. To gain advantage, processes are established governing the use – and cautioning against the misuse – of information.

The loyalty towards the organisation and its procedures and formalities for the sake of gaining advantage makes corporate memory an influential lever of power. Corporate memory power will yield the greatest benefit when it focuses on areas of best practice that may have been forgotten or ignored. In this way, skills that have fallen into disuse can be revived, particularly if those skills, or the relevant knowledge areas, were tacit. The way to use corporate memory power effectively is to bring the best of the past to the present, not to recall the past for its own sake.

SCOPE CONTEXT

In contrast, looking to the past to recapture former glory is a preoccupation for those in an organisation with an underlying culture of re-scoping and rethinking its future (Table 10.3). Here, those with an extensive corporate memory enjoy status and admiration. The organisation is driven by tradition. The values that have held the organisation together in the past

Table 10.3 Power levers in context: scope (Compiled by Andrew Kakabadse)

Reward	Role	Personal	Knowledge	Network	Information	Corporate memory
Extraordinary performance; status; financial; rapid promotion; can be 'politically' acquired; coercion for failure; coercion for those who do not fit.	Outwardly formal; be seen to respect accountabilities and responsibilities; do not overtly challenge structure; covertly negotiate; make deals; centralised.	Deals; double deals; charismatic; powerful leader; image important; promotes hope; does not damage or challenge the past.	Past expertise; maintenance of core values; delusion concerning worth of organisational knowledge; sensitive to criticism; critical of others; commodity.	Internal; high levels of dependency; reluctance to be exposed to external develop-ments; no 'tall poppies'.	Numbers driven; communicate in code; outwardly explicit; in reality implicit; preservation of past culture.	Long; tradition driven; past values necessary for future; war stories; former glory.

are considered necessary for a successful future. Those who can recall earlier triumphs are held in high esteem.

Building for the future while preserving the past, or at least not damaging it, provides the basis for reward power. Those who can lead the way forward through performance that is perceived as extraordinary are likely to be rewarded by rapid promotions, enhanced status and financial gain. Reward and personal power are interwoven. The powerful individual who promotes hope and does not challenge the past is rewarded for revitalising the organisation and enhancing its image and status. However, image and reality are two different perspectives. Being seen to be the leader is as important as providing a contribution towards the success of the organisation.

The reason the organisation has to re-scope and rethink its shape, identity and portfolio of goods and services is that it is uncompetitive. Radical change is needed to re-position the corporation. Fundamental change attacks the established values and traditions, which paradoxically the organisation clings to. Thus the charismatic leader is one who is also 'politically' astute (see Chapter 9) and can enter into deals. As rewards are given for success, no matter how it is achieved, coercion is equally applied for those seen to fail. But failure can be interpreted as failure to meet targets or failure to fit in. The truly charismatic leader, not hindered by current ideals and perceptions, is likely to be seen as too threatening and, although capable of achieving particular goals, as a liability to the organisation. They would be under pressure to depart.

Organisations that have reached the crisis point where they recognise the need to change but have no stomach for the necessary re-scoping can operate in an underhand manner, particularly through the use of role power. Outwardly formal, with everyone's accountabilities and responsibilities ostensibly respected, they often resort to covert practices. 'Understandings' and deals are commonplace. Depending on who is seen to be in or out of favour, varying standards are applied to accountability for performance and also to reward. Such inconsistency of approach to accountability and reward is a prime reason why the organisation is facing difficulties – there is one standard for those who are 'well in' and another for those who are not.

As the organisation struggles with the paradoxical demands of needing to move forward while still worshipping its past, the effective application of knowledge power faces the same dilemma. Knowledge power here mostly relates to past expertise and the maintenance of core values. Yet the knowledge power now needed to achieve competitive advantage is in scarce supply. Delusion sets in concerning the worth of the unique knowledge underlying the organisation.

Alongside the formal role structure stands the internal network of inter-relationships, some going back 30 years or more. This internal network is the way things get done. Those who are part of this internal network wield network power. These well-connected managers act as both barriers and gatekeepers for others, generating high levels of dependency. Everyone in the organisation knows who should not be challenged or offended. The network also acts as a barrier to unwelcome developments in the external world. Once the networks indicate that changing its ways of working is undesired, even though that decision contradicts the demands of the market, even senior management would be reluctant to challenge it. To voice disquiet with the organisation's ways of working is, by implication, to challenge the network. No 'tall poppies' are permitted.

Information power, like role power, is outwardly explicit. It is numbers-driven. Attention is paid to meeting targets and setting stringent goals, all as manifestation of the need to improve. Implicitly, however, the reluctance to contemplate fundamental changes betrays the 'deals in the background' culture. Targets that are not met, particularly by those held in high regard, are represented as unrealistic, or unexpected contingencies are advanced as reasons for the failure to achieve them. A similar level of understanding is unlikely to be shown to those not in favour with the network. As with all the other power levers, the prime aim of information power is the preservation of a past and culture held together by tradition.

COST DISCIPLINE CONTEXT

History has little influence in an organisation driven by a cost discipline identity (Table 10.4). In the cost disciplined organisation the difference between costs and revenue is the focal point of management's attention. Rewards are given for the attainment of ever-bigger profits. The greater the company's profitability the greater the reward in terms of promotion or financial gain through bonuses and share or share option schemes for the managers concerned. However, today's high performers may be unable to meet next year's targets for reasons not under their control. Memories are short and the individual may be pushed into resigning. Failure is not easily tolerated in an organisation at the commodity end of the market, competing against others with similar products and services. As substantial reward is given for success in meeting targets, considerable degrees of coercion can be applied for poor performance, the most likely being dismissal!

An organisation such as a low-cost airline, competing on price in highly competitive markets, needs to be focused on costs. The purpose of internal structures and procedures is to provide for ever greater market focus. To stay ahead of the competition, reorganisations are frequent. Under such circumstances, role power can be exercised formally or informally. What counts is the clarity of responsibilities and accountabilities in each person's role. Respect for success is greater than respect for the structure. If the hierarchy needs to be

Table 10.4 Power levers in context: cost discipline (Compiled by Andrew Kakabadse)

Reward	Role	Personal	Knowledge	Network	Information	Corporate memory
Extraordinary performance; financial; rapid promotion; target oriented; too busy for politics; highly coercive; no forgiveness for failure; here today, villain tomorrow.	Can be formal or informal; clear responsibilities, respect for success greater than respect for structure; bypass structure if necessary; decentralised; continuous re-organisation.	Powerful; charismatic; bully; drive through results; any means count; hit the numbers.	Numbers driven; commodity with no delusions; expendable; no understanding of unique knowledge; failure through knowledge based organisations acquisition.	Membership of any network; external networks as mechanisms for finding next job; relationship cold and distant; merger or acquisition driven; financial networks, Wall Street, City; those who fit are those who succeed.	Numbers; targets; explicit; costs as much as profit; margins driven.	Short; little or no corporate loyalty; loyalty to task at hand; people expendable.

bypassed, it will be. If successful, individuals are likely to be well rewarded. If not, then they may well lose their job, for both not being successful and circumventing their boss.

Personal power is a particularly potent lever in such organisations. The motto of a cost discipline context organisation is 'drive through', namely, drive through change, or drive through to success. Driving anything through requires strong leadership, which if success-ful is perceived as powerful or charismatic. If results are not achieved, exactly the same behaviours may be seen as distasteful and bullying. Virtually any means will be tolerated, as long as it is legal.

Knowledge power is synonymous with financial control and target setting. Knowledge power and information power are one and the same, in that both are numbers-driven. The organisation has reached commodity status and its staff and management are under no delusion about that fact. Just as any product, service or line of business is expendable, so too is the organisation itself. Apart from striving to meet financial targets, cost discipline based organisations have acquired knowledge-based, niche enterprises on the assumption that applying similar cost disciplines will make them even more profitable. Such acquisi-tions often end up as damaging failures. A cost discipline driven enterprise has no understanding of a more knowledge-based company and its tough approach is counter-cul-tural to the staff and management in the other organisation. The better employees leave. Furthermore, many of the niche organisation's customers, accustomed to far greater levels of personal service, have no desire for a 'cut price deal'.

The relationship between the organisation and its staff and management is distant. For most people, the organisation is 'just a job'. For many, tenure in cost discipline enterprises is short term. Hence, networking is as much concerned with making contacts to complete a project as it is to have avenues available to find a job elsewhere. For the senior management of the enterprise, networking takes on a different meaning. Access to investment bankers and analysts in Wall Street and the City of London represents a valuable set of relationships. Shareholders and analysts need to know that senior management is capable of meeting demanding targets. Access to capital for further acquisition, being personally known to investment bankers, who would vouch for the skills of any top manager, and credibility with the financial press are important attributes of leadership. Thus network power holds an entirely different meaning for top management in comparison to the other staff and management of the organisation. The networks, the formal organisation and the external contacts are in many ways rolled into one. The aim is to succeed. Those who fit are those who succeed; those who do not, leave and use their contacts to help them find other jobs.

Corporate memory is short. There is little or no corporate loyalty. The aim is to 'sweat the assets'. Historical recall is unnecessary, and could even be a hindrance. Corporate memory is respected when it is task-related. When it comes to meeting targets, the corporate memory that is valuable is one that shows how methods that succeeded in the past can be usefully applied today.

Levels of power sophistication

We have looked at the nature of power and the various power levers. One other aspect of power remains to be explored: the purpose and intentions of the power holder. Steven Lukes (1974) has identified three levels of power application.

LEVEL 1

The German philosopher Max Weber suggested that power was 'A' having power over 'B' to the extent that 'A' can get 'B' to do something that 'B' would not otherwise do. This interpretation was accepted by the early sociologists and those researching power in groups and communities. Most of the academic literature on power and politics, directly or indirectly, uses 'power' to mean level 1 power, and most people would interpret the word in this way. However, we can only confirm that level 1 power is operating after a careful examination of observable decisions. For example, 'A' must know what they want, what 'B' can offer and how far 'B' can be coerced. Power is conflict-based and overt conflict is emphasised. Decision choices are relatively clear-cut.

LEVEL 2

The view that power is simply 'A' getting 'B' to do what 'A' wants was challenged as it became evident that more sophisticated levels of power exist. Politicians in western society would not survive for long if they attempted constantly to force other people to do their bidding. They can be highly influential and their perceived power is achieved by their capacity to influence others of their own opinion on the key issues. Politicians' behaviour at election time provides a good example. They argue, debate and attempt to influence the electorate as to what the key issues are. One party offers one interpretation of the primary issues while the other offers a different programme of policies based on different assumptions and values. The party that convinces the electorate that their manifesto and leaders are the best wins the election. Level 2 power concentrates not on observable decisions and actions but on convincing others about issues, norms and values. In this way, certain issues are included in the discussion while others issues are left out of it.

Some financial policy and strategic planning techniques are a disguised form of level 2 power. The early Planning, Programming and Budgetary systems and current government concepts of 'best value' are undoubtedly techniques for making decisions, but they are also mechanisms for defining the key issues in the promotion of policy. Certain key issues may not be well understood by top management because of their complexity and technicality. Planning, Programming and Budgetary systems and best value can generate data to enhance understanding of the problem areas in order to improve the decision-making process. Of course, everything depends on how best value is applied. If best value has been deliberately programmed to concentrate on only certain types of data, other issues may be obscured. Unless people clearly understand both the technique and the way it has been applied, they will not be in a position to appreciate which data – and hence which potential problems – have been left out of the analysis. In fact, writers such as Aaron Wildavsky argue that these techniques are entirely power-based, for the results of applying them vary according to who is applying the technique and what is the objective.

The difference between level 1 power and level 2 power is that level 1 involves action and observable behaviour, whereas level 2 may involve no action. With level 2 power, if one or more individuals can convince others that they should pursue only one particular line of argument, by simply dropping another line of argument or not voting in favour of a particular policy, they are as powerful as if they had taken some specific action.

LEVEL 3

The idea that only two levels of power exist was challenged in its turn and a third level added. Creative and far-sighted people not only identify problems before they arise but are also capable of recognising potential issues. It is extremely difficult to be sufficiently forward-looking to identify problems that may threaten one's interests, but it is essential. Otherwise one would never know of the danger until it actually made itself felt. People with the capacity to examine short-, medium- and long-term trends, analyse the culture of their organisation and then predict the likely impact of economic and social trends on it, are using level 3 power. The Greek philosophers Socrates and Plato called such far-sightedness wisdom, or the ability to foresee what is likely to occur in the future and then consider whether the organisation's systems and structures are strong enough to meet the potential challenges.

Potential problems can be identified, and suitable action taken which most others would recognise as a benefit not a threat, even though they may not realise the implications. It is the ability to understand potential issues through an understanding of organisational norms that distinguishes level 3 power from the other two.

Power structure change

Certain changes, such as changes of leader and leadership style, a new acquisition, growth, contraction, reorganisation, singly or in combination, can alter the norms and values of the enterprise. As a consequence, the structure of relationships will alter. Changes in important cultural features will alter the power structure. If an organisation is driven largely by one person, then a change of leadership at the top will seriously affect the rest of the organisation. Those previously in favour may fall out of favour and vice versa. What is considered legitimate or illegitimate behaviour may change according to the style and philosophy of the new leader.

However, whether the changes are small or large, whatever is new must be consolidated into the fabric of the organisation. A programme of socialisation needs to be introduced to ensure that changes of power structure are accepted by a critical mass in the organisation (Figure 10.1). Socialisation is a process by which individuals accept changes of organisation and eventually consider them natural. Whatever discomfort the individual may have experienced, a well-managed programme of socialisation should enable them to feel more amenable and capable of interacting well in the new environment. The four stages of socialisation are: behaviour change, attitude change, internalisation and normative initial mass.

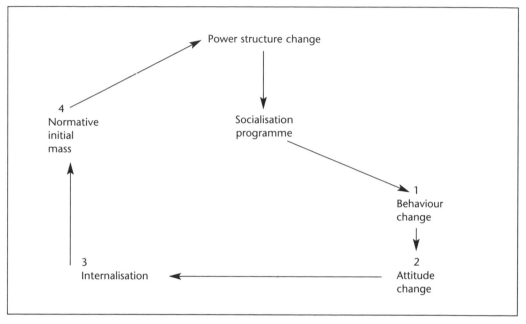

Figure 10.1 Assimilating power structure change into the organisation (*Source: Working in Organisations*, First Edition, 1987)

BEHAVIOUR CHANGE

Behaviour change means individuals doing something differently that could alter a previous acceptable behaviour pattern. If people discover for themselves that they can cope at work if they adopt new behaviours, then the links with the past are substantially weakened. Attempting to change people's behaviour patterns may mean introducing induction programmes that provide formal instruction in the new and desired practice and structures of the organisation. An induction programme could consist of training programmes lasting one day or more, or informal chats between individuals and a series of small groups, comprising those people whose acceptance of change is critical.

Alternatively, project groups or working parties could be formed, with a brief to examine better ways to introduce change. They should include people for and against the changes of power structure. The findings of these groups are likely to be of some value, not simply because a number of influential people are talking about how to improve the situation, but also because the groups also provide a sufficient critical mass to begin swaying opinion in the organisation.

Less ideally, coercion can be applied in addition to a cooperative approach. People may be allocated tasks they dislike or be harassed and punished for errors. Those who feel they cannot conform will probably leave the organisation. Those who adjust to the new power structures will probably feel an affinity with the organisation's new norms.

ATTITUDE CHANGE

A change of attitude will slowly come about as people adopt new behaviours and discard old practices. Either by support or by coercion, when people adopt different styles and approaches and use them for a while, their attitude towards the new power structure begins to alter. Constantly practising new behaviours reinforces the need to change one's views. If the behaviour change inputs are successful, then in time the resultant attitude changes are likely to be successful. However, one factor that can hinder attitude change even where the behavioural programme may be appropriate is dissonance.

Dissonance is the state of psychological discomfort we feel when we are subjected to two or more substantially different influences that we cannot accommodate. Most people experience mild forms of dissonance. A fashion-conscious person finds certain clothes attractive and asks a friend's opinion hoping for confirmation of their view, only to hear the friend criticise the garment. The individual is likely to experience a dissonance between acting on their own opinion and rejecting the clothes in compliance with the friend's opinion. A great deal will depend on the extent to which the person values the friend's views or even the friendship.

The highly successful play *Art* by Yasmina Reza (1996, London: Faber and Faber) centres on the dissonance experienced when one of the three protagonists purchases a 'white on white' painting for a huge sum of money, only to have his friend decry the value of the painting. The experience of cognitive dissonance can facilitate attitudinal change. A person may change his or her attitudes to meet the new behaviour that is the source of cognitive dissonance and thereby shake off the dissonance.

Managing change in organisations involves introducing change while attempting to reduce dissonance in others. Attempting to change behaviour by action groups, project groups or redesigning jobs can reduce dissonance. If people can do a new job or activity well, then they receive positive feedback about their skills and capabilities. Knowing that one can perform well relieves some of the anxieties associated with change. The more positive the feedback, the more the person will be sympathetic to the changes of power structure.

Simply allowing time for discussion, the opportunity for people to talk to each other and exchange views and experiences of recent problems, can be valuable. If the majority in a discussion group agree that the changes are valuable, then those not in favour of change will often alter their attitudes in line with the majority, or leave the group, or even the organisation. However, it is important to be fairly sure of the direction the discussion will take, for if the majority reject the changes, then the new power structure may collapse. To obtain the desired view, either the discussion in the group needs to be controlled, which can lead to further alienation if discovered, or the members of the group need to be vetted.

Finally, asking particular individuals publicly to commit their support to the new changes can be a powerful tool. Offering commitment publicly is synonymous with an admission of ownership that is difficult to disclaim. If a number of people openly commit themselves to a particular view or action, then it is impossible for them to say they are merely carrying out someone else's desires. In fact, they are likely to be seen as giving the orders rather than receiving them.

INTERNALISATION

Internalisation is the result of an individual having undergone behavioural change, attitude change and dissonance, and emerged from the experience with reshaped values, norms and practices. (Such personal change happens all the time. For example, a young student radical undertakes his or her first job in a merchant bank, buys a home and starts a family, soon becoming an upholder of the status quo even though the bank was once the target of early rebellion.) The person finds the changes acceptable and willingly attempts to promote further the changes of power structure. The person identifies with (has internalised) the new norms and practices.

NORMATIVE MASS

The phrase 'normative mass' is used to denote that majority of people who support the changes of power structure and regard the new norms and practices as an acceptable, natural part of the organisation's culture. Once such a critical mass of people has been reached, there is no further need to emphasise approaches to behaviour and attitude change: the change of power structure has been achieved.

Often people are not fully aware of the changes of attitude they have undergone, which becomes evident when they are confronted by someone who holds an 'outdated' view.

REALITY CHECK

JACK WELCH: MASTER OF POWER

Jack Welch has been hailed one of the greatest managers of his time. He is accredited with transforming General Electric, which was an already well run company, but considered by some as sluggish due to the numerous acquisitions that made it a major agglomerate. Welch was the outsider, 'the dark horse', whose family background and educational track record did not make him an 'Ivy Leaguer'. Equally, he had a reputation for abrasiveness, not as a matter of character but more due to the depth of passion he felt over issues of concern.

Even when he was just a rookie chief executive officer, he was already very sure of himself

and charismatic. Over the years, as his business success and reputation grew, he became more articulate, more visible, and even more charismatic, with an intensity that intimidated some and generated admiration in many others. His presence is so compelling that it would be easy to attribute his success to personal effectiveness, magnetism and personal power. He has those in no small measure, but viewing his 20 years as chief executive officer in retrospect, it is evident that he was also a master of identifying, capturing, and utilising the organisational levers of power. These levers are not so readily grasped, and are often left out of treatises on power in organisations.

Welch's view was that General Electric could not effectively grow due to its diverse interests. The aim was to become number one or number two in those areas which General Electric considered appropriate. Such discipline quickly enhanced his credibility with Wall Street and General Electric directors. It was that foundation of support that allowed Jack Welch to pursue innovative and radical change.

Early on, Welch replaced many top executives and built a new team, and restructured to take out layers of management. He also opened up communication in all directions by visiting management training programmes at Crotonville to create give-and-take sessions with managers, test new ideas, and preach his messages about what he expected. He introduced 360 degree feedback, and leveraged

what he later called the General Electric operating system, which included the planning and resource allocation processes, reviews of managerial talent (called Session C), and quarterly communication meetings to shape the company.

From this brief review, it is possible to see that Welch used directive and collaborative forms of power, with both structural and personal focus. His charisma and intelligence allowed him to drive many structural decisions that were not popular, as well as directly influencing many managers.

Source: Cohen, A.R. and Bradford, D.L. (2003), 'Power and influence', in Chowdhury, S. (Ed), *Organisation 21C*, New York: Financial Times: Prentice Hall.

Summary

Our analysis of power covered five different aspects.

POWER DEFINITION

Power is equated with the potential to do something, that is, a platform, a base from which to act. The application of power relies on the fact that an individual can (or cannot) muster sufficient resources to influence people to behave in particular ways. The concept of resources is crucial to the analysis of power. Resources can either be organisationally determined – that is, role-bound – or personally determined, that is, a feature of the individual's personality, skills and physical characteristics. The degree of dependency of others on these resources and the person wielding them will strongly influence how well the resources are deployed.

THE POWER LEVERS

The way an individual applies power is termed 'a power lever'. There are seven power levers:

- *Reward power*, the capacity to influence through the use of material and non-material rewards as well as through punishment. Reward and punishment can be applied to the individual, the team and the organisation.
- *Role power*, the application of control, principally through holding others to account and clarifying their responsibilities. Role power stems from the legitimate authority of an individual's position or role.

- **Personal power** involves the application of personal characteristics such as 'good looks', energy, charisma and flair, to influence the opinions, behaviours and attitudes of others.
- **Knowledge power** arises when an individual possesses specialist knowledge and skills that can give them at least the status of being more knowledgeable than others.
- **Network power** involves having access to individuals and groups inside and outside the organisation.
- **Information power** involves the ability to use information to support a particular point of view or alternatively to disprove other viewpoints.
- **Corporate memory power** involves gaining status and influence by having the capacity to recall events and circumstances from the past and thereby impress other people.

POWER LEVERS IN CONTEXT

The shared beliefs, attitudes and behaviours in any organisation mould its identity. Based on the analysis in Chapter 11 of how different organisational identities form, the four organisational contexts – creative, leverage, scope and cost discipline – were examined in terms of power lever application. The application of the seven power levers was explored in each of these four contexts. It was argued that not only is there a need to apply the power levers appropriately but also it is important to be selective as to which lever will be more suitable in any particular context. Further, the behaviours, values and attitudes of each individual need to adapt when moving from one organisational context to another if they are to be perceived as performing effectively in the new culture.

LEVELS OF POWER SOPHISTICATION

The application of power levers is related not only to the culture of organisation but also to the purpose of the individual power holder. Level 1 power concentrates on observable decisions and actions. Level 2 power emphasises the key issues, norms and values but does not necessarily concern itself with behaviour patterns. Level 3 power concentrates on latent issues and how an organisation's structure, systems and employees are capable of meeting future challenges.

POWER STRUCTURE CHANGE

To help people accept change, a four-stage socialisation programme is offered. Stage 1 involves inducing behaviour change in individuals so as to show that people can work just as well if they adopt new behaviours. If the new behaviours are found acceptable, then, at stage 2, attitude change will slowly come about as people adopt new behaviours and discard old practices. It is common for the individual to experience dissonance at this stage. At stage 3, the person emerges with, and tries to implement, reshaped values, norms and practices. This process is known as internalisation. A person at this stage is likely to find the changes acceptable and may willingly attempt to promote further changes of power structure. If a sufficient number of people undergo internalisation, then they are the critical mass (stage 4) who are likely to support the changes of power structure and wish to make any new norms and practices an acceptable part of the organisation's culture.

11 *Organisational Design*

The shape of an organisation, commonly known as its structure, is obvious to all those who encounter the enterprise. A new employee might regard structure as an imposed condition as soon as they are told to report to the manager. In a bureaucratic organisation most employees may associate structure with repetitive tasks and inflexible managers. In looser structures, innovative start ups or information technology companies, a career structure exists based on performance and flexibility, expertise and teamwork. Customers dealing with an organisation are faced by structure when they select goods to buy, or request a service to meet their needs. They may be seen by one employee, referred to a second, who it is thought can better satisfy their needs, and possibly charged for the service by a third. Every organisation operates within some sort of structure.

With the dramatic market shifts of the 1980s and 1990s a new form of organisational design emerged, based on integrated host organisation/supplier relationships. Instead of any organisation remaining self-sufficient, a series of relationships evolved between the host organisation (the client) and external suppliers who were considered to provide a service faster or more cost-effectively than the internal department of the host organisation. The traditional vertically integrated structure is now accompanied by a number of supplier relationships that can offer greater benefit through providing services previously undertaken in-house. Such a service is termed 'outsourcing'. Whether horizontally or vertically integrated, this form of organisational design provides value by harnessing resources to meet goals. Furthermore, the design affects the attitudes and performance of staff and management.

This chapter offers a broad-based analysis of organisational design. It looks at the three main influences on organisation: the factors that have produced the organisation's current shape, the various possible alternative structures and the degree to which outsourcing and needing to be flexible through the use of external suppliers now determine the profile and performance of the enterprise. The underlying assumption throughout this chapter is that organisational structure is a means to an end. It is the means by which strategy is pursued and resources harnessed so that desired outcomes (ends) can be achieved. A study of organisational design therefore allows for an analysis of the key considerations involved in creating appropriate structures that will in turn focus resources so as to achieve the desired ends.

Influences on design

Three primary influences give an organisation its shape. They are: determinants, configuration and the need to be flexible about the location of resources. Each of these factors affects the others so that it is the combination that provides the organisation with a shape, culture and identity that distinguish it from all others.

Determinants are forces that produce the current and future shape, size and structural pattern of the organisation. They act as a link between the past, present and future and strongly influence what changes are feasible. The seven key determinants are: size, history, geographic spread, the impact of technology (especially information technology), core competency assessment, habits and the effectiveness of management information systems. Configuration, or the formal role hierarchy, is the aspect of structure with which most managers are familiar. Who reports to whom and where each individual 'sits' are made clear by the organisation chart. We identify four organisational design blueprints for vertical working relationships: functional, product, divisional and matrix structures. Such structural alternatives fall into one school of thinking, namely the vertically integrated perspective, or the independent self-sufficient organisation, which emphasises drawing upon whatever services are needed in-house. However, over the last 15 years, another structural design format has developed in parallel to the vertically integrated perspective: the resource-flexible perspective, or that of outsourcing. Changes of structure within vertically integrated relationships, or in the pattern of outsourcing, will radically alter the pattern of decision-making, whether towards being more centralised or more decentralised. Changes in the design of the organisation will affect the way the enterprise functions. We look at how accountability will be exercised, and explore the role of customer satisfaction, employee morale and the impact on organisational culture.

The term accountability refers to the manner in which individuals exercise authority in their role and are judged according to the results of their endeavours. Changes in organisational design may require a different practice of accountability, so thought must be given to the individual's ability to cope with such changes as far as their accountability is concerned.

The relationship between determinants, configuration, and the impact of redesign is a dynamic one. It is important to recognise what determinants have produced the organisation's current shape and identity; what structural alternatives exist and how the maintenance or change of the present design can be enhanced through centralised or decentralised decision-making processes; and, finally, what effect any desired or undesired change will have on the organisation. On this basis, change and reorganisation are a never-ending process, interrupted by periods of stability (the length of which will vary from organisation to organisation). Changes of design introduced now will provide a basis for future reform and change. Today's reorganisation could become tomorrow's problem and hence a stimulus for further reconfiguration.

DETERMINANTS

Size

Size, as a determinant of organisational structure, has received substantial attention from researchers and management writers. The available evidence indicates that size is an important influence on the shape of an organisation. The following conclusions can be drawn:

- Larger organisations usually have more formal systems and procedures.
- Larger organisations tend to develop a network of complex inter-relations both internally and externally between a number of different groups.
- Larger organisations require extensive systems of coordination as much as of control.
- Size in itself does not determine either efficiency or quality of output.
- Size is an important determinant of employee attitudes (organisational culture).

As seen in Chapter 10, organisational culture refers to the attitudes, feelings and norms of behaviour shared by most in the organisation. Size strongly influences the structural design, which in turn helps to shape the attitudes and behavioural patterns exhibited by people in the organisation.

Historical background

The organisation's history, especially as regards issues such as ownership and control, will influence the present structure, culture and performance. Families who own and manage an organisation will probably maintain control over resources and distribution. Employees in the organisation may become too dependent on the key decision-makers in the organisation and hence find it difficult to think and act independently.

Large decentralised organisations may allow their divisions and subsidiaries substantial freedom. Such an organisation may be a combination of different cultures.

Morale and motivation among employees will be influenced by the management style of yesterday's as well as today's top management. A history of takeovers and constant change combined with an inability to define or control future direction can lead to despondency and low morale among the staff and management.

Mergers equally produce a particular structure–culture configuration. Historically, some mergers have involved a more aggressive organisation combining with a slower-moving, less energetic one. Yet, a decade later, employees may still identify with their original organisations. In fact, the procedures and structures of the two companies may never have been fully integrated, with the result that two separate systems are in operation. In such circumstances the organisation is unlikely to realise its full potential.

Irrespective of size and technology, the history of the organisation must be taken into account, especially if changes of structure, products or systems are contemplated. People's response to change is partly determined by history.

Geographic spread

The design of an organisation is further complicated by geographic location. An organisation whose units are widely dispersed may generate different structures and mechanisms for coordination and control from a similar-sized organisation operating in one area.

For example, sales managers attempting to meet customer needs may find it difficult to comply with head office requirements. The structure, systems and attitudes among employees vary according to market demands and local conditions. One motor manufacturing organisation in France recently transferred the whole manufacturing operation producing a high-status vehicle from a central location to the south of the country. The cost of such a move was enormous. Labour in the new locality was less militant, so that in the long run the transfer would result in greater stability of output. The move was made after systems and structures aimed at generating greater control and co-ordination of output on the original site had been unsuccessful.

The location of the profit centre is a key factor. Profit centre and cost centre may sometimes be difficult to distinguish but in theory they are substantially different concepts. Profit centres are points in the structure where the manager uses resources in order to achieve the profitability targets they have agreed to, or that have been set on their behalf. The purpose of a cost centre is to manage and control costs. A profit centre is also targeted to control costs. Although overlap does exist between the two, there is one crucial difference – the profit centre manager does not ask for permission to spend money or use resources but is held to account for the results achieved or not achieved. A cost centre manager asks for authority to spend money or use resources each time he wishes to do so. Thus locating the profit centre lower down the organisation promotes a decentralised or devolved style of decision making, even though the organisation may not be too geographically dispersed and its key managers for the country or even the region may be located in the same building. Alternatively, a cost-centre-based enterprise may be geographically spread out but its managers have limited discretion and require clearance to use resources, promoting a centralised decision-making pattern. Thus geographic spread, in combination with profit- or cost-centre modes of operating, strongly influences decision-making style. An added complication arises when a part of the organisation is run on profit-centre lines while another part adopts cost-centre controls, both in the context of extensive regional spread.

The impact of technology

Although management theory emerged from both a military and manufacturing background, little mention was made of technology until the late 1950s. One of the early researchers, Joan Woodward (1965), asserted that production technology is an important determinant of organisational structure. From her studies Woodward concluded that features such as length of line of command, spans of control, white or blue collar staff turnover and ratio of managers to operatives vary according to the technology of production in use. She hypothesised that efficient organisations are those whose structure fits the norm for their technology.

Research carried out in the 1960s and later by the Tavistock Institute in London found that changes of technology also involve substantial changes in work patterns, disrupting the relationships of those involved and sometimes reducing productivity. The phrase 'socio-technical systems' emerged to demonstrate that the structural design of the organisation must take into account the nature of the work and its impact on the people doing it.

Other researchers have taken quite different views. For example, the American researcher Charles Perrow (1976) suggested that several factors influence the impact of technology on the different aspects of organisational structure and goals. No single technology strongly affects the total structural configuration. The British researchers Derek Pugh and David Hickson (1977) concluded that a combination of technology and size is an important determinant of organisational structure. Alternatively, it was argued that there is little reliable evidence to show that structure is strongly affected by technology, as technology and structure are both multidimensional concepts and cannot be expected to relate in a simple manner.

The debate over the effect of technology on organisational design paled into insignificance with the information systems revolution of the 1990s. Epic in its scale, the impact of information systems on organisations is only slowly being understood. The emergence of the new information systems has not only altered the design of organisations, but has dramatically influenced patterns of interfacing and the nature of authority in the organisation. Information systems continuously create new possibilities that can benefit businesses and communities by providing multiple points of access to databases. The freedom that comes from being 'networked' is extensive. An individual can work from a local workstation and respond to various demands without being hampered by the systems and constraints of large organisations. E-mail, bulletin board-type infrastructure, the internet and intranets all allow interaction between remotely connected interests that would previously have had no contact with one another. Electronic communication has become an everyday affair. People no longer even need to acquire a computer, laptop or palm-held device. All they need is an internet address and with that they can log on at any station while having a cup of coffee. The internet café is almost as common as McDonald's. Further, becoming computer-literate is now easier than ever, with full computer facilities soon to be available through our television sets.

One consequence of readily accessible information is that status, authority and functional differentiation become blurred. Access to different data sources provides choice, making individuals less dependent on their bosses. And less dependence means less loyalty and a greater inclination to exercise mobility. If individuals feel uncomfortable where they work, through having greater access to information, they are more likely to 'move on', having identified other jobs and opportunities elsewhere.

On the other hand, new patterns of information access and sharing can equally create greater dependency. Maintaining databases is costly. As economies of scale apply to other parts of organisational life, so too do they apply to databases. It is cheaper and easier to manage databases on a centralised basis. By possessing critical information or by having privileged access to key databases, individuals in different parts of the organisation can increase their influence substantially. Hence the authority of the centre increases with greater surveillance and censorship. The organisational theorists of the 1960s and 1970s recognised such possibilities, and one in particular, John Child (1984), labelled the effect of this type of information management 're-centralisation' and predicted a negative and demotivating outcome.

Thus the potency of the information transformation was foreseen. Some commentators argued optimistically in terms of profit maximisation and improved cost control, while at the other end of the spectrum were those who saw a future of shrinking opportunities for employment as machines took over jobs as a new centralised elite emerged to control organisations. Whether in the past or now, technology was and is seen as a powerful determinant of organisational design. What, however, had not been foreseen was the extent to which decentralisation and centralisation would emerge simultaneously owing to the dynamics of the markets and each organisation's ability to respond through an assessment of its core competencies.

Core competencies

The progress of an organisation through its economic life cycle alters what differentiates the organisation from its competitors. The greater the competition, the more the downsizing, the faster the move to flatter organisations and the more flexible the organisation, the more each enterprise will be able to identify and develop competencies that distinguish it from others in the market place. Cost-effectiveness is critical. In the private sector, controlling costs is as much a route to profitability as increasing sales. In public service organisations, best-value criteria are now being applied by governments worldwide. Numerous theorists argue that best value concepts are more concerned with cost management than quality of service to the community. However, with developments in the market, what is core today may not be core tomorrow, so being disciplined over costs may be accompanied by a continuous search for alternative core competencies, varying from branding to exploiting new logistics channels. Elements of the organisation, divisions or strategic business units or even support functions such as human resources, can be moved, sold, purchased or outsourced and thus given to someone else to provide the service. With the maturing of markets and the vibrancy induced by ever greater innovation in information systems, core competency identification and leverage has taken on a dynamism that few expected. Flexibility of response to market needs and centralised control for the purposes of economies of scale have had a profound impact on organisational design.

Habits

Habits emerge from repeatedly undertaking the same activity. Repetition can turn a habit from a behaviour to a strongly held attitude. When habits become ingrained, they become difficult to break. Thus an organisation's habits can become as a powerful a determinant of behaviour as its structures. Rarely are habits strong enough to mould the design of an organisation. But by determining how structure is implemented and how new structures are resisted they may influence the way the organisation is managed.

The way people are moved in an organisation is often governed by habit. All organisations need to be sufficiently flexible to switch people from one role to another according to circumstances. Such moves do not necessarily involve promotion – they could involve simply transferring a person who is recognised as 'expert' to work in an area that requires their skills. Such mobility may mean redrawing lines of accountability. Each individual's responsibilities may need to be reassessed in the light of the new demands being made on the work unit in question. In a well-managed transfer, the incumbent and their new colleagues, subordinates and superiors have all been briefed as to the reasons for the move, accept the new arrangements and give their commitment and support to the new individual and their ways of working.

Organisations whose product life cycle is short and which therefore need to constantly re-examine their structures, or large organisations whose policy is to transfer managers to various parts of the organisation in order to develop them, may appoint key people on a contingency basis to manage particular projects or help line managers with a specific problem. Some organisations appoint internal consultants to help line managers with specific problems or even allocate them to certain departments or divisions for agreed periods of time. The internal consultant is a full-time employee of the organisation, but is not appointed to a particular position within an established hierarchy. Again, the introduction of new projects or consultants may stimulate a minor reorganisation within a specific part of the organisation.

Most British and American companies have long since dealt with overmanning by de-layering and redundancy. The danger now is not having sufficient slack in the system to respond to changed market conditions. In the continental European and Japanese economies, owing to laws of co-determination, labour legislation and social norms, many organisations still suffer from overmanning at shop floor and managerial levels. Consequently, people need to be found jobs, roles and titles. The problem is more acute in larger organisations that are well able to carry excess labour. Individuals who contribute little to the organisation still need to be accommodated in the short and, at times, longer term. Hence people who have to be placed somewhere in the organisation can strongly influence its structure. In European public service organisations, where security of employment is a predominant feature, role structures may be changed purely to accommodate particular people.

The manner of handling conflicts can also become a habit. Friction between managers can affect the way structure is used. Individuals who make a worthwhile contribution but find it difficult, or refuse to negotiate a reasonable working relationship with colleagues, subordinates or superiors, may be moved to another part of the organisation on a temporary or permanent basis. The organisation wishes to retain their services but does not know where to place them and so makes changes to a department's or division's structure.

People can be moved round the organisation for any of the above reasons, but also on an *ad hoc* basis that makes sense to the managers at the time. It may, for example, be felt that an individual merits on-the-job development. The most appropriate way to achieve that is to expose the individual to the activities of various functions, departments or divisions in the organisation. Or individuals may be moved round the organisation in response to expected demands, which never materialise. Senior management may also move individuals to different parts of the organisation because they do not know where best to place them. These individuals may not be sufficiently valued, but senior management does not wish to retire them or make them redundant. *Ad hoc*-ery in people placement can help to determine the level of trust in the structure.

The way an organisation manages its people can stimulate strong opinions among staff and management. People may feel that their organisation requires its managers to be competitive and assertive, and rewards high performers. As a result, the employees in the organisations may share certain attitudes, such as 'negotiate for what you want', 'you can always get what you want' or 'it does not matter how you get it – just get it'. Alternatively, people may feel that it is important to be supportive and helpful to one another, or more negative attitudes may predominate. The attitudes shared by people generate an organisational identity.

Every organisation has some sort of identity: something that makes it different from any other organisation even in the same industry. Newcomers to the organisation will quickly realise that they need to learn a number of unwritten dos and don'ts that form part of the organisation's culture. Cultures are the product of the combination of determinants and components of structure, that is, the impact that such a combination has had on the employees of the organisation. It is worth noting that the people and their attitudes become a determinant as well as an outcome of organisational design, in that the predominant attitudes and patterns of behaviour may strongly influence the manner in which a particular configuration is adopted.

Management Information Systems

Any organisation needs to ensure that the activities of its units, departments or divisions are well focused and coordinated. Focus and co-ordination can only be satisfactorily achieved by installing adequate communication and information systems. It follows that medium-sized and large organisations at least must develop an effective management information system. On this basis, the management information system becomes an additional determinant of how effectively organisational structure is used to improve the quality of decision making and problem solving. The technical challenges to developing an effective management information system have been largely overcome. Knowing what information is needed where, and winning acceptance of the system by the staff and management in the organisation, are now the issues. Problems to be resolved include:

- the resentment of countries or territories towards the centre,
- poor communication between those in the field and those in the centre, leading to misunderstandings concerning local market needs,

- mistrust of management,
- dynamic markets continuously promoting new needs which take time to recognise and
- lack of attention and investment to updating and growing databases, leading in turn to poor application of management information systems even when the necessary technical support is available.

Yet if such problems are overcome and an effective management information system is installed, the benefits that can be realised are immense. They include:

- *Improved responsiveness to market*. Improved market segmentation leading to a better understanding of customer needs allows for faster and more individually sensitive service.
- *Improved long-term planning*. Data for long-term planning are more accessible; sales data, for example, can be broken down by geographic area, or time taken for a range of products to be sold. In public service organisations, systematic recording and review systems provide important information on social activities, which senior management can easily use for long-term planning.
- *Improved managerial control*. Sometimes the speed with which information is provided may be more important than its accuracy. Management needs information quickly. An efficient management information system will provide management with the information it requires at the time it is needed and will be seen by those lower down the hierarchy as useful instead of yet another interference.
- *Reduction of conflict*. An information system that binds together everyone involved is likely to reduce the level of hostility between groups. First, all interested parties will know what is required of them and why. Second, individuals can plan their workload, for they know what type of information they have to gather and refer elsewhere. A common frustration at work is that people at all levels in the hierarchy may be asked to provide or find information without any prior warning. Sometimes they do not know where to begin to search and often they do not know why the information is needed. Working to a unified information system reduces such frustrations.
- *Improved motivation*. People who know what is expected of them can plan for future events and know that what they are doing is purposeful. They are motivated to work when they are more certain of their position. The more people know what is required of them, the less their need for continuous supervision.

CONFIGURATION

Depending on the organisation's mission and objectives and the combination of the seven determinants, the shape of the organisation will vary. As we have seen, changes in the market and the motivation and responsiveness of staff and management can result in considerable differences of design. However, as stated, design has two perspectives, the degree to which the organisation is integrated from top to bottom (vertically integrated) and the degree to which services or goods are provided by outside agents, thus making the location of resources flexible (resource-flexible). In this section, attention is given to examining the different ways of achieving effective critical integration.

It is uncontroversial to say that the allocation of responsibilities, the grouping of responsibilities, decision making, coordination and control are all fundamental to the continued operation of an organisation. What is hotly disputed is their combination, for from that derives the quality of an organisation's structure, which in turn affects both its day-to-day functioning and its long-term development. That quality is established by examining the configurational alternatives of the vertically integrated perspective.

In an organisation employing just a handful of people, there is little need to arrange people's roles and relationships formally. Individuals will conduct their business with each other face to face, especially the allocation of task responsibilities. Equally, the process of quality control is personalised as individuals are likely to praise or criticise one another's performance as the occasion arises.

The need to design formal structures increases with growing size and complexity. The formal structure refers to the manner in which people's roles are structured in a particular work unit. Management is required to control and coordinate the organisation's activities so as to achieve targets and outputs. The larger an organisation becomes, the more difficult it is for any one individual or group to control the activities of others. As direct control becomes problematic, so people pay greater attention to coordination.

John Child describes four models of role hierarchy designed to facilitate control and co-ordination:

- functional structure,
- product structure,
- divisional structure and
- matrix structure.

Functional structure

A functional structure is normally adopted once an organisation develops beyond a small size.

Usually activities are grouped into departments, with a department head, all contributing to a common mission. The work of these departments is coordinated through the appointment of a director, often supported by an executive committee or board (Figure 11.1).

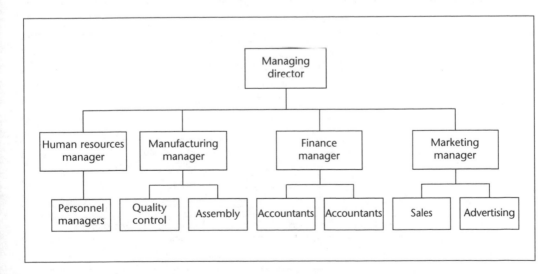

Figure 11.1 Functional structure (compiled by the authors)

If the organisation is not too large, there are advantages in employing a functional structure:

- There is less need for a large number of managers. Because of the relatively simple structure, coordination of activities is left to top managers.
- If experts are required to cope with certain problems, it is simpler and cheaper to request assistance from a single department. Grouping specialists together in one department increases the potential for the efficient utilisation of people across the whole organisation.
- There are easily recognised career paths, particularly for specialists. The specialist enjoys the satisfaction of working with colleagues with similar interests. From the organisation's point of view, managing such specialists is relatively simple. The opportunities for increased pay and status are already provided for in the career hierarchy and little else needs to be done to hire and retain specialists.

Problems occur with a functional structure once the organisation grows further or diversifies into new products, services or markets.

Product structure

With growth and expansion, the functional structure is unlikely to meet the demands placed on the organisation, especially the need to diversify into new products, markets or services. Managers operating under a functional structure are unlikely to be sufficiently motivated to make an impact with new products or services. Further, the market or service in question will not be the functional manager's prime area of responsibility and hence they will be unable to devote the necessary time and energy to managing its potential growth. In these circumstances a functional structure will be far less effective than a product structure.

The solution is to create a separate entity to manage each of the new processes. The product structure (Figure 11.2) is a more appropriate approach to grouping activities where an

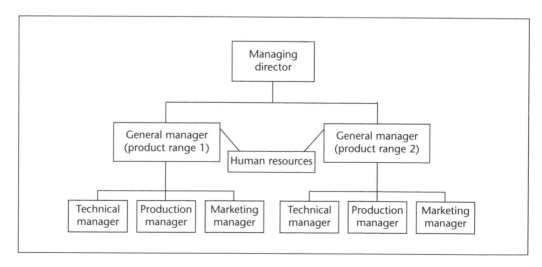

Figure 11.2 Product structure (compiled by the authors)

organisation has developed two or more ranges of products or types of service. Adopting a product structure will involve a duplication of services, as each range will have available its own specialists to service it. The advantage is that the greater the need for change in the products or services offered, the greater the pressure to respond to external changes by the managers and specialists of the organisation. Attention can be given to the needs of each product or service range according to market demands. With a greater number of specialists available to service a particular product or service, the demand for coordination and control will increase. Specialists will need to meet at regular intervals to examine the operational management and strategic development of each product range. Should, however, market demand for any product range dramatically decrease, then the organisation will be faced with the problem of whether or not to maintain a superfluous workforce.

Switching from a functional to product structure makes sense in growth market conditions. Problems arise when the market stabilises or declines, leaving the organisation no longer sufficiently flexible to find alternative employment for its line managers and staff specialists.

Divisional structure

Divisionalisation involves splitting the organisation into separate and sometimes virtually autonomous units where each division provides a total service for any one market. In effect, a number of smaller units, called 'divisions', are created within the organisation (Figure 11.3). Each division has at its head a divisional director, or managing director or chief executive officer. Below the divisional directors may be functional, product or even matrix structures. Each division may well have a different structure. An outcrop of divisionalisation is a structure concentrated around strategic business units, in which the relationship between the centre and the strategic business units is critically important. The fundamental difference between a divisional structure and one based on strategic business units is that the strategic business unit is treated more as a separate business entity, with profit-centre accountability.

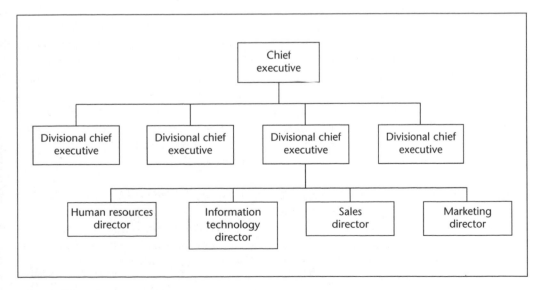

Figure 11.3 Divisional structure (compiled by the authors)

A divisional structure enjoys a number of advantages:

- Cost and profit issues are the direct responsibility of the divisional directors. The overall director of the organisation (that is, the chief executive) is not concerned with the day-to-day finances or the immediate operational demands of the division.
- The main function of the centre is identifying and implementing strategy, appraisal of policies and projects, and financial control. Planning for the future would be impossible if too many people become involved. Only the divisional directors and possibly certain corporate specialists, in conjunction with the chief executive of the organisation, are involved in considering future developments. Functions such as information technology, legal and human resources are likely to be located at the centre for reasons of economies of scale.
- Corporate and future planning would be committed to the development of the organisation as a whole rather than any individual division. It is inappropriate to identify only with the development of any one division unless that is of advantage to the whole group. Hence it is necessary to have an independently minded corporate structure above the divisional structures.
- A division can respond more freely to particular needs in certain local areas. Self-contained units operating within particular geographic localities or specific channels to market can meet emerging requirements, bearing in mind the budgetary constraints under which they operate.

Matrix structure

Matrix structure management is needed when an organisation has developed a somewhat unresponsive and inflexible culture, possibly through ever-increasing growth leading to a product structure or divisionalisation, but finds that various elements of its routine operations need to be integrated more closely. Matrix management is a way of generating greater flexibility in day-to-day activity and more market responsive attitudes among staff and managers (Figure 11.4).

Matrix management arose from the development of the aerospace industry in the USA in the 1960s. The US government had begun to demand that numerous companies work on projects that required substantial coordination and intricate inter-relationships within and between firms. Countless management and organisation consultants were hired to develop human relations training and form organisations into more closely-knit teams, thereby promoting a more open climate within the enterprise. It was recognised that serving two masters, each with quite different objectives and values, led to a number of dilemmas within the operating entity and a substantial degree of personal stress for the individuals concerned. Ralph Kingdon defined matrix management as:

> *An attempt to combine the advantages of functional specialisation with those of project management recognising that lateral negotiated relationships, complementary to superior-subordinate authority relationships, are essential for the performance of highly complex and interdependent technical tasks and for the promotion of organisational adaptiveness and flexibility. The key problem is to derive ways of implementing such relationships and reconciling them with the hierarchical order.*

Kingdon, D.R. (1973), *Matrix organisation: managing information technologies*, Tavistock, p 1.

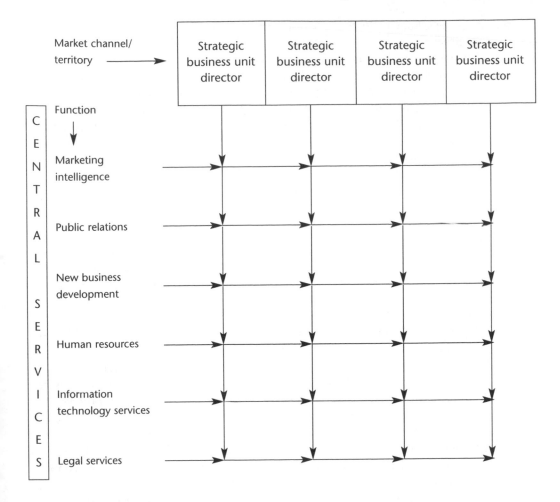

Figure 11.4 Matrix structure (compiled by the authors)

For some, the matrix management approach may seem paradoxical. On the one hand, people require control and coordination in order to work together on quite complex tasks. On the other hand, control can no longer be applied through hierarchical authority. In an attempt to increase coordination at the expense of control, certain private and public service organisations have introduced an additional resource to the structure – consultants. Their purpose is to respond to requests for help from people at any level in any organisational unit, if the problem area in question lies within their field of competence.

Whether consultants are used or not, the distinction between a matrix organisation, a complex organisation and a 'badly' organised and run organisation has more to do with the skills and attitudes of management and staff than the presence or absence of rules and regulations. Most organisations operate in a matrix manner, but it is the degree of recognition given to matrix development by senior management that is crucial. If higher-level management is attempting to impose an authority structure on what is essentially a matrix pattern of work relationships, then the matrix style will predominate but work performance will be poor. Subversive activity is likely to emerge at lower levels. Senior management will feel that its plans are being sabotaged by those beneath them and will attempt to introduce further controls. Eventually, even middle management will only pay lip service to procedures imposed from above. People at lower organisational levels will continue to inter-relate on a colleague basis in order to meet the requirements of their everyday tasks. The procedures imposed from above will be seen as hindrances to be bypassed. A substantial amount of time will be lost as senior management hold meetings to find ways of regaining control, while those at lower levels will be meeting to look for ways of continuing their work without management interference. In addition to loss of time, trust between employees at different organisational levels will diminish and conflict may become the most common form of interaction. Effective matrix organisations are as much a sign of the maturity of the people in the organisation as they are a type of organisational structure.

Innocence and ideal

The four structures just described – functional, product, divisional and matrix – emerged between the 1940s and the 1970s, driven by a belief that an ideal organisational format exists. The quest was based on the view that the purpose of structure was to harness resources so as to achieve particular goals and targets, assuming that the reason for doing so is clear to everyone in the organisation. The concept of clarity was extended from purpose and direction to role relationships in the organisation. Lyndall F. Urwick (1947) based his ideas of organisational design on the work of early management thinkers Henri Fayol, Chester Barnard and Mary Parker Follett, who were writing in the last decade of the nineteenth century and the first two decades of the twentieth century. Urwick concluded that logic and simplicity formed the basis for effective use of structures. The clearer the goals of the organisation, the more directly the structure is linked to those goals so that its logic is evident to those pursuing those goals and the simpler the structure, the more efficiently and effectively the goals will be achieved. He argued also that logic and simplicity motivate people strongly. Urwick felt that complexity generated 'bureaucracy' in that the more complex the organisation, the greater the need for clearer lines of authority and accountability, with each role needing formally specified areas of activity. Such thinking led to the popular adoption of job descriptions. Thus with greater specialisation or greater complexity, the more tightly defined the role, the greater the restriction on choice. In this way, clarity of purpose, linked to logical structure, brought about better decision making.

In the 1960s, thinkers such as the businessman Sir Geoffrey Vickers and John Child of the then Aston University Organisations Research Team, while acknowledging the clarity argument, were equally concerned with the issue of diversification. The need for clarity, and the procedural conformity that resulted from it for the purposes of ease of communication, monitoring and control, while allowing sufficient margin for flexible response to market changes, were re-examined in the context of the centralisation/decentralisation debate. John Child summarised the arguments in favour of each option as follows:

For centralisation
- Simplicity of coordination will occur if decisions are made at one point or among a small group.
- Senior management will have a broader perspective on developments in the organisation and maintain conformity of already established policies. They are better able to adjust to new developments in order to provide for the interests of the organisation. This will

avoid loss of control to people at lower levels who would be making decisions that are optimal for their group or unit but less than optimal for the organisation as a whole.

- Centralisation of control and procedures provides a way of helping the various functional areas in the organisation – research and development, information technology, human resources and finance – to maintain an appropriate balance. This is achieved by centralising decisions on resource allocation, functional policies, targets and human resource matters.

- Centralisation can reduce managerial overheads by avoiding duplication of activities or resources if similar activities are being carried out independently in divisions or sub-units.

- Because the segmentation of management to the lower levels of the organisation is prevented, there is greater justification for employing specialists who can provide support to the various functions and levels in the organisation. Expenditure on this service would be difficult to account for in a decentralised system, as there could be substantial duplication of specialist support resources.

- It is commonly held that the top managers have proved themselves by the time they reach a senior position. Although a point in favour of centralisation, there is a danger that management can adopt the attitude that because they are at the top, they are right.

- Crises often require strong leadership. Centralising power and control of procedures focuses on a key person or group, which facilitates speedy decision making and control over communication and co-ordination.

For decentralisation

- Delegation can reduce the amount of stress experienced by senior management, especially in large, complex organisations. It is well understood that when senior management becomes overloaded, then control tends to diminish. Delegation can remove some of the burden from senior management, allowing it to spend more time on policy issues and long-term planning. Delegation is not simply a decision by senior management to increase the number of decision-making tasks of managers at lower levels. It involves inviting other members of the management hierarchy to participate in decisions that senior management used to make.

- It had long been held by behavioural scientists that employee motivation improves with the degree of discretion and control they can apply to their work. The opportunity to make decisions and be involved can help to provide personal satisfaction and commitment for the individual. An assumption is made that with greater personal freedom, individual goals will broadly be in line with those of the company. Where power is delegated power, personal and corporate goals are more likely to match, but delegation can be severely tested where people's work is independent of each other. The problem then is to motivate people sufficiently to coordinate their activities without too much central direction.

- Organisations that are too large, or growing, need managers who can cope with uncertainty because of the number of complex tasks that need to be performed. It was considered impossible for one person or small groups of people to supervise such complex activities simultaneously. Delegation, therefore, was recognised as a contribution to the development of management by widening the on-the-job skills of managers and hence developing a number of people capable of undertaking senior management roles.

- Delegation generally allows for greater flexibility by providing for less rigid responses to change at operational levels in the organisation. Decisions do not have to be referred up the hierarchy.
- By establishing relatively independent units in an organisation where middle management are held accountable for operations, delegation can result in better controls and performance measurements. Separate spheres of responsibility can be identified and control systems applied to these units in order to provide appropriate feedback to higher management. Costs can be allocated to specific operations, facilitating accountability to the relevant people or units. Greater responsibility and self-direction are required of people in such circumstances.

Child and the theorists of the day recognised that a simple decision to centralise or decentralise would be impossible, for choices can only be made in the light of specific conditions and circumstances. These conditions will vary according to:

- the overall purpose of the organisation,
- the capacity of senior management to conceive a new type of organisation,
- the skills and attitudes of staff and middle management,
- the overall size, divisional size (if applicable) and geographic dispersion of the organisation,
- the efficiency and accuracy of the organisation's planning, control and information systems,
- the time constraints that apply to decisions made in the field or within the organisation. For example, is it appropriate for a decision to be made on the spot based on professional judgement, or is there time for a decision to be referred upwards to senior management?
- the degree to which subordinates can accept, and are motivated by, making their own decisions and
- conditions external to the organisation that will strongly influence its operation, such as government requirements, trade union objectives and local community conditions.

Urwick's straightforward view of organisations could not last. New realities called for new thinking. Where the world in which organisations operate is constantly changing, a level of personal influence is required that will make itself felt whatever the context, so that leadership – and with it organisational politics – emerges as a key issue. The era of the search for clarity, and the innocence that goes hand in hand with simplicity, has given way to one demanding a flexibility in the location and utilisation of resources that can sometimes resemble fragmentation.

RESOURCE-FLEXIBLE PERSPECTIVE

The impact of information technology, the maturing of many of the post World War II markets and the consequent need to control costs so as to compete on price, while simultaneously improving product or service quality, allows organisations to use a variety of approaches to maintain their competitiveness. The ever-growing demand for differentiation has raised an important question: why keep all resources in house? Why not concentrate on those activities that the organisation performs expertly and buy the other necessary services from someone else? Thus emerged the idea of outsourcing, based on the understanding that not all processes have to be owned by, and located in, the organisation.

Outsourcing is nothing new. The Romans outsourced the responsibility for tax collection to private enterprise. Governments in Victorian Britain outsourced the responsibility for prison management and refuse collection, just as today. For centuries enterprises have fluctuated between 'hierarchical governance' – maintaining direct control over all the resources needed – and 'market governance' – winning the best possible deal for any service or product from those most proficient at providing it.

The main reasons for outsourcing appear to be to achieve economies of scale and to gain strategic advantage based on core competencies. Many commentators maintain that western companies outsource primarily to save on overheads and introduce short-term cost savings. This argument has been applied above all to information technology, where continuous innovation has made it difficult for small and medium-sized enterprises to invest constantly in expensive hardware and software. Not surprisingly, the markets are awash with hardware and software suppliers, many of whom disappear as quickly as they came. Outsourcing to save cost is in fact a trade-off between production costs and monitoring costs: is it cheaper and more convenient to keep the relevant resources in-house? For example, whilst AT&T, British Telecom's global rival, was boasting about its fibre optic cable-laying capabilities to visitors to AT&T's Bell Laboratories in New Jersey, British Telecom took the decision to outsource the laying of its fibre optic cables along the floor of the Atlantic. Top executives at British Telecom no longer saw the installation of fibre optic cables as a core activity.

The concept of strategic outsourcing arises from the debate on core competencies. Deciding what is critical to the organisation and what can be passed to someone else has emerged as an important issue. With such a question comes the realisation that what is 'core' today may not be 'core' tomorrow. Furthermore, managing outsourcing relationships itself becomes a core skill of the organisation. Outsourcing as a lever of strategic re-positioning has now become so important that a recent study at Cranfield School of Management identified it as an item for boardroom debate. The strategic re-positioning of the organisation could involve harnessing the best-in-class strengths of key suppliers in order to achieve a competitive edge. Another motive for outsourcing may be a desire to improve incentives in the organisation by benchmarking against external standards of excellence. Whatever the reason for outsourcing, its purpose is to improve the position of the enterprise in the value chain by deploying its existing skills more effectively.

The advent of outsourcing has altered the nature of organisational design. The original four vertically integrative structures still survive in various forms, but with a management concerned as much with clarity of role relationships, accountabilities and responsibilities, as with the challenge of continuous change. Thus, the vertically integrative structures are managed hand in hand with a range of outsourced design features. The outsourcing arrangements vary according to the nature of the contract. Where the need for control is low and the need for flexibility is high between the host organisation and its suppliers, short-term contracts are useful, but where the opposite occurs, full ownership may be necessary. In between lie a myriad of alternative designs. The pros and cons of some of them are set out below:

- *Preferred, best-in-class supplier*. By far the most popular outsourcing arrangement in the USA and the UK is the single-supplier relationship, which is predicted to continue well into the future. The reason seems to be that it takes considerable time for the partners to become acquainted with, and develop a respect for, each other. No matter how tightly drawn the outsource contract, factors like understanding each other's culture, the leadership style of each organisation and how each reacts to unexpected changes in the contract, can make or break the relationship. Having evolved a competence in mutual understanding and collaboration, neither party is willing to contemplate a change of partner. The fourth of W. Edwards Deming's fourteen points to achieve total quality states: 'End the practice of awarding business on the basis of price alone. Instead require other meaningful measures of quality beyond price. Work to minimise total cost not just initial cost. Move towards a single supplier for any one item on a long-term relation of loyalty and trust.' (Bank, J. (2000), *The Essence of Total Quality Management*, Financial Times: Prentice Hall/Pearson Education, p 90).

- *Alliance arrangements* exist when a close relationship between client and provider is needed. Depending on the nature of the service and the competitive context, the relationship could vary from highly detailed contracts with specific targets to more flexible arrangements or even loose strategic initiatives. The more tightly defined the contract, the less need there is for positive relationships and high-quality communication between the parties. The looser the relationship, the greater the attention that needs to be paid to information-sharing and the attitudes of the people involved towards each other. Although looser arrangements tend to be viewed by theoreticians as more motivating, the evidence suggests that the tightly defined contract is preferred as being easier to manage.

- *The virtual organisation* involves managing relationships with multiple vendors and networks, where 'best-breed' services are required, all of whom possess different 'world class' capabilities. The host organisation could hand over a considerable number of its internal services and functions and become almost an agency drawing together varying skills in the market place and then, through the strength of its brand, marketing the products or services as if it were the manufacturer or service provider. Benetton falls into this category. So too would Marks & Spencer. Arrangements along these lines are the norm in the information and electronics industries and becoming the norm in financial services. Companies enter into such joint ventures for a variety of reasons, including making the most of the partners' respective strengths, locating financial support in places other than the markets or banks, the need to stay ahead of the competition and the fact that managing an extensive array of contracts has now become an important skill, irrespective of the origins of the organisation. The virtual organisation is not a small, discrete, almost anonymous entity, but an array of relationships focused on a central point.

- *Spin-offs*. In an attempt to make an internally provided service more competitive, some organisations expose it to market forces as a separately managed profit centre. In the information technology sector spin-offs have become commonplace, the outstanding example being EDS, which was previously the information technology department of General Motors. Similarly, Mercedes, now known as the Daimler Chrysler Group, undertook a joint venture with its internal information technology function to create Debis, a global provider of information technology, telecoms and financial services. Both EDS and Debis are now world leaders in information technology and related services. The only valid reason for a spin-off joint venture is that non-core activities have developed to a point where they can be turned into a profitable business.

- *Consortia and shared services*. One form of strategic alliance is consortia-based out-sourcing, popularly known as sourced service consortia. This is where a service such as information technology is outsourced and provided to the partners in the consortium. The savings are considerable as one central source provides a service to a number of organisations. However, consortia can be difficult to manage. Transparency between the partners is fundamental to making consortia arrangements work effectively. Information must be shared, but at the same time mechanisms must be in place that protect each partner's data. Philips, the Dutch electronics company, set up a joint venture, B.S. Origin, with BSO Beheer, the Dutch software enterprise. The move was so successful that other software providers were attracted to join the partnership thus extending the original joint venture into a sourced service consortia-based entity.
- *Information systems hosting*. The information technology revolution has spawned a market that only began to emerge in 1999; that of applications hosting. Apart from its other numerous advantages, the internet allows organisations to free themselves from the burden of purchasing and maintaining expensive computer systems by licensing access to information systems. Services such as accounting, personnel and payroll systems can now be rented on a fee-per-month basis. They can be tailored to meet the needs of a single organisation or an industry sector or be generically available. Access through the Web allows for services to be centralised at a single source, like electricity or gas, with each individual or organisation paying for usage without having to invest in the systems. These niche applications providers are commonly termed application service providers and offer Web hosting, e-commerce and network integration services. The options range from handing over complete information technology operations to a pay-as-you-go agreement for any one or more applications.

Advantages and disadvantages

As with the vertically integrated design perspective, the resource-flexible approach also presents opportunities and dangers.

Among the opportunities are:

- to concentrate on particular specialisms,
- to focus on achieving key strategic objectives,
- to improve the management of costs,
- to develop greater flexibility in responding to changing market conditions,
- to reduce the need for investment in expensive and rapidly changing technology,
- to reduce product or process design cycle times,
- to gain advantage by exploiting the skills of specialist suppliers, particularly in information technology and
- to improve cash flow by transforming fixed costs into variable costs. The organisation no longer has to own and maintain functions or particular information technology services – with someone else providing the service, the costs will vary according to usage or the specifics of the contract.

Possible dangers include:

- over-dependence on outside suppliers, thus losing both price and knowledge advantages,

- overlooking the hidden costs of any outsourced relationship that again means loss of the cost advantage,
- losing control of critical functions or processes,
- loss of morale of staff, and a management concerned about their future,
- loss of critical skills, and the prospect that in the medium to long term the wrong skills will be hired,
- loss of corporate memory and
- the prospect of having to manage relationships with a supplier that are turning, or have turned, sour.

Impact of redesign

Redefining organisational boundaries can involve financial and social gains and costs. In some circumstances the costs are transitory and can be mitigated through retraining, redeployment or merger, while the gains may be extensive and long-lasting. In other situations the costs may so outstrip the gains that the redesign is viewed as a damaging failure. In this section we discuss the impact of redesign in three important areas: accountability, customer satisfaction and morale and the social contract between employer and employee.

ACCOUNTABILITY

Balancing the accountabilities and responsibilities is important in the efficient operation of any of the vertically integrated structures. Responsibilities refer to the pursuit of an activity or initiative. Any individual may be responsible for a task, such as negotiating new supplier relationships in order to gain benefit from outsourcing or rethinking the brand portfolio of the company. On the other hand, being held accountable relates to being judged on the results of that activity: have the objectives been reached within the specified costs and time and to the level of the revenue expected? Only being held responsible is an opportunity to enjoy oneself, as new initiatives can be pursued or different approaches can be tried out, but with no real repercussions if all goes wrong. Being held accountable is demanding, especially if the individual has no direct responsibilities, as the person is being judged without necessarily having control over activities, projects or project members. Downsizing or delayering, creating an ever greater number of outsourcing relationships or moving the organisation closer to a matrix style, extends spans of control and can lead to increased responsibility rather than accountability. Flattening the organisation encourages the emergence of self-managed teams or just larger teams, with a greater need to exercise discretion. Flatter structures tend to strengthen responsibility, with less emphasis on accountabilities. The organisation can appear as a 'weave' of straight and dotted line relationships, in which one person (team leader, manager) is accountable for a greater number of people but relies on personal relationships rather than formal authority. Especially with employees possessing specialist skills who are therefore marketable, the manager uses personal influence and the building of trust. Where trust and openness have been established, the impact of the team can be powerful. However, if the team members have little desire to cooperate, they can 'outsmart' even an effective manager, resulting in poor relationships and deteriorating team performance. In summary, emphasising responsibilities at the expense of team skills and attitudes towards being held accountable, encourages immaturity and cynicism.

Allowing an imbalance in favour of responsibilities without clarifying roles and role bound-aries is likely to produce a climate in which the boss is blamed for 'everything'. Encouraging immature behaviour allows people to avoid feeling accountable for their own actions. So someone else must be to blame. Over-reliance on personal influence as compensation for ill-balanced accountabilities and responsibilities generates petulance.

CUSTOMER SATISFACTION

Re-drawing organisational boundaries is likely to affect one key relationship, namely that with the customer. A change to outsourcing can give rise to considerable customer dissatis-faction. A recent study at Cranfield School of Management found that, of a sample of over 740 companies, only 69 exhibited outsourcing best practice (Kakabadse, A. and Kakabadse, N. (2002), *Smart sourcing: international best practice*, Basingstoke: Palgrave). Most senior man-agers were not adequately focused on their goals, did not clearly communicate what was required of staff and management and did not balance the accountabilities and responsibil-ities in people's jobs, or at least show them where imbalance could be avoided. The conclusion was that focusing on organisational goals, consistently communicating how these goals are to be achieved and providing opportunities for staff and management to improve their skills, can reduce or eradicate the following areas of customer dissatisfaction:

- unrealistic expectations,
- unsatisfactory delivery,
- uncooperative supplier behaviour and
- Increases in costs.

As can be seen, any redesign needs to take account of the degree to which staff and man-agement reconsider how to manage their external relationships or be trained in new skills. The success of redesign can be ascertained by the degree of customer satisfaction that emerges.

MORALE AND THE SOCIAL CONTRACT

As highlighted in Chapter 1, research shows that downsizing, particularly where responsi-bility for certain activities is transferred to outside parties, can undermine employee loyalty. Just as the introduction of new skills and work practices are one of the benefits of outsourc-ing, so the disadvantage is that staff feel secondary to profit and improved stock prices. Emphasising shareholder value to the detriment of internal stakeholders erodes the social contract between the employee and the organisation (also see Chapter 3 on the new psy-chological contract). Feelings of belonging are replaced by short- to medium-term contracts specifying accountabilities, responsibilities and results. Operational improvements may be outweighed by a loss of loyalty and respect for management, making the flattened organi-sation difficult to manage. Insecurity reduces self-esteem, participation in the organisation's affairs and indeed overall effectiveness. The counter-argument is that employees become more self-reliant and career-resilient and can exercise greater discretion not only in terms of operational decisions but equally with advances in information technology or in working from home. For the individual, having more control over one's life, especially the home/work interface, allows them to determine their own leisure time. A Cranfield School of Management study on outsourcing suggests that in future the employment conditions for staff and management disrupted by outsourcing are unlikely to change. In effect, their

REALITY CHECK

A NEW TYPE OF STRUCTURE AT ST LUKE'S ADVERTISING AGENCY

Andy Law and the small team of employees who were running the London office of Chiat/Day were troubled to hear one day in 1995, that their advertising agency was sold to Omnicom. They decided collectively to disassociate themselves from this corporate deal and to start up their own advertising agency – St Luke's – as a new way of working together. They wanted to form a collective or cooperative in which each member of the team was valued for his or her talents as an equal. The equality of membership was reflected in the way ownership of the agency was structured through an employee share option scheme called QWEST (Qualifying Employee Share Ownership Trust). As Andy Law recounted in his book *Open Minds* (1998) charting the experiment, 'We formed a small group to devise a way to distribute the shares to everyone in proportion to their worth. But we found it very difficult to sort out why one person should be worth more than another.' (Law, A. *Open minds*, (1998), London: Orion in the UK; the same book was titled *Creative Company*, New York: Wiley in the USA). At first Andy Law was declared the only exception; as he was older than the others and the founder of the new agency, he was given a greater share – ten per cent – in the ownership to reflect this. But, on thinking about it, he gave up the ten per cent to be just like the other members of the team.

'I never owned the (original) company in the first place . . .' Law said. 'Taking a disproportionate share would have been theft of the sweat equity of everyone else. And this sweat equity was the very thing I was careful to unite because it was the honest contribution of the human capital in the workplace. It was the key to our specialness and difference. We have forced ourselves to take a different outlook on entrepreneurial ownership and constitutionally removed greed from the business. That I can tell you is our liberating force' (p 6).

They based their business in an old toffee factory near London's Euston station and soon established a world-reputation for running an advertising business differently. Instead of offices, staff 'hot-desked'; they set up 'brand rooms' and called receptionists 'hubsters'.

His mission to change things has been there from the start of St Luke's. As he put it: 'St Luke's is a small company. Noisy, fascinating, confusing, chaotic, successful and of course creative, but when all's said and done, small. But then our size (as I write, no more than 150 people in the UK, Sweden, India and France) has never deterred us from our mission (which we have held dear since we were just 30 people). Through the art of creativity, we wanted to put personal growth and development ahead of business growth and development and somewhere along the way invent a role for business as a force for good which seeks to add value to life rather than the bottom line' (Law, A. (2003), *Experiment at work*, London: Profile Books, p 16).

Eight years later, reflecting on St Luke's achievements as a new way of working, Law (2003) wrote in his new book, *Experiment at work*, 'Our contract of employment asserts the need to remain cooperative by outlawing fear, greed and ego, the unholy trinity that serves to foster selfishness in business. The teamwork structure institutionalises teamwork by fixing three or four participative meetings with everyone involved in the project – including the customer' (pp 43–44).

When challenged by an interviewer if this was possible – to ban fear, greed and ego –

since selfishness was at the root of human nature, Law said: 'You'd be laughed at (at St Luke's) if you talked about yourself as the greatest thing since sliced bread; you'd get severely criticised if you frightened people, and we cannot be greedy, there's no mechanism here for people to make excessive funds out of someone else' (Mendoza, M. (2003), 'Uncharted waters', *RSA Journal*, (February), p 41).

Law sees his organisation as an experiment against traditional capitalism. 'Advertising is at the apex of capitalism, it's the injection of steroids into its system. Isn't this where you want to be (if you want to change things)... on the inside?' (p 41). This radical structure with its emphasis on personal responsibility and exposure, its continually changing systems, creative demands and transparency, earned the cooperative the sobriquet of 'the most frightening company on earth' (Coutu, D. (2002), 'How resilience works' *Harvard Business Review*, (September–October), pp 49–50).

In March 2003 Andy Law resigned as chief executive officer of St Luke's and his deputy

Kate Stanners also resigned. Like many advertising agencies since 11 September, St Luke's had posted a pre-tax loss for 2001. Besides business, it had lost major clients such as IKEA, HSBC and BSkyB. According to the advertising industry magazine Campaign, there was a serious disagreement on the direction of the company between Law and Stammer and two managing directors he tried to make redundant. The two men, Neil Henderson, the accounts managing director and Phil Teer, the planning managing director, appealed to the members of the cooperative and kept their jobs. It must have been a case of irreconcilable differences between top members of the leadership. With Andy Law, the founder, spokesperson and charismatic leader of St Luke's gone, some observers are writing the obituary of the award-winning advertising agency. But others are backing the new leadership and the strategic plan they revealed on the seventh anniversary of the cooperative in the autumn of 2002.

(Rogers, D. (2003), 'Getting away from it all', *Financial Times, Creative Business*, (11 March), pp 8–9)

existing contract is simply taken over by someone else. Thus, although the morale of both staff and management drops when faced with the prospect of outsourcing, it is predicted that the fall will not be great. Keeping the fabric of the organisation together and preserving its positive habits is a worthwhile objective.

Summary

INFLUENCES ON DESIGN

Organisational design can be viewed from two perspectives. The traditional or 'vertically integrated' perspective is based on hierarchy. The growing practice of outsourcing processes, functions and activities to external suppliers represents an alternative, 'resource-flexible' perspective.

DETERMINANTS

Organisational design is influenced by seven 'determinants': size of organisation, historical background, geographic spread, impact of technology, core competencies, habits and management information systems.

CONFIGURATION

Four different structural blueprints fall within the vertically integrated perspective. These are functional, product, divisional and matrix structures.

Innocence and ideal

The period from the 1940s to the 1970s saw a search for the ideal organisational design, based on the assumption that clarifying people's roles and their accountabilities and responsibilities would ensure that staff and management in the organisation would know what to do according to specified standards. The same thinking applied in determining whether the organisation should be more centralised or decentralised.

RESOURCE FLEXIBLE PERSPECTIVE

When markets became more volatile, however, it was realised that the resources the organisation needs do not have to be located within the enterprise. Selected processes, functions and activities can be transferred to an external supplier offering a better quality of service at a lower cost than could be achieved internally. Possible outsourcing relationships include single-supplier relationships, alliance arrangements, the virtual organisation, spin-offs, consortia relationships and information systems hosting. As with the vertically integrated perspective, there are advantages and disadvantages to adopting any one or more of these differing relationships and arrangements.

IMPACT OF REDESIGN

Redesigning organisations affects the way accountabilities are managed, the morale and tenure expectations of staff and management, and customer satisfaction. Increased attention to cost reduction and outsourcing tends to weaken the 'social contract' between the organisation and its employees. As people become more 'expendable', so loyalty towards the organisation is reduced, irrespective of the blueprint of its structure.

12 *Governance*

Was the collapse of the US energy giant Enron, resulting in the accusation against Andersons (Enron's auditors), and the refusal of the American President to allow the federal prosecutor to pursue a line of enquiry exploring the relationship of George W. Bush with Enron, all attributable to poor governance? As questioned in Chapter 2, did the Enron way of doing things – their culture – and the intricate, interwoven network of relationships in Wall Street also contribute to such a dramatic collapse?

Percy Barnevick, charismatic founder and former Chairman of ABB, and Göran Lundahl, chief executive officer of ABB, agreed in March 2002 to return more than half of the controversial £98 million pension and severance benefits they each received on retiring from the Swiss-Swedish engineering group (Brown-Humes and Hall, 2002). These two top managers were pressured into returning the money by the bitter disputes that broke out at ABB board level, partly due to the size of the payments made to them, but also due to questions raised concerning ABB's internal controls. Apparently the board of directors had not been fully informed of the scale of their benefits.

Another scandal occurred at the same time at the Allied Irish Banks and their subsidiary, Allfirst (Mackintosh and Kirchgässner, 2002). Allfirst lost some US$691 million due to unfortunate currency trading. Media attention switched from John Rusnack, the currency trader, to Michael Buckley, AIB's chief executive officer – would he keep his job?

In all three companies – Enron, ABB and the Allied Irish Banks – the same two issues were raised. The first issue was about governance, which was labelled 'slack' in these organisations. Particularly in Enron and the Allied Irish Banks, governance procedures were reported as not being followed. The second issue was about the organisational cultures in the giant energy company, the global engineering firm and the Irish bank. 'Deception', 'mistrust', 'poor communication' were the words used to describe aspects of their organisational cultures.

For Enron, the image of a network of conspiracy has been portrayed, not only existing in the organisation itself, but also extending to Andersons and a trail of investment bankers. In ABB, the board seemingly was not aware of the full extent of the former chairman and the chief executive officer's pay off. The scope of the 'golden good-byes' smacked of deception. In all three organisations, undesired practices were supposedly unearthed. Slack governance was linked to organisational cultures that have been described as non-transparent, even deceitful, compounding the problems in full view of the public.

Particularly for international organisations, but also and less obvious, for more local ones, it is clear that observing governance is not just related to adherence to proper procedures but also to the more deeply embedded ways of doings things in the organisation – the culture.

In this chapter, we discuss the reasons why governance is becoming more prominent in the management of organisations. We explain how and why governance has become an important consideration in the transformational design of the organisation. We look at the historical positioning of governance and the contrasting interpretations of the term.

Mindful that governance has a regional flavour, we present and analyse two key governance models, the Anglo-American and continental European models. Both models hold contrasting philosophies, which promote different ways of viewing strategy and, in turn, acting upon strategic alternatives. We discuss why the Japanese model of governance is under strain. Our analysis of governance is at a geopolitical (that is, societal) and organisational level. We believe that directors of international organisations face challenges in reconciling the two models, as the levers of governance, transparency, audit, remuneration, procedures of control, risk assessment and concepts of social responsibility, hold different meanings. To conclude we highlight the role of the non-executive or external director, predicting that it will increase in importance, because the responsibility for integrating conflicting governance requirements with the operational reality of managing the organisation will fall more on that role.

Emergence of governance

The fact that governance is linked in the media to scandal and to the cultures of organisation is nothing new. Governance came into prominence in the 1970s with the movement to reform organisations in order to limit the self-interests of directors, particularly those involved in hostile takeovers. The wounded party were shareholders, particularly minority shareholders. Directors were dismissed for their wrongdoings and as the dismissals increased, so too did the volume of publications exemplifying the proper principles to pursue in terms of corporate governance. For example, the American Law Institute issued the 'principles of corporate governance' as an institutional guide for directors on how to manage their companies 'properly'. Hence, as the move for better governance gained momentum, so did the level of activism of investors. They began to criticise inefficient companies publicly. By the late 1980s, investors became a powerful force in their own right, demanding changes in many corporations. Yet, the more investors flexed their muscles, the more they recognised the destructive impact of certain of their interventions. The last thing they desired was for companies in which they had invested to go bankrupt. As certain companies did collapse, the energies of investors became redirected from public criticism to private dialogue, which, in turn, has also led to accusations of 'cover ups', as with the Enron saga. Today it is felt that managers of larger corporations and investors are too 'chummy' and, in fact, need to keep greater distance in order to maintain objectivity.

REALITY CHECK

CORRUPTION

Italy's *Moni Pulite*
In Italy prosecutions against top politician and businessmen have played out like a long-running soap opera. More than 4000 people have been investigated, about 1003 indicted and 460 convicted, including Bettino Crasci, a former two-time Prime Minister, and Gianni de Michelio, an ex-Foreign Minister.

Source: Walsh, J. (1998), 'A world War on Bribery', *Time*, **151**(25), (22 June), p 28.

Reform through governance sped from the USA to the UK, assisted by scandals, such as the collapse of the originally founded Turkish Cypriot company Polly Peck, Robert Maxwell's embezzlement of the Mirror Group's pension fund and the spectacular demise of the BCCI bank. Under the chairmanship of Sir Adrian Cadbury, a '19 Codes of Best Practice for Corporate Governance' was published, and is now used as a benchmark for companies listed on the London Stock Exchange.

Similar developments have taken place in continental Europe and Japan. In Germany, one scandal that caught the attention of the public was the loss of US\$1.8 billion by the mining company Metallgesellschaft, through their trading in oil futures (Kakabadse and Kakabadse, 2001). Business failures emerged in France, which brought demands from legislators for reform to the management of publicly listed corporations. France has always been unique due to its political and social structure, namely the extent of centralisation that exists since the time of Napoleon. By the mid-1990s, French reform was captured in two reports, the Vienot Report (1993) and the Marini Report (1996) (Lawren, A. (1999), Reforming French corporate governance, a return to the two-tier board?', *The George Washington Journal of International Law and Economics*, **32**(1), pp 1–72). Such initiatives forced through improvements in governance practice, in terms of internal protocols and the use of external directors. In fact, throughout the world, independent, external directors and non-executive directors have been and are being positioned to safeguard shareholder interests and to police the organisation, especially through audit, remuneration and nominations committees, or separate subcommittees of the board, chaired by an appropriate non-executive director (Monks and Minow, 1996). The interests of shareholders are being represented more fully by external part-time directors. As the appointment of directors and the remuneration of directors became more scrutinised and visible, in order to have an appropriate balance of power on the board, the roles of chief executive officer and board chairman were separated. Significant pressure in the UK and latterly in the USA was exerted to prevent the same individual holding both roles. The intent was to stop one person, with the power of both roles, from bullying the company into doing what they wanted.

Japan, where the post World War II model of economic recovery, the integrated Japanese corporation, or the 'keiretsu', has been under economic attack, is now following the lead of the USA and UK. The keiretsu is the vertically and horizontally linked company. It is vertically linked from top to bottom, in order to be self-sufficient, efficient and independent, and also provides the social platform for post World War II recovery, lifetime employment. But it is also horizontally linked, in that the mother company has evolved long-term contracts with a chain of suppliers who provide high quality goods and services, under the aegis of continuous improvement. Suppliers are able to leverage off the strength of the mother company, in terms of best practice and the investment capability, for continuous improvement. However, the inter-dependency elements of the keiretsu, once its strength, have become its weakness. Japanese banks, many of them deeply interlinked in the keiretsu network, began to make loans on the basis of network ties and relationships, rather than on the economic capability to generate return on capital. The dependence on cheap funding and unfortunate property speculation, led to a dramatic downturn in Japan's economic fortunes in the early 1990s, an experience from which the country has still not recovered.

Yet the bursting of the bubble has forced through fundamental changes to Japan's economy. Capital for investment is now being sought in the open market and not with banks that operate in a corporate world driven by networks of relationships. Further, changes to the issuing and structure of stock options in 1997 forced radical changes to the structure of Japanese boards. The size of boards was reduced. Sony, one of the first to list on the New York Stock Exchange, reduced the size of its board from 29 to nine directors, including two external, and later added a third external director (Kakabadse and Kakabadse, 2001). So a board of ten had three outsiders attending to the affairs of the Sony Corporation. Determining policy and overseeing the operations of the organisation has become the full responsibility of the Sony Board. Following suit, a considerable number of Japanese corporations have shrunk the sizes of their boards. They have also constituted nomination and remuneration sub-committees and have strengthened the audit functions.

In effect, throughout the world, including recent initiatives introduced into the Belgian and Amsterdam stock exchanges, the move has been towards the universal application of the Anglo American shareholder model of governance.

Definition of governance

The term governance originates from the ancient Greek word *Kivernitis*, meaning oarsman or helmsman, namely the person who steers the boat through stormy waters. True to this entomology, governance has not just been a concern with procedure and protocol but also with leadership and decision making (in the modern Greek, *Kivernisi* means government.) Yet, it is apparent from the media, and from academic writings that what constitutes government at the national level, or governance at a corporate level, differs from one country to another (Brenner and Cochran, 1991).

The Governance Working Group of the International Institute of Administrative Sciences, in 1996, defined governance as, 'the process whereby elements in society wield power and authority and influence and exact policies and discussions concerning public life.' (GWG IIAS (Governance Working Group of the International Institute of Administrative Sciences), (1996), *Governance: a working definition*, Brussels: International Institute of Administrative Sciences). One perception of governance is that of social diversity, adopting a broader notion of the interaction of citizens in the social and economic institutions of the state. Such a view of governance is focused on the promotion of employment and the inclusion of citizens in the affairs of the country, all to generate sound economic and financial policies that drive the economy for the benefit of its citizens.

History of governance

The alternative model of governance emerged from the forming of the first joint stock companies (firms) in response to the trading opportunities in the East and West Indies. The concept of the firm, namely a collective organisation, as a separate entity to that of the owner or operator, emerged in the Middle Ages, as protection against the dominance of royal autocrats. One outcome of organising collectivities was double-entry bookkeeping, so as to check on errors in accounting. So, from its Middle Ages roots emerged the entity known as the 'firm'. Those who managed a firm, or more precisely a joint stock company, in order to generate wealth from trade would regularly meet and conduct their business across a makeshift table which involved assembling around a long board supported by two saw horses. The people who managed the firm were called 'the board', and the leader of the board, who was distinguished by sitting on a chair, was referred to as 'the chairman', whilst others sat on stools. From such crude beginnings came the nomenclature still in use.

With the growing influence of trade in the Americas, early attempts to introduce governance processes and procedures in the New Jersey Legislature through Alexander Hamilton, the nation's first Secretary of Treasury, were made in order to introduce equity and 'fair play' in the production of clothing and men's and women's shoes. Hamilton established the first audit committee, and also the role of inspector who had the power to access and inspect a company's finances and review a company's affairs. Over the years, the influence of the shareholder model of governance grew in prominence, whereby the creation of wealth in itself is the critical goal, as long as third parties or society as a whole are not unduly burdened or disadvantaged. Hence, the two perspectives of governance, the stakeholder (or societal) model and the shareholder (liberal, wealth creation) model, today stand, increasingly uncomfortably, side by side.

Two governance models

SHAREHOLDER MODEL

The shareholder view of governance is that the corporation's prime function is the generation of wealth through the conduct of business. Those who wish to bear the risk of investment in business ventures but also share in any wealth that accrues, through dividends and capital gains, are known as shareholders, who in today's world charge the directors of the enterprise to oversee the wealth creation process. The phrase 'shareholder value', namely, that value shareholders will realise through their investments in terms of profit and wealth, brings their aims into sharp focus.

In the calculation of wealth, two fundamental measures are used. First, *asset value*, sometimes known as book value, comprises the total assets of the enterprise, namely offices, patents, manufacturing sites, people and skills. Even unrealised profit can be introduced into the calculation. The second measure is that of *option value*, a futuristic calculation, namely the total value that is expected to be created in the future. Asset value is determined through an audit procedure. Option value is an attribution awarded to the company by the market (that is, shareholders and their analysts) in terms of expectations. Is the strategy being pursued or the capability of the management and their quality of leadership such that greater than expected wealth is likely to arise in the future? One of the reasons that stocks have become ever more buoyant and volatile is because options value thinking has been applied. Of course, such wealth is not always realised, as was witnessed by the internet e-business crash beginning in the late 1990s, which had the knock on effect of damaging the value of other stock and other investments such as pensions.

Hence, shareholder value, in terms of wealth creation, is achieved if management perform beyond the expectations of shareholders, or at least can convince the markets that the strategies that they have in place will do so. One-off successful attainment of business targets is not sufficient. The promotion of shareholder value requires continuous success in terms of developing new value-adding strategies that can promote such confidence in the shareholders that they maintain their investment in the company. In this way, wealth creation and innovation become integrally linked. Shareholder wealth and the creativity applied to the development of products or services, or new ways of positioning and branding existing products and services go hand in hand. The greater the value that is promoted for customers, the greater the value that will ultimately be realised by shareholders in terms of rise of share price and enhanced dividends. In this way, governance mechanisms, creativity and corporate strategy are interwoven (Kilroy, 1999).

The greater the pressures for return on investments, the greater the reward, but equally the more vulnerable are executives who fail. Like highly paid Premier League football managers, they are expected to deliver the results that the club owners and fans demand. When they do not, they can expect to be fired. To compensate for the risk of losing one's job, extensive use is made of sharing future expected wealth through share options as one form of executive remuneration. A recent study by Towers Perrin highlights considerable remuneration differences for executives of medium sized companies throughout the world (Towers Perrin, (2002), *2001 Worldwide remuneration report*, www towersperrin.com/ hrservices). In 1996, the average USA chief executive officer's pay in a medium sized company was 325 times higher than the average operative. By the year 2000, the reported difference in the USA stood at 475 times, with figures of 525 times difference being bandied around for 2002. In contrast, such differences in year 2000 in Germany stood at 13:1 and in France at 12:1.

Overall, the important features of the Anglo-American model of governance include:

- The obligation to serve shareholder interests, thus maximising shareholder wealth.
- A single tier board structure comprising both executive and non-executive directors. The balance of members between the two varies company by company and between the USA and the UK. The trend in the USA is to have the chief executive officer or the vice president of finance representing the executive directors on a board, which could have up to eight non-executive (external) directors. Greater variation exists in the UK, ranging from a proportionate balance between executive and non-executive directors, to only the chief executive officer and finance director representing the executive body on the board. It is as rare in the UK for executive directors to outnumber the non-executives, as it is to have only the chief executive officer as the sole executive director on the board.
- Investment capital is obtained from a fluid global capital market.
- Governance processes and procedures are driven by guidelines laid down by the American Law Institute, the listing conditions on the New York Stock Exchange and their enforcement by the Stock Exchange Commission and the London Stock Exchange rules.
- In the USA (but not the UK) commercial banks were, until recently, prohibited from holding stocks (shares) in other enterprises.
- Shareholders are increasingly institutions and not private individuals. In Britain there are now fewer private shareholders than before the Thatcher era. Ironically, Margaret Thatcher has been acclaimed as the politician who made more wealth available to the ordinary citizen. The situation in the USA, Germany and Japan is similar: from 1970 to 1996, share ownership by private individuals in the USA dropped from 51 per cent to 49 per cent, in Germany from 28 per cent to 15 per cent and in Japan from 40 per cent to 20 per cent.
- The growing prominence of institutional shareholders and their exercise of power over the strategy pursued by companies. Through proxy voting or other means, institutional shareholders actively participate in the governance of the company and use such means to influence the price of stock.

- Transparency, or the disclosure of information concerning the company, its financial health and other matters, is now mandatory. Lack of transparency could mean damaging the confidence of shareholders in the company and share price consequently dipping.
- The continuous exposure of enterprises to the buffeting of market forces, whereby a slight change of fortune for the company could lead to friendly merger or hostile acquisition.
- The executive directors, and sometimes non-executive directors, are remunerated through both salary and share option schemes.
- In order to defend against hostile bids, reward high performing directors and invest to bolster up share price, the debt of corporations is on the increase. *The Economist* published an interesting article in 2000 which showed that between 1998 and 2000, corporate debt rose to US$900 billion, of which US$460 billion had been allocated to buying back the corporations' own shares and thus reducing the threat of hostile takeover (*The Economist*, (2000), 'Free to bloom', **354**(8157, 12 February), pp 19–21). However, such investments were not disclosed in the profit and loss accounts and hence the true health of the company was not transparent.
- The relationship between the corporation, the capital markets and the conduit to capital markets, the investment bank, has grown stronger and deeper. With Enron, the accusation was that Anderson lost its independence in 'policing' Enron's accounts.

REALITY CHECK

MY WAY

Enron senior management routinely brushed aside concerns raised by internal risk managers and outside auditors, resorted to bullying them to allow aggressive accounting treatments that made its loss-making business operations appear profitable.

The internal report says Anderson, Enron's long time auditor, was aware of the partnerships the company used to manipulate its earnings, and earned US$5.7m to advise on two of them.

Source: Hill, A., Chaffin, J., Spiegal, P. and McNulty, S. (2002), 'Criminal suspicions over Enron', *Financial Times* lead article (Monday, 4 February), p 1.

Consequently the Anglo-American governance model is generating greater wealth for an increasingly limited section of the community, the institutional investors. The pillars of the Anglo-American model, transparency, audit and remuneration, exist in order to let investors know what is really happening in the company, to check and control activities and to reward and motivate the managers in the firms to generate greater wealth. In the words of one well-known chief executive officer, heading a respected FTSE 100 company, 'I don't do strategy any more. It's done for me by those invisible arms outside the company. Until someone sits with me and watches me work, no one will believe how operational I am and, believe you me, that's not my preference.'

The 'invisible arms' referred to are shareholders and analysts. The added implication of this statement is that governance and strategy within the Anglo-American model are becoming integrally linked. Being ahead of competitors no longer just demands bringing to market new product or service innovations. As much, if not more, attention needs to be focused on the share price of competitors as a shift of market forces could induce volatility in share price that could trigger one or more hostile or friendly acquisitions, thereby altering the whole dynamic of the market. Investment in a new product or service portfolio is becoming less critical than access to the financial markets in order to raise capital for acquisitions.

Further, and as highlighted in Chapter 11, the greater majority of organisations need to be attentive to the management of costs. Building a logistics capability and recognising how to manage the supply chain could make a substantial difference to the fundamental profitability of the organisation. Hence, the quality of relationships with suppliers and, as Chapter 11 emphasises, displaying competence in outsourcing are now integral elements of strategy. The attention given to staff associations, trade unions and government (unless government is a customer) is likely to be minimal, as the prospect of generating shareholder wealth through these stakeholder groups is equally likely to be minimal.

The Anglo-American model of governance 'slip streams' strategy towards particular external stakeholder groups, shareholders, analysts or investment banks. In terms of responsiveness to internal stakeholders, the pattern varies considerably. The headline, 'Our most important assets are our people,' is a deeply felt sentiment in certain organisations to the point of being a philosophy that drives its vision and mission.

In other organisations the phrase is merely a headline. There the focus is on numbers. Meeting financial targets can lead to reducing the number of people in the organisation. Under such circumstances, it is not uncommon for one set of people to be retired simultaneously as another set with similar skills are hired. Those newly appointed are likely to be younger, less experienced but most of all cheaper. When the imperative is cost discipline, experience equates with being expensive as opposed to adding value. Under cost discipline circumstances, managing the logistics of the supply chain becomes more important than being attentive to the motivational needs of staff and management.

STAKEHOLDER MODEL

The shareholder model promotes an external orientation, known by some as the external control model, as external, independent agents monitor executive management in order to enhance the wealth prospects of investors. By contrast, the stakeholder model, or network system, shared by most European economies and Japan, promotes an internal control focus. The premise is that the firm will improve its performance and thereby provide favourable returns for shareholders if a more binding relationship of commitment can be engendered through the various groups who share an interest in the company. In turn, a positive and supportive environment stimulates the desire for greater innovation and the pursuit of opportunities. Thus, the two models of governance share two deeply held aspirations, the need to generate shareholder wealth and the pursuit of innovation.

The difference is that with the stakeholder model, numerous interest groups hold comparable status with shareholders and that the pursuit of innovation, particularly for the purposes of profit, may become secondary if these aims sharply conflict with broader stakeholder requirements. Simply put, the shareholder model is more preoccupied with wealth creation for investors, whilst the stakeholder model, although similarly inspirational, propounds the balancing of conflicting interests and a wider (re)distribution of wealth. The responsibility for aligning interests and for the monitoring of executive management rests with the firm's supervisory board, solely comprising external representatives of different stakeholders. The executive board, consisting of the senior managers of the enterprise, run the business. The supervisory board appoints key executive directors, monitors management and can remove the chairman and chief executive officer of the company. As in the shareholder model, the occupants of the two posts of chairman and chief executive officer (or president) are held to account by their respective boards. Unlike the shareholder model, it is acceptable practice within stakeholder governance for supervisory board members to be invited, more often than not informally by their colleague board members, to sit on each other's supervisory boards. Stakeholder governance fosters networks of interlocking relationships, thus preventing the interests of any stakeholder group from being unduly undermined.

The important features of the stakeholder model are:

- The continuous balancing of shareholder and stakeholder interests.
- The provision of investment capital principally from commercial banks and not capital markets. In the late 19th century, the financial heart of Germany lay along the river Rhine, where private banks provided long-term loans for major projects as well as other services of fiduciary administration. For example, many bank managers acted as the finance manager for the company to whom they had issued a loan. Through the intimate involvement of banks with companies, their current accounts were managed by the banks in order to safeguard their investments. Despite the emergence of the Frankfurt Stock Exchange to fund corporate needs, German banks remained the dominant source of investment capital. Japan progressed in a similar fashion, whereby the banking sector was initially focused to mobilise funds for the defence industry, but then extended to all aspects of the economy.
- Investment for the purposes of wealth is meant for the whole community.
- Legislation, rather than self-regulation, has shaped corporate governance structures, resulting in two tier boards (supervisory board and executive board).
- The supervisory board, composed of external (non executive) directors, represents relevant interest groups, including the workforce and determines the future of the executive directors.
- The supervisory board selects the members of the executive board.
- It is mandatory that there should be no overlap between the supervisory board and the executive board in terms of membership or function.
- The tradition of loans from commercial banks for the purposes of investment, places banks in a strong position to be represented on the supervisory board through the exercise of their voting rights.
- Through German law, union representatives occupy half of the supervisory board positions.
- Only relatively few companies are publicly listed on the Frankfurt Stock Exchange, the reason being that a substantial proportion of shares are owned by families who do not wish to release information concerning the health of the firm they own.

As the essence of governance in continental Europe, typified by Germany, is of a social market economy, with labour legally linked to the corporation, investment and disinvestment decisions emerge as a result of co-operative bargaining amongst an array of stakeholders. The sources of financing that are the core differentiator between the Anglo-American model and continental European models provide a powerful knock on effect in terms of economic and social repercussions. Liquidity of capital, the hallmark of the Anglo-American model, is matched by the continental European model by low interest rates from banks allowing firms the opportunity to spread payments on borrowings. Germans save in banks and building societies and as savings accounts attract low interest rates, so too do loans. Such a system is held together by banks that are required to make only nominal profit margins. Although certain variations exist in France which allows companies to choose a single or two-tier structure, and in Japan, which has a more intricate relationship between board members, executive directors and the audit function but still operates on a two-tier basis, the dominance of loan based commercial banking for investment remains.

The difference in the pursuit of strategy between organisations that have adopted the continental European model as opposed to the Anglo-American model is the level of consideration and attention given to stakeholders. Far greater nurture of relationships between the enterprise and its variety of stakeholders takes place within continental European governance driven organisations, particularly of staff, trade unions, lobby groups and government. Workers' councils represent the views of the labour force, thus emphasising the strategic importance of directives from the workforce. Organisations that are not publicly listed or that may be but have no desire to dilute their ownership would obtain capital from financial institutions but not offer shares for sale in the markets. Equally, many organisations wish to remain as distinct entities and would not enter into outsourcing relationships, although this practice is now rapidly changing both in Japan and Europe. Thus, irrespective of government owning shares in the enterprise, which is a particular characteristic of France, the notion of the large corporation within the continental European model of governance is more that of the 'public vessel' promoting the public interest.

The shareholder value model with its need for liquidity of finance promotes a 'quick time' way of operating, namely, realise the value from the investment and then reinvest, often elsewhere. The continental European model favours 'slow time', as investments are more project based and assessed according to national economic and social impact. A quick time way of working promotes greater concentration of wealth in fewer hands. Why? Because speed of decision making is of the essence. To miss or miscalculate an acquisition opportunity, irrespective of the technical or professional skills of the organisation, could mean loss. Thus corporate entrepreneurship is rewarded through options and share schemes. In continental European governance based enterprises, salary, status and also job security are the elements of the remuneration package. In fact, to make money personally in a company at the expense of others losing their jobs is seen by many in continental Europe as immoral.

Contrasts of meanings

As can be seen, terms such as transparency, remuneration, ethics, mobility, loyalty and identity hold substantially different meanings within these two models.

Enquiries conducted in the UK, such as those of Cadbury, Tricker, Turnbull, Greenbury and Myners, examined aspects of governance ranging from the need for greater transparency to how better to remunerate management and how to enhance risk assessment

Table 12.1 Contrasts of governance levers (developed by Andrew Kakabadse)

Levers	Anglo-American	Continental European
Transparency	Financial; investor based	Spread of director interests
Remuneration	Options, bonus based additional to salary but performance driven	Salary, status, promotion, security of tenure
Loyalty	Oneself, profession	Organisation
Values	Self-generated wealth	Public good
Conduct	Self-disciplined; codes of conduct as models	Legislation
Identity	Own initiatives; self developed; mobility	Community or organisational; broader based initiatives; less mobile
Risk assessment	Executive, non-executive director responsibility; needs attention; formally given attention	Executive, external director responsibility; needs attention; formally given attention

capability. However, as already highlighted, transparency in the Anglo-American model refers to financially based information that would be of interest to investors, whereas under the European model that adopts a more community networked orientation, transparency relates to information concerning the spread of interest of directors on supervisory boards (Table 12.1). In a more community networked society, the secrecy concerning who sits on whose board can substantially damage the credibility of the individual and the organisation. The orientation of the Anglo-American model towards the creation of wealth favours management utilising their discretion to pursue opportunities. Such a system, which promotes flexibility, has personal and organisational repercussions. In order not to inhibit management realising wealth creating opportunities, codes of conduct emphasise self-discipline. Consequently, loyalty is to one's self and one's own abilities.

On such a basis, the structure of remuneration is directly geared to the achievements of the individual through performance targeting. In contrast, the continental European model, in promoting the platform of public good, limits discretion at the individual and organisational level in order to guarantee equity across a whole society and relies far more on legislation to determine governance practice. Living within such an environment promotes a community-based identity, whereby loyalty to the organisation and to the broader community, become integral. The spread of wealth for the purposes of public good equally limits mobility, in terms of being quick to respond both upwardly and geographically. Being seen to be too ambitious is as unacceptable as moving home too often in the pursuit of either business or career opportunities. Hence, within the continental European model, wealth holds a contrasting meaning in that recognition by one's peers or community is of almost equal status to tangible, financial based wealth. Status can be as powerful a motivator as income.

The fundamental reasons for such differences of values and orientation date back to the emergence of the United States of America, a country that sharply resented the British and European concept of centrally concentrated political sovereignty, initially through absolute monarchy and then through Parliament. The decentralised political structure of the USA promoted courts and local parties more than a national bureaucracy that promoted national interests. On this basis, the political opinion of the day determined the structure of the USA more than was the case in continental Europe or Japan. Hence, particular powerful political personalities such as Hoover and his New Deal of the 1930s encouraged the emergence of certain social insurance programmes, such as unemployment, pension and industrial accident but not comprehensive health coverage. A centralist, but more consistent spread of public programmes, dominated the late nineteenth and twentieth centuries in the UK, continental Europe and Japan. As various researchers show, 400 years of evolution and a substantial volume of legislation has generated a level of difference between the two governance models that is deep (Batten and Waller, 2001).

However, whatever the differences, the leadership of the enterprise and the organisation's continued survival and prosperity remain as practical shared challenges. Risk assessment, therefore, is a critical consideration for executive and non-executive/external directors in both models. In fact, a view emerging from the UK's Institute of Directors is that risk assessment and risk management are a fundamental aspect of the contributions of the external director, whether sitting on a single-tier or two-tier board.

Boundary spanners

As governance concerns have increased within both the Anglo-American and continental European models, so too has the importance of the external director. A recent study of non-executive directors on boards of companies on the Financial Times 200 companies index (FTSE 200) highlights that the capabilities required for effective performance include (Kakabadse and Kakabadse, 2001):

- a range of functional skills, principally financial, marketing and branding,
- sector expertise,
- linkages with the investment community,
- experience of leading through change, in terms of re-organisation, mergers, acquisitions.
- being a supportive mentor and coach, and
- having independence of mind.

Of all of the capabilities, non-executive directors rated independence of mind as one of the most valuable. The personal strength to offer unwelcome opinion, or to challenge or even to resign from the board, make the critical difference particularly in hostile circumstances. However, the level of capability of non-executive directors emerged as substantially varied. The study shows that approaches to governance involved:

- for many, little more than procedural box ticking,
- a reluctance to proceed with further codification,
- for the few, a mechanism for nurturing an opportunity-oriented environment in the organisation, and
- promoting greater transparency.

Unfortunately, even some of the more capable non-executive directors all too often entered into 'cover your back' behaviour as opposed to confronting the challenge of promoting greater transparency, ethical behaviour and procedural justice. Part of the reason for a seeming inability to improve governance is the question of who drives the governance agenda? If the chairman and chief executive officer promote good governance, the non-executive director is in a better position than if the chairman and/or chief executive officer undermine governance reform. Despite splitting the roles of chairman and chief executive officer, the influence of either or both of these individuals is viewed as predominant.

REALITY CHECK

ENDANGERED SPECIES

It's 30 years since the two giant pandas Chia-Chia and Ling-Ling failed to reproduce . . . Tomorrow, Derrick Higgs will launch a campaign to boost the population of another endangered species, the non-executive director. Harried by increasingly large work loads, criticisms of their ineffectiveness and the looming prospect of being sued for getting things wrong, there is a danger that too few of these ancient beasts will be around to perform the task required of them.

Source: Nisse, J. (2003), 'Ling-Ling . . . giant pandas ring a bell with the fate of non-executives', *The Independent on Sunday, Business, The Ideas Exchange*, (19 January), p 2.

However, that and subsequent studies raise an important question. What is the value-adding contribution of non-executive directors? Ruth Barratt, a doctoral candidate at Cranfield School of Management, has adopted the phrase 'boundary spanner', namely that non-executive directors straddle a number of boundaries and interfaces between a variety of stakeholders and the organisation (Barratt, 2002). The presumption is that in addition to their functional contribution, their network of contacts, experience of managing demanding challenges and personal skills as coaches, non-executive directors should focus on reconciling 'boundary spanning tensions'. Boundary spanning involves reconciling operational requirements with the strategy being pursued with the pragmatic demands of disparate internal and external constituents, all with the aim of enhancing corporate reputation. The assumption is that effective boundary spanning emphasises corporate social performance, whereby the pragmatism of operational reality is well aligned with the notion of the social responsibility of the corporation. The reality emerging from research is that all too many non-executive and external directors do not recognise the nature of, or feel able to provide, a competent boundary spanning service. Hence, the tensions of governance are likely to continue for the foreseeable future, particularly for those international organisations that have interests across North America, continental Europe and Southeast Asia.

Summary

EMERGENCE OF GOVERNANCE

With the emergence of scandals involving directors of public companies promoting their self-interests, either illegally or at the expense of particularly shareholders, attention to corporate governance grew in prominence. Codes of governance practice and procedures in order to safeguard the interests of shareholders and other stakeholders emerged in the USA, UK, Germany, France and Japan.

TWO GOVERNANCE MODELS

With the growing interest in governance, the realisation is only just coming to the surface that two distinctly different models of governance stand side by side, namely, the Anglo-American and continental European models.

The Anglo-American model is characterised by:

- equity based financing,
- a single-tier board structure,
- the generation of wealth for the benefit of shareholders and
- a share of that wealth for the managers of the corporation through extensive bonuses and options share schemes.

The continental European model is characterised by:

- loan based financing from commercial banks,
- a two-tier board structure,
- a supervisory board of external directors who monitor the board of full-time executive directors,
- the generation of wealth for the benefit of all interested stakeholders,
- a remuneration philosophy based on salary and tenure of employment in return for loyalty to the corporation and
- a strategic orientation attentive to the needs of multiple stakeholders.

CONTRASTS OF MEANING

With such contrasting differences of approach to governance, entirely different meanings are attached to terms as transparency, audit, remuneration, risk assessment and wealth distribution.

BOUNDARY SPANNERS

Particularly for international organisations, resolving governance and strategic differences so as to meaningfully focus the organisation to achieve its goals in a cohesive manner is demanding. It is considered that the role and contribution of the external director or non-executive director, as a boundary spanner attempting to reconcile such differences, will become, in the future, an ever more important role. However, the level of awareness amongst external directors concerning the boundary spanning challenges is postulated as low.

Bibliography

Anonymous, (1996), *Primary colors: a novel of politics*, New York: Random House.

Alderfer, C.P. (1972), *Existence, relatedness and growth: human needs in organisational settings*, Boston: Free Press.

Argyris, C. (1957), *Personality and organisation*, New York: Harper Collins.

Auger, P. and Palmer, J. (2002), *The rise of the player manager: how professionals manage while they work*, Harmondsworth: Penguin.

Bank, J. (2000), *The essence of total quality management*, Harlow, Essex: Pearson Education, p 90.

Barratt, R. (2002), 'The role and contribution of non-executive directors to corporate social performance', *First doctoral review paper* (unpublished), Cranfield, UK: Cranfield University, School of Management.

Barnard, C. (1948), *Organization and management*, Boston: Harvard University Press.

Bass, B.M. (1985), *Leadership and performance beyond expectations*, New York: Free Press.

Batten, M. and Waller, D. (2001), 'Europe's models – a business view', *European Business Forum*, (Issue 5, Spring), pp 37–40.

Bauby, J-D. (1998), *The diving-bell and the butterfly*, London: Fourth Estate Limited, p 11–14.

BBC *Panorama* Broadcast, (1986), 'The Dream That Fell Out of the Sky', (28 April).

Belbin R.M. (1981), *Management teams: why they succeed or fail*, London: Heinemann.

Belbin, R.M. (1993), *Team roles at work*, Oxford: Butterworth-Heinemann.

Bion, W.R. (1968), *Experiences in groups*, London: Tavistock Publishing.

Black, O. (1996), 'Addressing the issue of good communication', *People Management*, 2(155), pp 4–44.

Blake, R.R. and Mouton, J.S. (1964), *The Managerial Grid*, 3rd Edition, Houston: Gulf Publishing Company.

Bonington, C. (1996), *Mountaineer: thirty years of climbing on the world's great peaks*, London: Baton Wicks.

Boring, E.G. (1930), 'A new ambiguous figure', *American Journal of Psychology*, **42**, p 444.

Bower, T. (2000), *Branson*, London: Forth Estate, p 15.

Boyatzis, R.E. (1982), *The competent manager*, London: Wiley.

Brennar, S. and Cochran, P. (1991), 'The stakeholder theory of the firm: implications for business and society, theory and research', *JABS Proceedings*, pp 449–67.

Brown-Humes, C. and Hall, W. (2002), 'Former ABB chiefs to forego big part of £98m in benefits', *Financial Times, Companies and Markets*. (Monday, 11 March), pp 25–27.

Buckley, N. (2003), 'Amazon reports higher profits than expected', *The Financial Times Companies & Finance The Americans Edn*, (24 Jan).

Building Industry Association, (1993), '*The four hour house*', video, San Diego, California.

Cadbury, A., Sir, (1990), *The company chairman*, Cambridge: Fitzwilliam Publishing.

Calaman, P. (2003), 'Eerie echoes of Challenger disaster', *Toronto Star*, (2 February), p B04.

Cannon-Bowers, J.A. and Salas, E. (1997), 'A framework for developing team performance measures in training', in: Brannick, T., Salas, E. and Prince, C., (eds), *Team performance, assessment, and measurement: theory, methods and applications*, Mahwah, NJ: Lawrence Erlbaum Associates.

Cascio, W.F. (1993), 'Downsizing, what do we know? What have we learnt?', *Academy of Management Executive*, 17(1), pp 95–104.

Chaffin, J. (2003), 'US banks day of reckoning after 'betrayal' of investors', *Financial Times*, (29 April), p 1.

Child, J. (1984), *Organization: a guide to problems and practice* 2nd edition, New York: Harper and Row.

Cohen, A.R. and Bradford, D.L. (1999), 'Power and influence', in: Chowdhury, S. (Ed), *Organisation 21C*, New York: Financial Times: Prentice Hall.

Columbia Accident Investigation Board Report, (2003), Volume 1, Limited first printing by the Columbia Accident Investigation. Subsequent printing and distribution by the National Aeronautics and Space Administration and the Government Printing Office, Washington, DC.

Colvin, G. (2001), 'Shaking hands on the Web', *Fortune European Edition*, **25**(14 May).

Coutu, D. (2002), 'How resilience works', *Harvard Business Review*, **80**(10), pp 49–50.

Dearborn, D.C. and Simon, H.A. (1985), 'Selective perception: a note on the department identification of executives'. *Sociometry*, **21**(2), p 144.

De Geus, A. (1999), *The living company: growth, learning and longevity in business*, London: Nicholas Brealey, pp 225–226.

Doherty, N., Bank, J. and Vinnicombe, S. (1996), 'Managing survivors: the experience of survivors in BT and the British financial section', *Journal of Managerial Psychology*, **11**(7), pp 51–60.

Drucker, P. (1990), *The new realities*, New York: Harper and Row.

Dyson, J. (1997), *Against the odds: autobiography*, London: Orion Business Books.

Eisenhardt, K.M., Kahwajy, J.L. and Bourgeois III, L.J. (1997), 'How management teams can have a good fight', *Harvard Business Review*, **75**(4), pp 77–85.

Equal Opportunities Commission (EOC) (2002), *Women and men in Britain: management*, Manchester: EOC.

Evans, Sir R. and Price, C. (1999), *Vertical take-off: the inside story of British Aerospace's comeback from crisis to world class*, London: Nicholas Brealey Publishing, pp 94–95.

Ewing, M.T., Pitt, L.F., de Bussy, N.M. and Berthon, P. (2002), 'Employment branding in the knowledge economy', *International Journal of Advertising*, **21**(1), pp 3–22.

Eysenck, H.J., Arnold, W. and Meili, R. (1972), *Encyclopaedia of Psychology* 2, London: Continuum International Publishing Group-Burns and Oates.

Fast, J. (1971), *Body language*, New York: Pocket Books, pp 7–8.

Fayol, H.G. (1916), 'Administration industrielle et generale – Prevoyance, organisation, commodidement, coordination, controle', *Bulletin de la Societe de l'Industrie Minerale*.

Fiedler, F.E. (1967), *Theory of leadership effectiveness*, Ohio: McGraw-Hill.

Fisher, R. and Ury, W. (1991), *Getting to yes negotiating an agreement without giving in*, London: Business Books Ltd (Random Century).

Fitz-Gibbon, S. (2001), *The history and mythology of the battle of Goose Green*, Cambridge: The Lutterworth Press.

Follett, M.P. (1924), *The creative experience*, Boston: Longman Publishing.

Gardenswartz, L. and Rowe, A. (1998), *Managing diversity: a complete desk reference and planning guide*, Ohio: McGraw-Hill.

Gates, B. (1996), *The road ahead*, London: Penguin Books.

Gates, B. (1999), *Business @ the speed of thought: using a digital nervous system*, Harmondsworth: Penguin Books.

Giuliani, R.W. with Kurson, K. (2002), *Leadership*, London: Little Brown.

Goleman, D. (1996), *Emotional intelligence*, London: Bloomsbury.

Gregersen, H.B. and Dyer, J.H. (2002), 'Lockheed Martin Chairman and CEO Vance Coffman on achieving mission success interview', *Academy of Management Executive*, **16**(3).

Gowler, D. and Legge, K. (1989), 'Rhetoric in bureaucratic careers: managing the meaning of management success', in: Authur, M.B., Hall, D.T. and Lawrence, B.S. (Eds) *Handbook of Career Theory*, Cambridge: Cambridge University Press.

GWG IIAS (Governance Working Group of the International Institute of Administrative Sciences), (1996), *Governance: a working definition* (Brussels: International Institute of Administrative Sciences).

Hackman, J.R. (Ed.) (1989), *Groups that work (and those that don't): creating conditions for effective teamwork*, San Francisco, CA: Jossey-Bass.

Hackman, J.R. and Oldham, G. (1980), *Work redesign*, Massachusetts: Addison-Wesley.

Hall, D.T. and Associates (1996), *The career is dead, long live the career: a relational approach to careers*, San Francisco: Jossey-Bass, pp 1, 20, 21, 344.

Handy, C. (1976), *Understanding organizations*, London: Penguin Educational Series, pp 177.

Hare, D. (2000), *My zinc bed*, London: Faber & Faber.

Hersey, P. and Blanchard, K. (1976), *Situational leadership, centre for creative leadership*, Internal Paper, USA.

Herzberg, F., Mausner, B. and Snyderman, B. (1959), *The motivation to work*, London: Wiley.

Hewett, C. (2003), 'Wilkinson refuses to rest in quest to be perfect ten', *The Independent, Rugby World Cup*, (4 October), p 13.

Hill, A., Chaffin, J., Speigal, P. and McNulty, S. (2002), 'Criminal suspicions over Europe', *Financial Times*, (4 February), p 1.

Hiltrop, J.M. (1995), 'The changing psychological contract: the human resource challenge of the 1990s', *European Management Journal*, **13**(3), pp 286–294.

Hofstede, G. (1980), 'Motivation, leadership and organisation: do American theories apply abroad?' *Organisational Dynamics*, 9(1), pp 42–63.

House, R.J. (1997), 'A 1976 theory of charismatic leadership', in: Hunt, J.G. and Larson L.L.I. (Eds), *Leadership: the cutting edge*, Carbondale: Southern Illinois University Press, pp 76–94.

Hunt, B. (2002), 'Getting bigger even faster: view from the top: Jeff Bezos of Amazon'. *Financial Times*, (4 December), FT Report// FTIT // Asian IT, edn, 8.

Internal Control Working Party of the Institute of Chartered Accountants in England and Wales (Nigel Turnbull, Chair), (1999), *Internal control: guidance for directors on the combined code*, (September), London: The Institute of Chartered Accountants in England and Wales.

Jaques, E. (1951), *The changing culture of the factory*, London: Tavistock.

Janis, I.L. (1973), *Victims of group-think*, Boston: Houghton Mifflin.

Johnson, R.S. (1998), 'The 50 best companies for Asians, blacks and Hispanics', *Fortune* 138(3, 3 August), pp 94–96.

Kakabadse, A. (1983), *The politics of management*, Aldershot: Gower.

Kakabadse, A. and Kakabadse, N. (2001), *The geopolitics of governance: the impact of contrasting philosophies*, Basingstoke: Palgrave.

Kakabadse, A.P. and Kakabadse, N. (2002), *Smart sourcing: international best practice*, Basingstoke: Palgrave.

Kaneira, N. (2003), 'Gulf news – Cancun's fallout – greater US leverage', *Financial Times*, (20 September).

Kanter, R.M. (1995), *World class: thriving locally in the global economy*, New York: Simon & Schuster.

Kanter, R.M. (1997), *Men and women of the corporation*, New York: Basic Books.

Keefe, C. (2003), 'Jeff Bezos: founder and CEO, Amazon.com', *Dealerscope*, 45(1), p 76.

Keegan, J. (1988), *The mask of command*, Harmondsworth: Penguin Books.

Kets de Vries, M.F.R. (1989), *Prisoners of leadership*, New York: John Wiley.

Kidder, R. (1999), 'Global ethics and individual responsibility', *RSA Journal*, (1 April).

Kilroy, D.B. (1999), 'Creating the future: how creativity and innovation drive shareholder wealth', *Management Decision*, 37(4), pp 74–79.

Kingdon, D.R. (1973), *Matrix organisation: managing information technologies*, London: Tavistock Publications, p 1.

Kirkman, B.L., Rosen, B., Gibson, C.B., Tesluk, P.E. and McPherson, S.O. (2002), 'Five challenges to virtual team success: lessons from Sabre, Inc.', *The Academy of Management Executive*, 16(3), p 70.

Klein, N. (2002), *Fences and windows: dispatches from the front lines of the globalization debate*, London: Flamingo, HarperCollins.

Kobassa, S.C., Maddi, S.R. and Khan, S. (1982), 'Hardiness and health: a prospective study', *Journal of Personality and Social Psychology*, 42(1), pp 168–177.

Kolb, D.A., (1984), *Experiential learning: experience as the source of learning and development*, Englewood Cliffs, NJ: Prentice-Hall.

Kuhn, T.S. (1970), *The structure of scientific revolutions*, 2nd Edition, Chicago: The University of Chicago Press.

Larsen, J.K. and Rogers, E.M. (1984), *Silicon Valley fever: growth of high-technology culture*, London: George Allen and Unwin.

Lasserre, P. (2003), *Global strategic management*, Basingstoke, Hampshire: Palgrave Macmillan.

Law, A. (1998), *Open minds*, London: Orion.

Law, A. (1998), *Creative company*, New York: John Wiley.

Law, A. (2003), *Experiment at work*, London: Profile Books.

Lawless, D.J. (1979), *Organisational behaviour: the psychology of effective management*, 2nd edition, Englewood Cliffs: Prentice-Hall.

Lawren, A. (1999), 'Reforming French corporate governance, a return to the two-tier board?', *The George Washington Journal of International Law and Economics*, 32(1), pp 1–72.

Leavitt, H.J. and Lipman-Blumen, J. (1995), 'Hot groups', *Harvard Business Review*, 73(4), pp 109–116.

Lewis, R. (2002), 'The CEO's lot is not a happy one', *Academy of Management Executive*, 16(4), pp 37–42.

Likert, R. (1965), *The human organisation*, New York: McGraw-Hill.

Lipnack, J. and Stamps, J. (2000), *Virtual teams: people working across boundaries with technology*, 2 Edition, New York: Wiley.

Louis, M., Posner, B. and Powell, G. (1983), 'The availability and helpfulness of socialization practices', *Personnel Psychology*, 36(4), pp 857–866.

Luft, J. and Ingram, H. (1955), 'The Johari window: a graphic model of interpersonal awareness, *Proceedings of the Western Training Laboratory in Group Development*, Los Angeles: UCLA Extension Office.

Lukes, S. (1974), *Power: a radical view*, Macmillan.

Mackintosh, J. and Kirachgässner, S. (2002), 'AIB chief called for trading probe in May', *Financial Times, Companies and Markets*, (Monday, 11 March), p 25.

Marcel, G. (1960), *The mystery of being*, Chicago: Regnery.

Marcouse, G. I., Martin, B., Surridge, M. and Wall, N. (1999), 'Business studies', in, Gillespie, M.I., Martin, B., Surridge, M. and Wall, N. (Eds), *Business Studies*, Abingdon: Hodder and Stoughton, pp 242.

Maslow, A. H. (1954), *Motivation of personality*, New York: Harper and Row.

Mayo, E. (1947), *The political problems of an industrial society*, Harvard: Harvard University Press.

McClelland, D. (1965), 'Achievement motivation can be developed', *Harvard Business Review*, **43**(6), pp 6, 11.

McGregor, D. (1960), *The human side of enterprise*, New York: McGraw-Hill.

McGoldrick, J. and Stewart, J. (1996), *The HRM-HRD nexus*, London: Pitman Publishing.

Mendoza, M. (2003), 'Uncharted waters', *RSA Journal*, (February), p 41.

Mills, T. and Tyson S. (2001), 'Organisational renewal: challenging human resource management', presented on 15 November 2001 at the HRM Network Conference, Nijmegen School of Management, The Netherlands, p 1.

Mintowt-Czyz, L. (2003), 'Boss who's taking 119 of his staff on holiday', *Daily Mail*, (8 April).

Mintzberg, H. (1994), 'Rounding out the manager's job', *Sloan Management Review*, **36**(1).

Mintzberg, H. (1975), 'The manager's job: folklore and fact', *Harvard Business Review*, **53**(4).

Monks, R.A.G. and Minow, N. (1996), *Watching the watchers: corporate governance for the 21st century*, Cambridge: Basil Blackwell.

Morrell, M. and Capparell, S. (2002), *Shackleton's way*, Harmondsworth: Penguin Books, p 163.

Morrow, (1993), 'Relationships among five forms of commitment: an empirical assessment'. *Journal of Organizational Behaviour*, **20**, pp 285–308.

Myners, P. (2001), *Institutional investment in the United Kingdom: a review*, Report to the HM Treasury, 6 March, London.

Nadler, D.A. and Lawler III, E.E. (1997), 'Motivation: a diagnostic approach', in: Hackman, J.R., Lawler III, E.E. and Protek, L.W., *Perspectives on behaviour in organisations*, McGraw-Hill, p 23.

Nierenberg, R. (1999), 'The music paradigm', *Money Programme* Lecture, BBC Videos for Education and Training, London.

Nietzsche, F. (1969), *The will to power*, New York: Vintage.

Nisse, J. (2003), 'Ling-Ling ... giant pandas ring a bell with the fate of non-executives', *The Independent on Sunday, Business, The Ideas Exchange*, (19 January), p 2.

Owen, H. (1996), 'Creating top flight teams: the unique teambuilding techniques of the RAF Red Arrows', *The hungry spirit: beyond capitalism a quest for purpose in the modern world*, London: Kogan Page.

Parker, C. and Lewis, R. (1980), 'Moving up...how to handle transitions to senior levels successfully', *Occasional Paper*, Cranfield: Cranfield School of Management.

Perrow, C. (1976), 'A framework for the comparative analysis of organizations', *American Sociological Review*, **32**(2), pp 194–208.

Pfeffer J. (1992), *Managing with power: politics and influence in organizations*, Boston: Harvard Business School Press.

Pugh, D.S. and Hickson, D.J. (1977), *Organizational structure: extensions and reflections: the Aston programme II*, Massachusetts: Saxon House/Lexington Books.

Ragins, B.R. and Cotton, J. (1991), 'Easier said than done: gender differences in perceived barriers to gaining a mentor', *Academy of Management Journal*, **34**(4), pp 939–951.

Ragins, B.R., Townsend, B. and Matthis, M. (1998), 'Gender gap in the executives suite: CEOs and female executives report on breaking the glass ceiling', *Academy of Management Executive*, **12**(1).

Rayport, J.F. (1999), 'The truth about internet business models', *Strategy & Business*, (16, 3rd Quarter).

Reeve, C. (1997), *Still me*, New York: Random House, pp 297–298 .

Report to the Presidential Commission on the Space Shuttle Challenger Accident, 1986, (6 June), Washington, DC.

Reza, Y. (1996), *Art*, London: Faber & Faber.

Roach, S.S. (1999), 'A new competitive dilemma', Euromoney Conference: The Global Borrowers and Investors Forum, 18 June, London, UK.

Roddick, A. (2000), 'Beautiful business', *RSA Journal*, (4 April).

Roddick, A. (2001), *Take it personally: how globalisation affects you and powerful ways to challenge it*, London: Harper Collins.

Rogers, C. (1961), *On becoming a person: a therapist's view of psychotherapy*, Boston, Mass: Houghton Mifflin.

Rogers, D. (2003), 'Getting away from it all', *Financial Times, Creative Business*, (11 March), pp 8–9.

Roosevelt Jr., R.T. (1990), 'Affirmative action to affirming diversity', *Harvard Business Review*, **68**(2), p 113.

Rosener, J.B. (1990), 'Ways women lead', *Harvard Business Review*, **68**(6), pp 119–125.

Sahdev, K. and Vinnicombe, S. (1998), 'Downsizing and the survivor syndrome: a study of HR's perceptions of survivors' responses', *Cranfield Working Paper*, (Abstract).

Schein, E.H. (1978), *Career dynamics: matching individual and organisational needs*, Reading, Mass: Addison-Wesley.

Schein, E.H. (1989), 'Corporate teams and totems', *Across the Board*, **26**(5), pp 12–17.

Schlender, B. (2001), 'Steve Jobs: the graying prince of a shrinking kingdom', *Fortune*, (14 May).

Sellers, P. (2003), 'Most powerful women in business, power: do women really want it?', *Fortune*, (13 October), pp 1–2.

Singh, V., Schiuma, G. and Vinnicombe, S. (2002), 'Assessing diversity management', *3rd International conference on theory and practice in performance measurement and management*, Boston, (17–19 July).

Stein, N. (2002), 'Crisis in a coffee cup', *Fortune*, (16 December).

Stern, S. (2002), Interview with Marjorie Scardino, CEO of Pearson, The Global Media Company, *RSA Journal*, (1 October).

Stiglitz, J. (2002), *Globalization and its discontents*, London: Penguin.

Stroh, L.K., Northcraft, G.B. and Neale, M.A. (2001), *Organizational behavior: a management challenge*, 3rd Edition, Mahwah, New Jersey: Lawrence Erlbaum Associates, p 7.

Sturges, J. (1999), 'What it means to succeed: Personal conceptions of career success held by male and female managers at different ages', *British Journal of Management*, **10**(3), pp 239–252.

Sunday Times, (2003), '100 best companies to work for 2003', (2 March).

Sunday Times Magazine, 'Rich list', (27 April 2003).

Taylor, F.W. (1911), *The principles of scientific management*, Harper and Row.

The Economist, (2000), 'Free to bloom', **354**(8157), (12 February), pp 19–21.

The Independent, (2003), 'We do our best for the world's poor', (10 September), p 1 headline.

The Study Group on Directors' Remuneration (Chaired by Greenbury, R.), (1995), *Directors' remuneration – report of a study group chaired by Sir Richard Greenbury*, London: The Study Group on Directors' Remuneration and Gee Publishing Ltd, (July).

Thomas, K.W. and Kilmann, R.H. (1974), *Conflict mode instrument*, CPP, Inc. 3803 E. Bayshore Road, Palo Alto, CA 94303.

Time Magazine (2003), 'The Year of the Whistleblowers', (30 December), p 8.

Tonge, A., Greer, L. and Lawton, A. (2003), 'The Enron story, you can fool some of the people some of the time', *Business Ethics: a European Review*, 12(1), (January).

Towers Perrin, (2002), 2001 World wide total remuneration report, http//www.towersperrin.com/hrservices/webcache/towers/United_States/publications/Reports/2001_02_WorldwideRemun/WWTR_2001_English.pdf.

Tricker, R.I. (1996), *Pocket director*, London: The Economist Books.

Tuckman, B.C. (1965), 'Development sequence in small groups', *Psychological Bulletin*, **63**(6), pp 384–99.

Tuckman, B.C. and Jensen, M.C. (1977), 'Stages of small group development revisited', *Group and Organization Studies*, **2**(4), pp 419–27.

Tulgan, B. (2003), 'Winning the talent wars', *Newsletter* 97th Edition, (30 April).

Urwick, L.F. (1947), *The elements of administration*, London: Pitman.

US House Committee on Science and Technology (1986), Investigation on the Challenger accident report, Washington, DC: Government Printing Office.

Van Maanen, J. (1978), 'People processing: strategies of organisational socialisation', *Organisational Dynamics*, **7**(1).

Vaughan, D. (1996), *The Challenger launch decision: risky technology, culture and deviance at NASA*, Chicago: The University of Chicago Press.

Vinnicombe, S. and Bank, J. (2003), *Women with attitude: lessons for career management*, London: Routledge.

Vroom, V.H. and Yetton, P.W. (1973), *Leadership and decision making*, Pittsburg, USA: University of Pittsburg Press.

Waller, D. (2001), *Wheels on fire, the amazing inside story of the Daimler Chrysler merger*, London: Hodder & Stoughton, pp 13–16.

Walsh, J. (1998), 'A World War on Bribery', *Time*, **151**(25, 22 June), p 28.

Waples, J. (1998), 'Library suit backfires on Bottomley', *The Sunday Times*, (26 July).

Weber, M. (1968), On charisma and institution building, Chicago: University of Chicago Press.

White, J.E. (1996), 'Texaco's high-octane racism problems', *Time*, (25 November).

Wildavsky A. (1968), 'Budgeting as a political process', in: Sills, D.A., (Ed.), *The interventionists' encyclopedia of the social services*, Collier Macmillan, pp 192–9.

Wilensky, H.L. (1961), 'Life cycle, work situation, and participation in formal associations', in: Kleemeie, R.W. (Ed), *Aging and leisure: research perspectives on the meaningful use of time*, New York: Oxford University Press, pp 213–242.

Wilensky, H.L. (1961), 'Orderly careers and social participation: The impact of work history on social integration in the middle mass', *American Sociological Review*, (26), pp 521–539.

Wolfe, T. (1979), *The right stuff*, London: Cape.

Woodward, J. (1965), *Industrial organization*, Oxford: Oxford University Press.

Index

Andrew Kakabadse

BSC MA PHD AAPSW FBPS FIAM FBAM

Deputy Director, Cranfield School of Management

Professor of International Management Development

Andrew Kakabadse is Professor of International Management Development and Deputy Director of the School of Management. He was ACT Visiting Professor at the Australian National University, Canberra, Visiting Professor at Hangzhou University, China, is Visiting Fellow at Babson College, Boston, USA and was Honorary Professorial Fellow, Curtin University of Technology, Perth. He is a Fellow of the International Academy of Management, a Fellow of the British Psychology Society and a Fellow of the British Academy of Management.

Andrew has consulted and lectured in the UK, Europe, the USA, Southeast Asia, China, Japan, Russia, Georgia, the Gulf States and Australia. He was also Vice Chancellor of the International Academy of Management and was Chairman of the Division of Occupational Psychology of the British Psychological Society in 2001. His current areas of interest focus on improving the performance of top executives and top executive teams, excellence in consultancy practice, corporate governance and conflict resolution and international relations. His top team database covers 17 nations and many thousands of private and public sector organisations. The study of the strategic skills of top teams has now extended into Japan, China, Hong Kong and the USA. He has published 21 books, over 132 articles and 14 monographs, including the best-selling books *Essence of leadership*, *Politics of management*, *Working in organisations* (first edition) and *The wealth creators*. His two new books are entitled *Geopolitics of governance* and, just released, *Smart sourcing: international best practice*. Andrew has just been awarded a substantial research grant to study board effectiveness, the role and contribution of non-executive directors, governance and corporate social responsibility practice. He is about to embark on an extensive global survey of international governance. He holds positions on the boards of a number of companies. He is editor of the *Journal of Management Development* and sits on the editorial board of the *Journal of Managerial Psychology* and the *Leadership and Organisation Development Journal*. He has also been adviser to a Channel 4 business series. Andrew is married to a fellow academic, Professor Nada Kakabadse of University College Northampton in the UK.

a.p.kakabadse@cranfield.ac.uk

JOHN BANK

BA MA

Consultant and Lecturer in Human Resource Management

John took his BA and MA in Philosophy in his native USA. His first job was as a freelance journalist specialising in industrial relations. He spent five years as aide to Cesar Chavez, the National President of the United Farm Workers of America, AFL-CIO, in building up the national farm workers' union.

From 1975 to 1979, he undertook preparatory research for a PhD and was a visiting lecturer in Industrial Relations at London Business School. His book, *Worker directors speak*, based on research work in the British Steel Corporation, was published by Gower in 1978. It contributed to the debate on industrial democracy.

He joined Cranfield School of Management in 1979, to lecture in Industrial relations. He teaches on a variety of executive development programmes and MBA courses. He introduced the use of outdoor activities at Cranfield. His book *Outdoor development for managers* (Gower) was the first to research the use of outdoor activities for management development.

He specialised in total quality management. A new edition of his *The essence of total quality management* (first published in May 1992) was published by Prentice Hall/Pearson in 2000. It was translated into many foreign languages. His book *Creating a resilient workforce: managing the upside of downsizing* with Kusum Sahdev and Susan Vinnicombe was published in 2001 by the Financial Times/Prentice Hall as part of the *Knowledge into action* series.

His book with Susan Vinnicombe *Women with attitude: lessons for career management* was published by Routledge in 2003. It profiles 19 women who have won the Veuve Clicquot Business Woman of the Year Award. He is writing a textbook on *Managing workforce diversity: a global challenge*, to be published by Pearson in 2004.

He has worked for a number of organisations in the public sector in the UK including the Metropolitan Police, the Housing Corporation and the Civil Service College. He was an adjunct faculty member of IBM's Corporate Education Programme in New York. He worked with IBM worldwide. He was a total quality management consultant registered with the Department of Trade & Industry's Quality Initiative. For over 15 years he has served as a consultant and management educator for companies in the Arabian Gulf in Kuwait, Oman and the United Arab Emirates. He is senior partner in Strategic Human Resources Partnership based in London, having recently retired from Cranfield School of Management.

j.bank@cranfield.ac.uk

SUE VINNICOMBE

MA PHD MCIM FRSA

Professor of Organisational Behaviour and
Diversity Management
Director of Graduate Research
Director of the Centre for Women Business
Leaders

Susan completed her MA in Marketing at Lancaster
University and her Doctorate in Organisational
Behaviour at Manchester Business School. She has held
positions in Thomas De La Rue International, British
Airways and Imperial College of Technology, London
before joining Cranfield.

She teaches in a variety of programmes at Cranfield,
including the MBA, and directed the Senior Managers' Programme. She runs the leading
edge executive programme for senior women managers, called *Women as Leaders*, as well as
launching a consortium programme for high potential women managers in 2004. In addition, she runs customised programmes for women managers, which have won three
national awards.

Susan's particular research interests are women's leadership styles, the issues involved in
women developing their managerial careers and sex diversity on corporate boards. Her
Research Centre is unique in the UK, with its focus on women leaders and the annual
Female FTSE 100 Index is regarded as the UK's premier research resource on women directors.

She has written seven books and numerous articles. Her most recent book was *Women
with attitude: lessons for career management* (with John Bank), Routledge, 2003, and she is currently working on a new book with Cambridge University Press on how women managers
can advance their careers.

Susan has consulted for organisations across the globe on how best to attract, retain and
develop women managers. Susan ran the first programme for women managers in South
Korea, the United Arab Emirates and the Philippines.

Susan is regularly interviewed in the press and on the radio and television for her expert
views on women directors. She is on the editorial board of *Group and organization management* and *Women in management review*. She is a director of the Strategic Human Resources
Partnership, which is based in London.

s.m.vinnicombe@cranfield.ac.uk